Reader's Guide
to
JOHN DRYDEN

Reader's Guide
to
JOHN DRYDEN

S. Dorsch

CENTRUM PRESS
NEW DELHI-110002 (INDIA)

CENTRUM PRESS
H.O.: 4360/4, Ansari Road, Daryaganj,
New Delhi-110 002 (India)
Ph.: 23278000, 23261597

B.O.: No. 1015, Ist Main Road, BSK IIIrd Stage
IIIrd Phase, IIIrd Block,
Bangalore - 560 085 (India)
Tel.: 080-41723429
Visit us at: www.centrumpress.com

Reader's Guide to John Dryden

First Edition, 2009

ISBN 978-93-80106-59-5

PRINTED IN INDIA

Printed at Salasar Imaging Systems, Delhi-110035 (India)

Contents

Preface

Dryden occupies a peculiar place in the history of the drama. He had no great genius for the theater, and yet he imposed his ideas upon the English play-going world. He was that unusual product, a politician with a poetical mind. For a time he was attached to the Puritans, and wrote an ode on the death of Cromwell; but, on the accession of Charles, he found no difficulty in transferring his muse to the royalist party. Towards the end of his stormy life he became a Roman Catholic. Soon after the accession of William and Mary, the queen, as a mark of honor to the poet, ordered a performance of *The Spanish Fryar,* one of his best comedies.

Although Dryden began his career as a playwright with the production of two or three comedies, yet it was in heroic drama that he achieved his great popularity. Dryden tried his hand at opera, one of his efforts being the arrangement of Milton's *Paradise Lost* for a musical setting. Some of this work was composed by the celebrated Englishman, Henry Purcell.

Dryden abandoned the heroic couplet and used blank verse; he also reconstructed the original play in such a way as to make it conform to the three unities. About 1678 he gave up the use of the heroic couplet altogether. His version of *Oedipus,* in collaboration with Nathaniel Lee, was too ghastly and horrible for stage production, even in those days of strong nerves.

Author

Chapter 1

Introduction

John Dryden, (1631-1700), English poet, literary critic, dramatist and leader in Restoration comedy wrote the comedic play *Marriage A-la-Mode* (1672), and the tragedy *All for Love* (1678). John Dryden was born in Aldwinkle, Northamptonshire, England, the eldest of fourteen children of Erasmus Dryden (c.1602–1654) and Mary Pickering (d. 1676). Dryden was a King's scholar studying the classics at Westminster. He contributed to the collection of tributes to honour Henry, Lord Hastings, an elegy in *Lachrymæ Musarum* (1649).

He entered Trinity College, Cambridge in 1650, graduating in February of 1654, the same year his father died. While living in London in 1657 Dryden started working with the civil service and began in earnest writing plays of heroic tragedy and satires of varying success.

Heroic Stanzas (1658), on the death of Oliver Cromwell is his first important work. With the protectorate crumbling, Dryden sought other work including writing for a bookseller. With the return of Charles II he celebrated the King's divine right with, among other works, his poem *Astræa Redux* (1660). *To His Sacred Maj0esty, a Panegyrick on his Coronation* (1661) came next, Dryden courting favour with the new regime which would later bring allegations of insincere and self-serving allegiance.

On 1 December 1663 Dryden married the daughter of the Earl of Berkshire, Lady Elizabeth Howard (c.1638–1714), with whom he would have three sons. His first play *The Wild Gallant* was first staged in 1662. *The Rival Ladies* (1663) also had Spanish influences. Attached to it is one of his famous Prefaces where he describes his principles of dramatic criticism. His first successful play, written in heroic couplets was *The Indian Emperor* (1665). The same year of the Great Fire in London, *Annus Mirabilis* (1666) celebrates the English Navy's victory over the Dutch. Dryden had retired to the country with the plague threat, where his first son was born, and he continued to write. *The Maiden Queen* composed in blank verse, rhyming couplets and prose and *The Assignation, or Love in a Nunnery* were produced in 1667.

An Essay of Dramatic Poesy (1668) was written two years after the Restoration with the reopening of the theatres. Dryden entered into a contract in 1668 with the King's Theatre Company in which he would produce three plays a year. For his efforts the Archbishop of Canterbury awarded him an M.A. in 1668. The same year he became Poet Laureate and in 1670 Royal Historiographer which would provide a stable income for him.

The play *Marriage A-la-Mode* (1672) was followed by his unsuccessful work on the theme of Paradise Lost, *The State of Innocence*, staged in 1674. After 1676, he began to use blank verse, and he produced his best play, *All for Love* in 1678. It is Dryden's most famous masterpiece based on Anthony and Cleopatra.

He had mastered the art of comparative criticism, using prose and dialogue for debate, and wit and satire to illustrate disparities between church and state. A year later Dryden was beaten by thugs, an attack that had been ordered by the Earl of Rochester when Dryden was suspected of collaboration on *An Essay upon Satire*, which vilified various prominent figures, of which the real author was never realised.

The well-known political satire of Shaftesbury under the transparent guise of the Old Testament, *Absalom and Achitophel*, Dryden's allegorical poem appeared in 1681 and his didactic poem *Religio Laici* (1682) followed, which argues the case for Anglicanism. *Threnodia Arigustalis* (1685) is an ode to Charles II. *The Hind and the Panther* (1687) marked Dryden's final conversion to Roman Catholicism.

After the Revolution of 1688 he lost his Laureateship with

the accession of William III. Refusing to take an oath of allegiance, his politics and religion left him out of favour with the court, and his sole source of income was from his plays and translations of poetry from Latin and Greek. The tragi-comedy *Don Sebastian* (1690) was on a par with *All for Love.* Another tragi-comedy *Love Triumphant* (1694) would be his last play. Included in his ensuing critical essays was *A Discourse concerning the Original and Progress of Satire.*

Dryden would also take on the massive task of translating the works of Virgil to prose. John Dryden died on 12 May 1700 from inflammation caused by gout. He is buried in the Poet's Corner of Westminster Abbey, London, England, nearby to his longtime friend William Congreve.

"Genius must be born, and never can be taught." ~ John Dryden

John Dryden was born at the vicarage of Aldwinkle, Northamptonshire, on August 9, 1631, son of Erasmus Dryden and Mary Pickering. His family were Parliamentary supporters with Puritan leanings. He attended Westminster School as a king's scholar under Richard Busby, and was an avid student of the classics. While at Westminster, Dryden published his first verses, an elegy "Upon the Death of Lord Hastings", in *Lachrymæ Musarum* (1649).

He entered Trinity College, Cambridge, in 1650, and took a BA in 1654. Dryden moved to London around 1657, and first gained notice with his 'Heroic Stanzas' (1659) on the death of Lord Protector Cromwell. In the Royalist climate of the Restoration, he sensibly wrote *Astraea Redux* (1660) to celebrate the return of King Charles II. For the coronation, Dryden wrote "To His Sacred Majesty, A Panegyric" (1661). In 1662, Dryden wrote verses "To My Lord Chancellor" Clarendon, and was elected to the Royal Society.

The theatres had been reopened, demand for entertainments was high, and Dryden set to writing plays. In 1663, Dryden married Lady Elizabeth Howard, the sister of his theatrical partner Sir Robert Howard, and the eldest daughter of the Earl of Berkshire. His first play was the prose comedy of humours *A Wild Gallant* (1663), a wholly unremarkable piece, followed by the tragicomedy *The Rival Ladies* (1664) and *The Indian Queen* (1664). In 1665, the theatres were closed down because of the plague that raged in London, and the King's court relocated to Oxford. There, Dryden finally established a reputation as a playwright with *The Indian Emperor* (1665), a heroic drama. The year 1666 was eventful in English history, including both the naval war with the Dutch, and the Great Fire of London.

Dryden commemorated this 'year of wonders" in his long poem, *Annus Mirabilis,* in 1667. This poem secured him the position of Poet Laureate on the death of William D'Avenant in 1668. The same year, he was also given the degree of M. A. by the Archbishop of Canterbury. As a fellow of the Royal Society, he was furthermore made Historiographer Royal in 1670, which brought him an annual income of £200.

In 1668, Dryden began a fruitful period of both critical and dramatic writing. His first major critical work was the *Essay of Dramatic Poesy* (1668), followed by *A Defence of an Essay* (1668), and *Essay of Heroic Plays* (1672). His plays from this period include the comedy *Secret Love* (1667); the heroic drama *Tyrannic Love* (1669); the two-part *The Conquest of Granada* (1670-71); and the comedy *Marriage á la Mode* (1672). In 1674, Dryden published a tribute to Milton in the form of a musical adaptation of *Paradise Lost,* entitled *The State of Innocence*—it was never performed.

The tragedy *Aureng-Zebe* (1676) was Dryden's first play in blank verse, followed by his masterpiece All for Love (1678), based on the story of Anthony and Cleopatra. The success and fame Dryden enjoyed naturally garnered him enemies. He was ridiculed in Buckingham's *The Rehearsal* (1671), and brutally beaten in an attack in Rose Alley, Covent Garden, on December 18, 1679. It has been suggested, though never proved, that Lord Rochester had a hand in hiring the ruffians responsible for the attack. Rochester had lampooned Dryden earlier, and had in turn suspected of Dryden for complicity in ridiculing him in Lord Mulgrave's *Essay on Satire.*

With the the unsuccessful prose comedy "Limberham" (1678), the poor adaptation of *Troilus and Cressida* (1679), and the play "Spanish Friar" (1681), Dryden left his career as dramatist for a time and turned his attention to satire. His political satire on Monmouth and Shaftesbury, *Absalom and Achitophel,* appeared in 1681.

It is one of the great English satires, and it brought him further favor with Charles II, who was pleased at this attack against the Whigs during the Exclusion Crisis. Dryden dutifully wrote the *Second Part of Absalom and Achitophel* in collaboration with Nahum Tate, as well as another attack on Shaftesbury's supporters, *The Medal* (1682).

These naturally provoked counterattacks, including Thomas Shadwell's *The Medal of John Bayes*. Dryden in turn responded *Mac Flecknoe,* full of ridicule for Shadwell, perhaps his most entertaining poem, pirated in 1682, and officially printed in 1684. Dryden also had a keen interest in theology, and this resulted first in the publication of *Religio Laici* (1682). This work, the title of which translates as "A Layman's Faith", was a long religious poem arguing Christianity over Deism, the Bible as the guide to salvation, and the Anglican Church over the Catholic Church.

This period saw some of Dryden's best poems, the Pindaric ode "Threnodia Augustalis" (1685) at the death of Charles II, the beautiful lyrical ode "To the Pious Memory... of Mrs Anne Killigrew" (1686) written to commemorate a painter who drowned in the Thames, and "A Song for Saint Cecilia's Day" (1687).

Dryden had long grappled with religious uncertainty, and converted into Roman Catholicism in 1686, the year after the ascension to the throne of King James II, a Catholic. In 1687, Dryden published *The Hind and the Panther,* an allegorical fable criticizing the Anglican church. Dryden suffered for this almost immediately. The Revolution of 1688, which placed the Protestant William III on the throne, caused him to be deprived of his laureateship, and what was worse, he was replaced by his old enemy, Shadwell.

Dryden returned to the theatre. He wrote the libretto to Purcell's opera *King Arthur* (1691); a tragicomedy, *Don Sebastian* (1690); a comedy of errors, *Amphitryon* (1690); and

Cleomenes: the Spartan Hero (1692). Dryden's *Love Triumphant* (1694), the prologue of which announced it as his last play, was a failure. Dryden turned to writing translations, including the satires of Perseus and Juvenal (1693) and Virgil's *Aeneid* (1697). He also wrote more poetry, including "An Ode, on the death of Mr Henry Purcell" (1696) commemorating the composer, a second ode for St. Cecilia's Day, "Alexander's Feast" (1697), which was later incorporated into his *Fables Ancient and Modern* (1700), paraphrases of Ovid, Boccaccio, and Chaucer.

Dryden died on April 30, 1700, soon after the publication of the *Fables*, of inflammation caused by gout. He was buried in Westminster Abbey. Dryden was a good playwright and poet, a fine translator, a solid critic, and an excellent satirist whose works are still worthy of much admiration. Regarded by many scholars as the father of modern English poetry and criticism, Dryden dominated literary life in England during the last four decades of the seventeenth century.

By deliberately and comprehensively refining language, Dryden developed an expressive, universal diction which has had a profound impact on the evolution of speech and writing in the English-speaking world.

Although initially famous for his comedies and heroic tragedies, among Dryden's other accomplishments are critical essays as well as translations of works by Virgil, Chaucer, and Boccaccio. Today he is also highly regarded for his satirical and didactic poems, notably *Absalom and Achitophel, The Hind and the Panther*, and *Religio Laici*. In poems such as these, Dryden displayed an irrepressible wit and forceful line of argument which later satirists adopted as their model.

The eldest son of a large, socially prominent Puritan family, Dryden was born in Aldwinkle, Northamptonshire. Little is known about his early years, except that as a young boy he received a classical education at Westminster School through a royal scholarship. While there he published his first poem, *Upon the Death of the Lord Hastings*, commemorating the life of a schoolmate who had recently died of smallpox.

In 1650 Dryden began attending Trinity College,

Cambridge, where he earned a bachelor of arts degree. Shortly afterward his father died, leaving him to oversee the affairs of his family and of his own small estate.

Dryden's activities and whereabouts during the next several years are unknown; in 1659, however, following the death of Oliver Cromwell, Lord Protector of England, Dryden returned to writing and published *Heroique Stanzas,* a group of complimentary verses which portray Cromwell as architect of a great new age. In the following years, Dryden continued to publish politically oriented poems, of which the most notable are *Astraea Redux* and *Annus Mirabilis: the Year of Wonders, 1666.*

The former, which celebrated the exiled Charles II's restoration to the English crown, incited condemnation in later years from those who charged Dryden with political inconsistency and selfish motivation. Since then, historians have argued that Dryden maintained throughout his life a belief in religious tolerance and moderate government and switched allegiance from the republicans to the royalists in keeping with the majority of the English people.

In 1663, following his marriage to Lady Elizabeth Howard, Dryden debuted as a playwright, a career which at the time held the most financial promise for an aspiring writer in England.

His first play proved unsuccessful, but later endeavors, in particular *The Indian Emperour* (1665), was popular and established Dryden's reputation in drama, a field which he increasingly dominated during the next fifteen years. In 1668 Dryden became poet laureate of England, and shortly thereafter, received the title of historiographer royal. In 1685, during the first year of the reign of Catholic monarch James II, Dryden converted to Catholicism.

He did not renounce this conversion after the abdication of James or with the accession in 1689 of Protestant rulers William and Mary. Dryden died in London in 1700 and was buried in Westminster Abbey. Throughout the years, Dryden's detractors have focused on his shifts from Protestantism to Catholicism and from republicanism to monarchism as proof of the poet's flair for political expediency. Generally, however, Dryden is recognized as someone who in his time was an extremely popular literary figure, who believed in religious moderation, and who influenced heavily the tastes of his age.

MAJOR WORKS

Apart from the encomiums or complimentary poems of his early years, Dryden is well-known for his satirical verse. The Popish Plot (1678-81), a thwarted attempt by the Earl of Shaftesbury and others to exclude Charles's Catholic brother, James, from his right of succession to the throne, provided Dryden with the topic for what critics consider his greatest work, *Absalom and Achitophel,* a satirical attack on Shaftesbury and his confederates.

This work inaugurated a phase of satirical and didactic verse which directly influenced the development of Augustan poetry in the next century, especially that of Alexander Pope. The poem was followed in 1682 by *Mac Flecknoe,* a mockheroic poem which was directed at the poet Thomas Shadwell, a literary antagonist of Dryden.

Allied to *Absalom and Achitophel* in tone, *Mac Flecknoe* displays Dryden's mastery of rhythm and cunning verbal attack. The same year there also appeared a shorter, more serious satiric poem titled *The Medall,* which again was aimed at Shaftesbury.

Political and religious matters repeatedly overlapped in Dryden's time, an era much vexed with the question of whether Protestant or Roman Catholic monarchs were the legitimate rulers of Britain; accordingly, Dryden also began to address religious issues in his poetry. *Religio Laici; or, a Layman's Faith* (1682) appeared when Whig plots to assassinate King Charles II were being formed.

In this didactic poem, which also contains religious and metaphysical insights, Dryden advocated a compromise between Protestant Anglican exclusivism and Roman Catholic belief in absolute papal authority, articulating the king's stance in favor of religious toleration. Dryden's later, allegorical poem, *The Hind and the Panther* (1687), a three-part work written in beast-fable form, was published after the poet's conversion to Catholicism, but like *Religio Laici,* it argues for moderation between the two churches. Dryden's odes represent his final poetic period. They include *A Song for St. Cecilia's Day, 1687,* and *Alexander's Feast.* Today, they are widely anthologized, and they attest to Dryden's skill at incorporating musical composition into his poetry.

CRITICAL RECEPTION

The eighteenth-century English author Samuel Johnson regarded Dryden as a poet who crystallized the potential for beauty and majesty in the English language by effectively shaping rough words into refined verse. Dryden first began developing his poetic style while writing his early, laudatory verses, experimenting as he wrote them with the traditional hexameter form.

Although recognized for their artistic promise and innovation, these poems have since been faulted for misplaced or excessive conceits and similes. Ultimately, the best of this early poetic period is represented by *Annus Mirabilis,* an inspirational, heroic treatment of the great fire in London and of the AngloDutch naval war.

Years later, with *Absalom and Achitophel,* Dryden displayed his mastery of the heroic couplet and the suitability of his streamlined verse for political satire. Cloaked in allusive language and based on the biblical story of King David's rebellious son, this mockheroic poem addresses the explosive political climate of the time through a string of character portraits, narrative, and speeches.

Dryden's portrayals of Charles II, an inveterate philanderer; his illegitimate son Monmouth, who planned to dethrone his father; and Shaftesbury, the chief orchestrator of the Popish Plot; are admired by critics not only for their liveliness but for the judicious manner in which they are presented. Scholars have remarked that the relentless movement of the poem, its delightful yet pointed commentary on the crucial situation, and its timeless appeal establish it as one of the highest achievements in the heroic couplet form.

That Dryden was an exemplary poet of public events and was able to infuse even the most ordinary incident with dignified, original art is not disputed. However, his poems have been charged with displaying a disturbing impersonality. Nevertheless, several modern critics have detected a clear, confessional tone in Dryden's later poems, *Religio Laici* and *The Hind and the Panther*. Although the theological viewpoints in them are disparate, critics have observed that both these works forcefully document the poet's personal reactions to the political milieu as well as to the power of religious faith in his era.

THE PLAYS

The heroic drama of the Restoration period is glorious extravaganza written for a special audience: to enjoy it today—and this is true to a lesser extent of the comedies—is perhaps to indulge an acquired vice. Largely outside the tradition of the English theatre, in it the loose Shakespearian method is continually at war with the French neo-classical form, to which the courtiers exiled during the Commonwealth had become accustomed.

Emotions, states of mind, which are to the final degree romantic are tailored into, or at least partly wear, severe classical garb. It is, in short, baroque—dynamic, sometimes fantastic ornament being added to a formalized structure. As Dryden himself remarked, "'tis unjust that they who have not the least notion of heroic writing, should therefore condemn the pleasure which others receive from it, because they cannot comprehend it"; and he was careful to add that he would not "dispute the preference of Tragedy; let every man enjoy his taste."

Certainly, to read these plays, or to go to see them, in the expectation of being plunged into the abundant life of the Elizabethan theatre, or to meet the realism of a later period, is to court disappointment. We may even find them grotesque, susceptible to rollicking parody, as Buckingham, Sprat, and others found when they gleefully concocted *The Rehearsal*.

But accept the *données* of each play, be prepared to enter

a world of absolute emotions—the heroism, the ideas of honour and of love, the Romanism and so forth—these dramas can give a piquantly flavoured pleasure, if only, and markedly with Dryden, from the sheer virtuosity of the performance, the flamboyance—that quality which so largely faded from our literature as it grew older.

A play was a heroic poem, an epic in little, and its business, Hobbes had asserted, was 'to raise admiration, principally for three virtues, valour, beauty, and love'. Artificial? Of course, why not? Heroic drama is consciously artificed: and with Dryden you often feel that he is standing aside, with a twinkle in his eye, watching himself perform.

Thus however bombastic the sentiments may be, Dryden's handling is firmly secure; he can even produce effects of prettiness, which as he places them are not at all destructive, but, on the contrary charmingly enhancing of the result. Moreover, inserted in the plays are the enormously varied songs, prosodically delightful, ranging from those breathing nostalgia or the futility of human endeavour, to the frankly, and so harmlessly, erotic. From *The Indian Emperour* (1667) we get:

Ah fading joy, how quickly art thou past!
Yet we thy ruin haste.
As if the cares of human life were few,
We seek out new:
And follow fate, which would too fast pursue...
Hark, hark, the waters fall, fall, fall,
And with a murmuring sound
Dash, dash upon the ground
To gentle slumbers call.

From Tyrannick Love (1670) the song beginning:

Ah how sweet it is to love!
Ah how gay is young desire!

And from *King Arthur* (1691), the famous patriotic lyric disguised as a Song of Venus:

Fairest isle, all isles excelling,
Seat of pleasures and of loves;
Venus here will choose her dwelling,

And forsake her Cyprian groves.
Cupid from his favourite nation
Care and envy will remove;
Jealousy, that poisons passion,
And despair, that dies for love...

which Purcell set to such dulcet, singable melody. With the plays go also the equally varied Prologues and Epilogues, in which Dryden enters into an evidently friendly relation with his audiences, sometimes chaffing them, sometimes scolding, even a little scornfully upbraiding, now and again indulging in acute, pertinent criticism. There is a characteristic captivating vigour about them all, and, with the laughter they provoke, a dominant persuasiveness.

Yet the plays will be widely read only by devotees of the history of drama; not all even of Dryden enthusiasts will tackle them wholesale; for indeed they are not all easy to read, thanks to the sudden reversals of fortune in the tragedies, and the intricacy of the plots in the comedies, which are apt to be bewildering in the study.

They would clarify on the stage, certainly, for the playwrights of those days had a lively dramatic sense. Yet even in the reading such a play as *The Conquest of Granada* in two parts (1670-1671), the high point of the heroic bubbles with special interests.

The same will be found with *The State of Innocence* (1677), the quite individual rendering in rhyme of *Paradise Lost*; the Shakespeare adaptations; or, to go to the other extreme, the purposefully blunt *Mr. Limberham* (1678). But there are two tragedies at least, and one comedy, of abundant general appeal, which serve to round off the canon.

For all its slightly exotic flavour, its heroic sentiments, its too ingenious plot, *Aureng-Zebe* (1676), the last of the rhymed plays, is moving and actual, if only for the emotive quality of the speeches, of which the most famous, if not the deepest reaching, is the haunting:

When I consider life, 'tis all a cheat;
Yet, fooled with hope, men favour the deceit;
Trust on, and think tomorrow will repay:

Tomorrow's falser than the former day;
Lies worse; and while it says, we shall be blest
With some new joys, cuts off what we possest.
Strange cozenage! none would live past years again,
Yet all hope pleasure in what yet remain;
And from the dregs of life, think to receive
What the first sprightly running could not give.
I'm tired with waiting for this Chymick gold,
Which fools us young, and beggars us when old. (IV. i.)

There is the mastery of rhyme, never dictating the sense, never interfering with the run of the phrase.

But by now Dryden had satisfied his instinct to conquer the couplet for stage purposes. His prologue declares:

Our author by experience, finds it true,
'Tis much more hard to please himself than you;
And out of no feigned modesty this day,
Damns his laborious trifle of a play;
Not that it's worse than what before he writ,
But now he has another taste of wit;
And, to confess a truth, (though out of time,)
Grows weary of his long-loved mistress, Rhyme.

So in his next great venture, *All for Love* (1678), in which he handled the story of Anthony and Cleopatra in his own original way—you feel he is wholly involved· confessedly it was the one play he wrote to please himself—in his style he 'professed to imitate the divine Shakespeare', that is, he 'disencumbered himself from rhyme'.

The result is the best dramatic blank verse since Shakespeare, at once concise and rich, flexible, capable of grandeur and also of lightness. It can achieve:

How I loved
Witness, ye days and nights, and all your hours,
That danced away with down upon your feet...

equally with:

O horror, horror!
Egypt has been; our latest hour is come:
The queen of nations from her ancient seat,
is sunk for ever in the dark abyss:

Time has unrolled her glories to the last,
And how closed up the volume.
and the monosyllabic simplicity of:
Farewell! Ever my leader, even in death!
My queen and thou have got the start of me,
And I'm the lag of honour.

In this proud and lovely masterpiece, this sombre tragedy as it has been called, we are held and swayed by the interplay of the emotions, of all the characters, as well as of the chief ones, though more especially by the revulsions of feeling in Antony.

At first plunged in the depths of despair till roused by the goading urgency of Ventidius (in a scene Dryden thought the best he had written), he is later torn between his pride, his passion for Cleopatra, his sense of duty towards Octavia; and the conduct of the play builds it up into an integrated whole, fused together by Antony's inner conflicts, the unities being 'more exactly preserved, than, perhaps, the English theatre requires'. The accents are always human, free of rant, with a minimum of high-flying imagery.

Take, for example, the beautifully moulded speech of Cleopatra struggling to maintain her hold of Antony:

How shall I plead my cause, when you, my judge,
Already have condemned me? Shall I bring
The love you bore me for my advocate?
That now is turned against me, that destroys me;
For love, once past, is at the best forgotten,
But oftner sours to hate: 'twill please my lord
To ruin me, and therefore I'll be guilty.
But, could I once have thought it would have pleased you,
That you would pry, with narrow searching eyes
Into my faults, severe to my destruction:
And watching all advantages with care
That serve to make me wretched? Speak, my lord,
For I end here. Though I deserve this usage,
Was it like you to give it?

Nor is the play lacking those sententiae, the great commonplaces, without which no seventeenth-century play was complete, though as the century progressed they became less and less Senecan. No one would claim that Dryden's phrases, however memorable, compare with the tremendous platitudes that Shakespeare well-nigh sears us with: nevertheless they are a measure. In this play we have the once well-known 'Men are but children of a larger growth...' or:

O that I less could fear to lose this being,
which, like a snow-ball, in my coward hand,
The more 'tis grasped, the faster melts away.
Poor reason! what a wretched aid art thou!
For still, in spite of thee,
These two long lovers, soul and body, dread
Their final separation.

The play, to be sure, has echoes—but they are only echoes— from Shakespeare and Daniel, especially where Plutarch is invoked: but it exists in its own full-blooded right as an individual contribution to the corpus of English tragedy, and is still, from time to time, acted.

So is the most lively of his comedies, the yet sparkling *Marriage a-la-Mode* (1673) embodying the quintessence of Restoration comedy, the sex-antagonism so delicately handled by Congreve. Many of the Court and its hangers-on at that period were engaged in the desperate attempt to rationalize love, trying to conduct their lives on the assumption that sexual attraction was easily separable from affection, that jealousy was ridiculous, and that a husband was, almost by definition, a fool whose obvious destiny was to be cuckolded.

A large part of the game of Restoration comedy was to show how disastrous, how contrary to common sense, the assumptions were; for this comedy was in the main classical 'critical' comedy intent upon 'curing excess'. Far from being 'artificial' as it is commonly dubbed, it was very nakedly down to earth, and had a direct bearing upon how life was lived.

Dryden states the theme at once with the song:

Why should a foolish Marriage Vow,
Which long ago was made,
oblige us to each other now,
When Passion is decayed?

We loved, and we loved, as long as we could,
Till our love was loved out in us both;
But our Marriage is dead, when the Pleasure is fled:
'Twas Pleasure first made it an Oath.
If I have Pleasures for a Friend,
And farther Love in store,
What wrong has he whose joys did end,
And who could give no more?
'Tis a Madness that he
Should be jealous of me,
Or that I should bar him of another:
For all we can gain,
Is to give ourselves Pain,
When neither can hinder the other.

The play is conducted with a romping gaiety throughout, till, schooled by bitter stark experience, the would-be erring couples agree to give over their frolics, and make a' firm league not to invade each other's property'.

The epilogue, full of delicious mockery, drives the point home. And parallel with the brisk comedy there runs a modulated, almost serene heroic pastoral play, which, a little sadly treats of the theme of constancy on another level. This different tinge of feeling gives an added depth to the pure critical comedy, the two plays not jarring with each other, but making an emotionally coherent whole.

Dryden did not altogether abandon playwriting till 1694; but there was a large gap, which he did not regret. He never felt himself very fitted for the theatre, least of all for comedy, on account, he said, of the 'sullenness' of his temper; indeed most of his comedies tend to become uproarious farces of incident. As for his tragedies, at one moment he carelessly cast off the remark, 'they were bad enough to please'.

Yet in some ways his later work, in which he very considerably modified the heroic strain, is preferable to his earlier. In the comedies there is his version of *Amphytrion* (1690), in opera *King Arthur* (1691), and in tragedy, as opposed to heroic drama, the moving, and often tense *Don Sebastian* (1690) and *Cleomenes* (1692).

And whatever he did, the vigour is always there, the amplitude of mind, and the confident versification.

THE POETRY

Dryden's poetry can roughly be classified in three groups, the occasional, comprising the greater odes, the epistles, elegies, and complimentary addresses; the politico-religious; and the translations, though the second group is also in the proper sense occasional. Though he wrote few direct satires (he translated several) a strong vein of satirical comment runs through the body of his verse, and indeed flickers intermittently in his play.

But apart from what he may have been writing about, his verse is always characteristic, moulded partly by what he thought a poet ought to be, and what he should accomplish. As to the former he stated--to quote one of his passages on this theme: Mere poets and mere muscians are as sottish as mere drunkards are, who live in a continual mist, without seeing or judging anything clearly.

A man should be learned in several sciences, and should have a reasonable, philosophic, and in some measure a mathematical head, to be a complete and excellent poet: and besides this, should have experience in all sorts of humours and manners of men, should be thoroughly skilled in conversation, and should have a great knowledge of mankind in general. (*Notes and Observations on The Empress of Morocco.*)

In another place he says that he thinks little of a poet who cannot argue well. His poetry, then, deals with what is common experience, not, of course, omitting spiritual experience. There is, then, in his poetry, none of the yearning of the Romantics, the reachings out after the impalpable in the attempt to grasp the inapprehensible: his vivid, actual imagination plays around the actions and passions of men and women as they live out their lives, in soul as well as in body.

He does not confront us with profound, searching sentiment making us face the innermost nature of our being: but he has a firm grasp over a wide field, handling at no despicable level the eternal religious issues, and the scientific development of his age. His diction is in tune with his ideas; he disciplines himself to use the precise word rather than the word with a vague aura of association, endeavouring always, to express as clearly and firmly as possible what he means to say. In a way, moreover, that is pleasantly acceptable.

'Would not Donne's *Satires*, which abound with so much wit, appear more charming, if he had taken care of his words, and of his numbers?' For the musician in the poet was not to be ignored, as he might have seemed to suggest in the passage quoted above. For:

by the harmony of words we elevate the mind to a sense of devotion as our solemn music, which is inarticulate poesy, does in churches'

Here, of course, is the eternal question of pleasure and profit, of the aesthetic as against the moral. 'Delight', he said in the *Defence of the Essay of Dramatick Poesie* (1668), 'is the chief. if not the only, end of poesy: instruction can be admitted but in the second place, for only instructs as it delights'; though a few pages later 'We says that poetry must 'resemble natural truth, but it must be ethical'. He sums up his attitude best in his *Discourse* on satire (1693):

They who will not grant me, that pleasure is one of the ends of poetry, but that it is only a means of compassing the only end, which is instruction, must yet allow, that, without the means of pleasure, the instruction is but bare and dry philosophy: a crude preparation of morals, which we may have from Aristotle or Epictetus, with more profit than from any poet.

But words, he held, were only the colouring of the poem-picture; what was important was the idea, and the structure, though the colouring was what first struck the eye. So whatever words he uses, his is still the language that might be spoken by men to men. It is never, pejoratively speaking, 'poetic'.

That is one of his great triumphs. Even in his most grandiose odes or addresses he keeps his colloquial phrasing: there is no tortuousness, none of the 'exhausting nagging after effect' (as Mr. George Barker has called it) of the Metaphysicals.

It was because he saw his main task as the redeeming of English verse from obfuscation that he insisted so much upon rhyme, since this 'bounds and circumscribes the fancy. For imagination in a poet is a faculty so wild and lawless, that, like an high-ranking spaniel, it must have clogs tied to it, lest it outrun the judgement.'

Fancy and judgement—those were the faculties a poet must ever try to balance, so as to bring out the richest thoughts; fancy being what we call imagination, moving the sleeping images of things towards the light'. That was a view put forward in 1664 (*Dedication of the Rival Ladies*), and maintained in 1697 (*Dedication of the Æneis*):

And whereas poems which are produced by the vigour of the imagination only have a gloss upon them at the first which time wears off, the works of judgment are like the diamond; the more they are polished, the more lustre they receive.

As to 'numbers', namely mellifluous prosody, he considered Denham and Waller to be the fathers of English poetry, with Spenser as a forbear, admiring their 'smoothness' as opposed to the rugosities of Donne. Smoothness of course is not enough; it can be overdone, as critics a generation later were to find, Pope himself saying:

Waller was smooth; but Dryden taught to join
The varying verse, the full resounding line,
The long majestic march, and energy divine:

Or, as Coleridge put it; the wheels take fire from the mere rapidity of their motion'. What we get from Dryden, then is an invigoration of being, such as tends to release the imagination.

His attack [approach] is always superb; plunging you straight into the sweeping movement of his theme, as, for instance, in the first of his three wide-embracing occasional pieces, *Absalom and Achitophel*.

This, called by him simply 'A Poem', and best described by Dr. Ian Jack as a 'witty heroic poem', was written for the purpose of setting public feeling against Lord Shaftesbury, leader of the Whig faction scheming to exclude the Catholic

Duke of York from the succession, and perhaps put the King's natural son, the Duke of Monmouth, on the throne.

Thus Dryden opens with a deliciously bland excuse for Charles II's virile manifestations:

In pious times, ere priestcraft did begin,
Before polygamy was made a sin;
When man on many multiplied his kind,
Ere one to one was cursedly confined...
Then Israel's monarch after Heaven's own heart,
His vigorous warmth did variously impart
To wives and slaves; and, wide as his command,
Scattered his Maker's image thro' the land.

and then we are led into the story, or, rather, situation. Though the poem is not primarily a satire the satirical element soon appears—in the biting description of the English, the Jews of the story:

God's pampered people, whom, debauched with ease,
No king could govern, nor no God could please;
(Gods they had tried of every shape and size,
That god-smiths could produce, or priests devise).

Only a modicum of historical knowledge is needed to enjoy the poem; the drama unrolls itself to culminate in the great temptation scene, where Achitophel (Shaftesbury) lures Absalom (Monmouth) to his doom, pricking him into saying:

Why am I scanted by a niggard birth?
My soul disclaims the kindred of her earth;
And made for empire, whispers me within,
'Desire for greatness is a godlike sin.'

Achitophel's reaction to his triumph is pressed home with deliberate Miltonism:

Him staggering so when hell's dire agent found,
While fainting Virtue scarce maintained her ground
He pours fresh forces in, and thus replies...

the grip never being relaxed through the more than thousand lines.

Yet Dryden, always in control, orders the rise and fall, eases the tension as he will, partly by pace, but largely by the 'characters', in the main satirically drawn. The most famous is that of Achitophel, though he himself thought that of Zimri (Buckingham) 'worth the whole poem', since it was 'not bloody, but ridiculous enough', in fact more subtle as being raillery rather than bludgeoning.

Yet Shaftesbury must always be the favourite, as it contains more poetic power:

For close designs and crooked counsels fit;
Sagacious, bold, and turbulent of wit;
Restless, unfixed in principles and place;
In power unpleased, impatient of disgrace:
A fiery soul, which, working out its way,
Fretted the pigmy body to decay,
And o'er informed the tenement of clay...

the pressure continuing for some fifty lines without a hint of monotony, the caesuras [pauses] being brilliantly varied in depth as well as position as stroke follows devastating stroke. Other personages crowd upon the scene, treated bitterly, scornfully, or disdainfully as occasion serves, sometimes with one or two deft shafts of ridicule, as, for instance, Shimei (Bethell) who:

Did wisely from expensive sins refrain,
And never broke the Sabbath, but for gain...

The religious sects receive due buffeting, as do the petty political intriguers together with the deluded populace. Not for a moment does the poem fail in pungency: and through it pierces Dryden's innate conservatism, summed up in one phrase, 'For innovation is the blow of fate'.

Very different is *The Medal*, again directed against Shaftesbury, where Dryden achieved sheer Juvenalian satire; *MacFlecknoe*, on the other hand, is a gloriously comic mock-heroic, the first in the language, in which Dryden lampooned Shadwell, treated with equal contempt in the second part of *Absalom and Achitophel.*

The opening is delusively magniloquent:

All human things are subject to decay,
And when fate summons, monarchs must obey...

the account of the enthronement of Shadwell as successor to the throne of *Nonsense* proceeding with a gorgeous pomposity. The piece is variegated by parodied echoes of other poets all the while that the low is exalted, and fantastic absurdities rocketed to dazzling heights. The poem is more poetically sensuous than Tassoni's *La Secchia Rapita,* more wittily barbed than Boileau's *Le Lutrin.*

The first great debating poem, *Religio Laici,* is not difficult to follow, being mostly written in the plainest language, since 'a man is to be cheated into passion, but to be reasoned into truth'. It is an argument for adherence to the national religion; political stability demands a commonly held faith: and what, he asks, is wrong with Anglicanism?

No sublimity is demanded, since finite cannot reach infinity (a favourite phrase of his); the stress is again and again on *needful* faith. As always he is contemptuous of those who 'barter solid quiet to obtain the windy satisfactions of the brain'. After all:

The unlettered Christian, who believes in gross
Plods on to Heaven, and never is at a loss.
Too many men, however, itch to expound:
... crowds unlearned, with rude devotion warm,
About the sacred viands buzz and swarm,
The fly-blown text creates a crawling brood,
And turn to maggots what was meant for food.

Satire, whetted by Dryden's stubborn dislike of priests, is never long absent, and makes the argument spin along briskly. And though 'unpolished, rugged verse [he] chose, As fittest for discourse and nearest prose', there are passages that sweep along with compelling poetic pulse.

Take the exordium:

Dim as the borrowed beam of moon and stars
To lonely, weary, wandering travellers,
Is Reason to the soul; and, as on high
Those rolling fires discover but the sky,
Not light us here, so Reason's glimmering ray
Was lent, not to assure our doubtful way,
But guide us upward to a better day.
And as those nightly tapers disappear,
When day's bright lord ascends our hemisphere;

So pale grows Reason at Religion's sight,
So dies, and so dissolves in supernatural light...

Are we, after all, we ask ourselves, to be reasoned into truth?

Wholly to grasp *The Hind and the Panther,* essentially a plea for toleration, demands rather more background knowledge, both of the political situation, 'when the nation was in a high ferment', and of the claims of the various religions and sects.

Early in the poem, in one passage among many in these two poems that establish Dryden as a noteworthy religious poet, we get the statement of Dryden's submission to the Roman communion:

What weight of ancient witness can prevail
If private reason hold the public scale?
But, gracious God, how well dost thou provide
For erring judgments an unerring guide!
Thy throne is darkness in the abyss of light,
A blaze of glory that forbids the sight.
And what had 'the monster breed' of Protestants accomplished?
Such wars, such waste, such fiery tracks of dearth
Their zeal has left.

Bitter experience had shown that:

Of all the tyrannies on humankind.
The worst is that which persecutes the mind

Every here and there occur memorable phrases, moulded by the driving force of conviction, made aphoristic by great poetic power:

Revenge, the bloody minister of ill,
With all the lean tormentors of the will.

A great deal of nonsense has been talked about the fable form being unsuitable; but if rats can talk about the virtue of dining peaceably, why should not nobler animals discuss religion? At all events, we soon accept the framework of the fabular, which at least gives Dryden a chance of characterizing the religions. The milk-white Hind, immortal and unchanged, is, of course, Roman Catholicism; the Panther, fairest creature of the spotted kind, is the Anglican Church; we have the bloody Bear, the Independent beast, the buffoon Ape who stands for the atheists, the Calvinistic Wolf who pricks up his predestinating ears, the Baptist Boar who with fat pollutions fills the sacred place, and so on.

The conversation moves vigorously, and has its dramatic moments, as when the Panther threatens the Hind with the gallows: the third part ensconces the two vivid fables within the fable, those of the swallows and of the pigeons, each a beautiful little poem in itself, apart from the political implications. The astonishing thing is that though now and then we encounter some tedious passages of outmoded argumentation, the total impact is poetic rather than philosophical.

The most triumphant of Dryden's other poems were written late in life: the Elegy on Oldham in 1684; that richly baroque picture-frame, the Anne Killigrew Ode in 1686; the Saint Cecilia Ode in 1687; 'Alexander's Feast' in 1697. Though the poems differ enormously, the success of all is due partly to his making words that we do not generally use in great numbers in ordinary speech, sound perfectly natural even when densely packed.

Take some of the lines I have quoted. In prose the words would become turgid, but in Dryden's verse thay have wings:

Sagacious, bold, and turbulent of wit.

or

O sharp convulsive pangs of, agonising pride.

Sometime the commonplace expression jostles the more ceremonius, as in his rendering of *Veni Creator Spiritus*:

Our frailties help, our vice control,
Submit the senses to the soul;
And when rebellious they are grown,
Then lay thy hand, and hold 'em down.

His words are just as forceful as Donne's, of whom he said that he gave us deep thoughts, in common language.

The ideas were not necessarily startling. The lines on Oldham are composed of clichés, or references one might think outworn, and which in anybody else's hands would be jaded: but the result is an acknowledged gem, expressive of just so much emotion, of personal feeling, as the relationship between the two poets required. An altogether different matter is the second Saint Cecilia Ode, 'Alexander's Feast'. Outrageous, one might think, in conception, flaunting in its prosody, verging on the burlesque in its imagery—it has been called 'immortal ragtime'—his contemporaries acclaimed it as his best poem.

Perhaps its most unexpected feat is to bring the rushing, tumultuous movement to the quiet close of:

Let old Timotheus yield the prize,
Or both divide the crown;
He raised a mortal to the skies;
She drew an angel down.

Maybe it was the unexpectedness of the poem, its imaginative originality, that captivated his contemporaries, familiar as they were with the Ode of ten years earlier, far more normally conceived, graceful, sensuous, and conventionally religious in tone. Of his translations there is little room to speak, though they form the great bulk of his work.

His task, he felt, lay in 'the maintaining the character of an author, which distinguishes him from all others'. Yet his own distinctive quality is always there. In a sense, then, these 'paraphrases' become original poems, as is inescapably felt when reading his Lucretius on the fear of death.

A few of his versions, some of Horace, a good deal of Virgil, maintain their place as renderings that are still alive and actual: but translations must inevitably be for their own age, couched in the idiom of their day.

The fashion changes, and they become outmoded, a fate that has inevitably overtaken Dryden's work in this field. But part of his purpose was to make great European literature familiar to the many, and here he succeeded within the limits he set himself. He may not be at the summit of Parnassus, but he is very near it. He was humble enough about it in all conscience. 'I do not know', he is reported to have said, 'if posterity will think me a great poet; they will not be able to deny that I was a good versifier.'

CRITICISM

As with his poetry, most of Dryden's prose is occasional.

The exception is his *Essay of Dramatick Poesy,* a dialogue platonic in its framework and general conduct.

Otherwise it is made up of dedications and prefaces, the former sometimes becoming critical essays, as the latter always are. The dedications we tend to regard as fulsome; they are addressed for the more part to noble patrons, even to royalty, and may seem to us ludicrously, or shamefully, laudatory: but then the dedication was a *genre* of its own, with its laws and traditions.

Nobody—least of all, one imagines, the addressees—took them literally. Dryden's, beautifully phrased, always graceful, sometimes witty, invariably retain a perfect balance, the tribute paid never being wholly undeserved. But they need not detain us here. The prefaces are another matter. They are full of meat, lively, to the point, still of vital interest to any writer who takes his craft seriously.

They are never stiff or pedantic; they border on looseness, for a preface, Dryden held, should be a rambling sort of affair, never wholly in the way, nor ever wholly out of it. No one, Dr. Johnson pronounced, ever found them tedious. Sometimes Dryden attacks; sometimes he defends himself; but for the greater part he is thinking aloud as an artist handling his material.

Dryden, to quote Johnson again, 'may properly be considered as the father of English criticism'. There had, of course, been critics before him, but their approach was sectional, dealing either with philosophic ideas or narrow technique. Dryden not only combined and broadened the two, but was the first critic to define, by practice rather than by precept, what were the important things to talk about. Take, for instance, the *Essay of Dramatick Poesy*. The important things to talk about, then, now, and always, are structure and diction, and his characters talked about them.

We may not go hand in hand with the debaters there; we approach the matter a little differently: but here as everywhere he puts the issues squarely before us, not attempting to dragoon us into one opinion or another. He stimulates our thoughts to make up our own minds; for after all, we are all unalike, and 'our minds are perpetually wrought on by the temperament of our bodies'. So long as he is writing plays, he discusses the drama: but when he engages in other forms he divagates upon those, as satires in *The Original and Progress of Satire*; and when he comes to translation he talks about that, especially when prefacing his *AEneis*. But in his tremendous, easy discourses, those to the various Miscellanies known as *The Preface to Sylvae* (1685), the *Dedication of Examen Poeticum* (1693), and the final *Preface to the Fables*, and others, he tries to get at the heart of the writers he is criticizing.

This seems to come in incidentally, as when he is explaining why he translates various authors in different ways, how he is striving to get at their being before deciding how they would have said in English in the late seventeenth century what they said in their own tongue in their own age. To choose a little at random:

If I am not mistaken, the distinguishing character of Lucretius (I mean of his soul and genius) is a certain kind of noble pride, and positive assertion of his opinions... From this sublime and daring genius of his, it must of necessity come to pass that his thoughts must be masculine, full of argumentation, and that sufficiently warm.

From the same fiery temper proceeds the loftiness of his expressions and the perpetual torrent of his verse, where the barrenness of his subject does not too much constrain the quickness of his fancy...

That is discriminatory criticism; we understand Lucretius: and think also of the implications of Dryden's seemingly casual remarks. Or look at what he says about Chaucer, some of whose work he modernized from his desire to keep him in the tradition of English literature. In his day many judges, including Cowley, regarded Chaucer as 'a dry, old-fashioned wit, not worth reviving', or on the other hand held him in such 'veneration due to his old language... that it [was] little less than profanation and sacrilege to alter it'. But Dryden wanted Chaucer to be read.

As he is the father of English poetry, so I hold him in the same degree of veneration as the Grecians held Homer, or the

Romans Virgil. He is a perpetual fountain of good sense; learned in all sciences; and therefore speaks properly on all subjects: As he knew what he wanted to say, so he knows also when to leave off; a continence which is practised by few writers...

He must have been a man of a most wonderful comprehensive nature, because, as has been truly observed of him, he has taken into the compass of his *Canterbury Tales* the various manners and humours (as we now call them) of the whole English nation in his age... 'tis sufficient to say, according to the old proverb, that here is God's plenty.

He was always eager to pay tribute to his giant predecessors, which is not only part of his humility towards those who have done superbly the task he assigned himself, but proof of his extraordinary judgement. It is easy enough for us to regard Chaucer, Spenser, Shakespeare, Milton, as towering figures; but it was Dryden who first declared they were so. As early as the *Essay of Dramatick Poesy* he could write:

To begin then with Shakespeare. He was the man who of all modern, and perhaps ancient poets, had the largest and most comprehensive soul. All images of Nature were still present to him, and he drew them, not laboriously, but luckily; when he describes any thing, you more than see it, you feel it too. Those who accuse him to have wanted learning, give him the greater commendation: he was naturally learned; he needed not the spectacles of books to read Nature; he looked inwards, and found her there.

There is hardly anything more to be said: but Dryden said it at a time when Shakespeare was dubiously regarded, looked upon as a barbarous author, who did indeed want learning. That he needed trimming Dryden agreed with Ben Jonson in thinking; he also knew that for his plays to be popular they must be infused a little with the sense of the new age; Dryden was the first to appreciate that different ages have different needs.

What is more remarkable still for a practising poet, he could pay homage to a near contemporary working towards different ends by methods other than his own: earliest among critical contemporaries he hailed *Paradise Lost* as 'undoubtedly one of the greatest, most sublime poems which either this age or nation has produced'.

For with his wide comprehensiveness he regarded all literature as one, a gift given to creative writers, but unavoidably a little foreign to the academic mind, intent upon separating, reluctant to believe with Dryden that 'Mankind is ever the same, and nothing lost out of Nature, though every thing is altered'. And throughout he reveals a superb common sense, in itself amounting to genius: he never allows an idea to rush him into extravagance; he merely sets forth his own at the time.

'I have only laid down,' he ends *The Author's Apology for Heroic Poetry and Poetic Licence,* 'and that superficially enough, my present thoughts; and shall be glad to be taught better by those who pretend to reform our poetry.' He does not presume to constrict anything so fluid, so *divers et ondoyant* as the great human activity of literature into rigid compartments, emaciating by definitions, strangling by categories. For after all—from the same essay—

'they wholly mistake the nature of criticism who think its business is principally to find fault. Criticism... was meant a standard of judging well; the chiefest part of which is, to observe those excellencies which should delight a reasonable reader.'

It is perhaps natural that the picture most of us have of Dryden should be that of the Monarch of Will's Coffee House, the old giant surrounded by the lesser fry and the young aspirants, for that is the best documented. It slips us too easily that he spent the larger proportion of his life in the country, to which he was devoted, especially where fishing was to be had, and that his most taking epistle is the Horatian one to his kinsman John Driden in praise of the rural pieties.

We forget earlier struggles, the squabbles with Howard and with Settle, and, properly, the gossip, unsubstantiated as it is, about his private life. The best portrait is that sketched by his young friend Congreve, whom he praised, we may think, beyond his merit, as he certainly did Addison. He was of a nature exceedingly humane and compassionate, ready to forgive injuries, and capable of a sincere reconciliation with those that had offended him. His friendship, where he professed it, went beyond his professions. He was of very pleasing access; but somewhat slow, and, as it were, diffident in his advances to others... He was extremely ready and gentle in his correction of the errors of any writer who thought fit to consult him, and full as ready and patient to admit of the reprehension of others, in respect of his own oversights and mistakes.

But his last years were far from placid. Battered by political circumstance, without hope of quiet leisure, condemned to write more and more to sustain his mentally deranged wife and his ailing son; he 'felt impelled to write:

What Virgil wrote in the vigour of his age, in plenty and at ease, I have undertaken to translate in my declining years; struggling with wants, oppressed by sickness, curbed in my genius, liable to be misconstrued in all I write; and my judges, if they are not very equitable, already prejudiced against me by the lying character which has been given them of my morals. Yet steady to my principles, and not dispirited by my afflictions, I have by the blessing of God on my endeavours, overcome all difficulties, and, in some measure, acquitted myself of the debt which I owed the public when I undertook this work.

Sanity, balance, these marked him to the last, and the zest which eabled him when nearly seventy, to brush off his forehead with a gesture of magnificent assurance such petty rivals as Milbourne and Blackmore, while with splendid dignity firmly drawing the limit of his error in the matter of the obscenity with which Collier had charged him. The non-juring parson had attacked him in his notorious *Short View of the Stage*, and though Dryden pleads guilty to the use of certain expressions, he asserts that Collier has traduced him:

Besides that, he is too much given to horse-play in his raillery: and comes to battle, like a dictator from the plough. I will not say, the Zeal of God's House has eaten him up; but I am sure it has devoured some part of his good manners and civility.

This might imply little were it not coupled with the homage he was always ready to pay to those who do things well, as good craftsmen, or good poets. One of the engaging things about him is the absence of rancour against the younger generation that would tread him down.

In thinking of Dryden it is a sense of overall greatness that remains; he is the superb all-round man. His influence has been enormous, but this is always a difficult matter to assess. It does, however, seem to be undoubted that he made the Ode live on as an English form, which he made shapely rather than formalized.

It is certain that his Saint Cecilia Odes, 'Anne Killigrew', and perhaps others, prepared the ground for the odes of Collins and Gray, and made possible Wordsworth's 'Immortality Ode' (which Dryden would have disliked for its imprecision) and the 'Ode to Duty'.

By his example he sustained the variety of the lyric, and without him, for better or for worse, eighteenth-century poetry would have been very different from what it is: to begin with, one may say, No Dryden, no Pope', with all that that involves. It may be noted further that poets have turned to him in their distress, as Keats began to do when he found that Milton failed him. Craftsmen in poetry—that is to say good poets—even now are not slow to salute him; and those of us who venture upon the other harmony find ourselves echoing Matthew Arnold:

'Here at last we have the true English prose, a prose such as we would all gladly use if only we knew how.'

Chapter 2

The Restoration Dramatist

In the history of the drama Dryden occupies a peculiar place. He had no great genius for the theater, and yet he imposed his ideas upon the English play-going world. He was that unusual product, a politician with a poetical mind. For a time he was attached to the Puritans, and wrote an ode on the death of Cromwell; but, on the accession of Charles, he found no difficulty in transferring his muse to the royalist party. Towards the end of his stormy life he became a Roman Catholic.

Soon after the accession of William and Mary, the queen, as a mark of honor to the poet, ordered a performance of *The Spanish Fryar*, one of his best comedies. Among his last writings is rather an apologetic answer to Jeremy Collier's attack upon the stage. He died in May, 1700, and was buried in Westminster Abbey in the grave of Chaucer. He bequeathed his "dramatic laurels" to William Congreve.

Although Dryden began his career as a playwright with the production of two or three comedies, yet it was in heroic drama that he achieved his great popularity. A brother-in-law, Sir Robert Howard, wrote a play called *The Indian Queen*, which had an absurd plot with a picturesque setting. Dryden assisted in its revision; and its success was such as to encourage him to write a sequel, *The Indian Imperor, or the Conquest of Mexico by the Spaniards*, which took the stage by storm.

Later came *The Conquest of Granada*, in two parts with five acts each, the scene laid in unknown regions, and the story full of intrigues, battles, bull fights, revenge, ghosts and murders. Three distinct love affairs are threaded together.

Another piece of this type, *Tyrannick Love,* has for its subject the persecution of the Christians by the Emperor Maximin and the sufferings of Saint Catherine.

Dryden tried his hand at opera, one of his efforts being the arrangement of Milton's *Paradise Lost* for a musical setting. Some of this work was composed by the celebrated Englishman, Henry Purcell. Dryden and Davenant together re-wrote *The Tempest,* giving Caliban and Ariel each a sister for some unknown reason.

Romeo and Juliet, revised by Dryden and his brother-in-law James Howard, had a happy ending, and was performed on alternate nights with the original play. In *All for Love, or the World Well Lost,* a revision of Shakespeare's *Antony and Cleopatra,* Dryden abandoned the heroic couplet and used blank verse; he also reconstructed the original play in such a way as to make it conform to the three unities. About 1678 he gave up the use of the heroic couplet altogether. His version of *Oedipus,* in collaboration with Nathaniel Lee, was too ghastly and horrible for stage production, even in those days of strong nerves.

Dryden's influence was greater than would be thought possible from a study of any one of his dramas. As a playwright he did not consider himself wholly a success, and expressed his dislike and contempt of the stage more than once. Of certain of his plays he said, "I knew they were bad enough to please, even when I wrote them." He had no sense of the ridiculous, nor any conception of a natural, sincere portrayal of human nature. Ranting and absurd imagery often lie beside passages of real beauty.

Dr. Johnson described his style as a "false magnificence." One comedy, *The Spanish Fryar,* and one tragedy, *All for Love,* deserve to be remembered. Far more interesting than the plays, however, are Dryden's discussions of dramatic questions. Like George Bernard Shaw, he had the habit of writing long prefaces and comments as an accompaniment to the text. In these dissertations are to be found many sound principles, including the idea that dramatic rules should be deduced from a study of plays rather than from abstract speculation.

John Dryden, an English poet and dramatist who would dominate literary efforts of The Restoration, was born on August 19, 1631, in Aldwinkle, Northamptonshire, England. He received a classical education at Westminster School and Trinity College, Cambridge, then moved to London in 1657 to commence his career as a professional writer. His first play, *The Wild Gallant* (1663), was a failure when first presented, but Dryden soon found more success with *The Indian Queen* (1664) which he co-authored with Sir Robert Howard and which served as his initial attempt to found a new theatrical genre, the heroic tragedy.

Although George Villiers' *The Rehearsal*, a vicious satire of heroic tragedy, brought a quick end to the form, Dryden still managed to produce a number of successful works in this genre including *The Indian Emperor* (1665) and *Secret Love* (1667) which mixed heroic tragedy with contemporary comedy.

The young playwright's reputation grew quickly, and in 1668, only ten years after his move to London, Dryden was appointed Poet Laureate of England. (He was later stripped of the title because of religious differences when William and Mary came into power.) That same year, he agreed to write exclusively for Thomas Killigrew's theatrical company and became a shareholder.

Both his first offering, *Tyrannick Love* (1669), and his successful follow-up, *The Conquest of Granada by the Spaniards* (1670), are examples of heroic tragedy. In 1672, however, perhaps sensing the demise of his short-lived genre, Dryden turned his hand to comedy and produced *Marriage A-la-Mode*, a brilliant battle of the sexes.

Dryden's relationship with Killigrew's company continued until 1678 at which point he broke with the theatre (which was floundering in debt) and offered his latest play, *Oedipus*, a drama he had co-authored with Nathaniel Lee, to another company.

In his later years, Dryden turned to poetry and solidified his reputation as the leading writer of the day with such masterpieces as *Absalom and Achitophel*. However, he continued to write for the theatre, producing such plays as *Don Sebastian*

(1689), the story of a king who abdicates his throne after discovering that he has committed incest, and *Amphitryon* (1690), a brilliant retelling of the classic myth. He also adapted a number of Shakespeare's plays icluding *The Tempest* and *All for Love* (1677), a retelling of *Antony and Cleopatra.* In addition, he wrote the libretto for several operas including *The State of Innocence* (1677) (an adaptation of Milton's *Paradise Lost*) and *King Arthur* (1691) with music by Purcell.

John Dryden died in London on May 12, 1700, and was buried in Westminster Abbey next to Chaucer. He left behind almost 30 works for the stage as well as a major critical study (*An Essay on Dramatic Poesy*) and a number of translations including the works of Virgil.

Then came the gallant protest of the Restoration, when Wycherley and his successors in drama commenced to write of contemporary life in much the spirit of modern musical comedy.... A new style of comedy was improvised, which, for lack of a better term, we may agree to call the comedy of Gallantry, and which Etherege, Shadwell, and Davenant, and Crowne, and Wycherley, and divers others, labored painstakingly to perfect.

They probably exercised to the full reach of their powers when they hammered into grossness their too fine witticisms just smuggled out of France, mixed them with additional breaches of decorum, and divided the results into five acts. For Gallantry, it must be repeated, was yet in its crude youth.... For Wycherley and his confreres were the first Englishmen to depict mankind as leading an existence with no moral outcome. It was their sorry distinction to be the first of English authors to present a world of unscrupulous persons who entertained no special prejudices, one way or the other, as touched ethical matters."

From 1642 onward for eighteen years, the theaters of England remained nominally closed. There was of course evasion of the law; but whatever performances were offered had to be given in secrecy, before small companies in private houses, or in taverns located three or four miles out of town. No actor or spectator was safe, especially during the early days of the Puritan rule. Least of all was there any inspiration for dramatists. In 1660 the Stuart dynasty was restored to the throne of England. Charles II, the king, had been in France during the greater part of the Protectorate, together with many of the royalist party, all of whom were familiar with Paris and its fashions.

Thus it was natural, upon the return of the court, that French influence should be felt, particularly in the theater. In August, 1660, Charles issued patents for two companies of players, and performances immediately began. Certain writers, in the field before the civil war, survived the period of theatrical eclipse, and now had their chance. Among these were Thomas Killigrew and William Davenant, who were quickly provided with fine playhouses.

APPEARANCE OF WOMEN ON THE ENGLISH STAGE

It will be remembered that great indignation was aroused among the English by the appearance of French actresses in 1629. London must have learned to accept this innovation, however, for in one of the semi-private entertainments given during the Protectorate at Rutland House, the actress Mrs. Coleman took the principal part.

The Siege of Rhodes, a huge spectacle designed by Davenant in 1656 (arranged in part with a view of evading the restrictions against theatrical plays) is generally noted as marking the entrance of women upon the English stage. It is also remembered for its use of movable machinery, which was something of an innovation. The panorama of *The Siege* offered five changes of scene, presenting "the fleet of Solyman the Magnificent, his army, the Island of Rhodes, and the varieties attending the siege of the city."

DISAPPEARANCE OF NATIONAL TYPES

By the time the theaters were reopened in England, Corneille and Racine in France had established the neo-classic standard for tragedy, and Molière was in the full tide of his success. These playwrights, with Quinault and others, for a time supplied the English with plots. The first French opera, *Cadmus and Hermione,* by Lully and Quinault, performed in Paris in 1673, crossed the channel almost immediately, influencing Dryden in his attempts at opera.

The romantic, semi-historical romances of Madame Scudéry and the Countess de la Fayette afforded a second supply of story material, while Spanish plays and tales opened up still another. Sometimes the plots of Calderón or Lope de Vega came to the English at second-hand through French versions.

Whatever the case, it was now evident that the national type of play had ceased to be written. From this time on every European nation was influence by, and exerted an influence upon, the drama of every other nation. Characters, situations, plots, themes—these things traveled from country to country, always modifying and sometimes supplanting the home product.

PERSISTENCE OF ELIZABETHAN PLAYS

With this influx of foreign drama, there was still a steady production of the masterpieces of the Elizabethan and Jacobean periods. The diarist Samuel Pepys, an ardent lover of the theater, relates that during the first three years after the opening of the playhouses he saw *Othello, Henry IV, A Midsummer Night's Dream,* two plays by Ben Jonson, and others by Beaumont, Fletcher, Middleton, Shirley, and Massinger. It must have been about this time that the practice of "improving" Shakespeare was begun, and his plays were often altered so as to be almost beyond recognition.

From the time of the Restoration actors and managers, also dramatists, were good royalists; and new pieces, or refurbished old ones, were likely to acquire a political slant. The Puritans were satirized, the monarch and his wishes were flattered, and the royal order thoroughly supported by the people of the stage. Richard Boyle, Earl of Orrery (1621-1679), seems to have the doubtful glory of re-introducing the use of rhymed verse. Boyle was a statesman, as well as a soldier and a dramatist. During the ten years or so following the Restoration, he wrote at least four tragedies on historical or legendary subjects, using the ten-syllabled rhymed couplet which (at the moment) he borrowed from France. It runs like this:

"Reason's a staff for age, when nature's gone;
But youth is strong enough to walk alone."

No more stilted sort of verse could well be contrived for dialogue. Monotonous as well as prosy, it was well suited to Orrery's plots. He took a semi-historical story, filled it with bombastic sentiments and strutting figures, producing what was known as "heroic drama." Dryden, who identified himself with this type of play, described it as concerned not with probabilities but with love and valor.

A good heroic play is exciting, with perpetual bustle and commotion. The characters are extricated out of their amazing situations only by violence. Deaths are numerous. The more remote and unfamiliar the setting the better; and the speech should be suited to the action: hence the "heroic couplet." Pepys saw *Guzman*, by Orrery, and with his engaging frankness said it was as mean a thing as had been seen on the stage for a great while.

PARODY OF HEROIC DRAMA

Other writers, Davenant, Etherege, and Sir Robert Howard, had also produced specimens of heroic plays, and by the time *The Conquest of Granada* reached the stage these clever gentlemen had grown tired of the species. Compared to Dryden they were nobodies in the literary world; but among them they contrived a hilarious burlesque called *The Rehearsal*, in which these showy but shallow productions were smartly ridiculed.

Dryden is represented as Bayes (in reference to his position as poet laureate), and his peculiarities of speech and plot are amusingly derided. Though *The Rehearsal* was condemned as "scurrilous and ill-bred," yet it served a useful turn in puncturing an empty and overblown style.

NATURE OF RESTORATION COMEDY

In almost every important respect, Restoration drama

was far inferior to the Elizabethan. Where the earlier playwrights created powerful and original characters, the Restoration writers were content to portray repeatedly a few artificial types; where the former were imaginative, the latter were clever and ingenious. The Elizabethan dramatists were steeped in poetry, the later ones in the sophistication of the fashionable world.

The drama of Wycherley and Congreve was the reflection of a small section of life, and it was like life in the same sense that the mirage is like the oasis. It had polish, an edge, a perfection in its own field; but both its perfection and its naughtiness now seem unreal. The heroes of the Restoration comedies were lively gentlemen of the city, profligates and loose livers, with a strong tendency to make love to their neighbors' wives. Husbands and fathers were dull, stupid creatures.

The heroines, for the most part, were lovely and pert, too frail for any purpose beyond the glittering tinsel in which they were clothed. Their companions were busybodies and gossips, amorous widows or jealous wives. The intrigues which occupy them are not, on the whole, of so low a nature as those depicted in the Italian court comedies; but still they are sufficiently coarse. Over all the action is the gloss of superficial good breeding and social ease.

Only rarely do these creatures betray the traits of sympathy, faithfulness, kindness, honesty, or loyalty. They follow a life of pleasure, bored, but yawning behind a delicate fan or a kerchief of lace. Millamant and Mirabell, in Congreve's *Way of the World*, are among the most charming of these Watteau figures.

Everywhere in the Restoration plays are traces of European influence. *The Plain Dealer* of Wycherley was an English version of *The Misanthrope* of Molière; and there are many admirable qualities in the French play which are lacking in the English. *The Double Dealer* recalls scenes from *The Learned Ladies (Les femmes savantes)*; and Mr. Bluffe, in *The Old Bachelor*, is none other than our old friend Miles Gloriosus, who has traveled through Latin, Italian and French comedy.

The national taste was coming into harmony, to a considerable extent, with the standards of Europe. Eccentricities were curbed; ideas, characters, and story material were interchanged. The plays, however, were not often mere imitations; in the majority of them there is original observation and independence of thought. It was this drama that kept the doors of the theater open and the love of the theater alive in the face of great public opposition.

WOMEN PLAYWRIGHTS

Soon after the Restoration women began to appear as writers of drama. Mrs. Aphra Behn (1640-1689) was one of the first and most industrious of English women playwrights. Her family name was Amis (some writers say Johnson). As the wife of a wealthy Dutch merchant she lived for some time in Surinam (British Guiana). Her novel, *Oroonooko,* furnished Southerne with the plot for a play of the same name. After the death of her husband, Mrs. Behn was for a time employed by the British government in a political capacity.

She was the author of eighteen plays, most of them highly successful and fully as indecent as any by Wycherley or Vanbrugh. Mrs. Manly and Mrs. Susannah Centlivre, both of whom lived until well into the eighteenth century, also achieved success as playwrights. The adaptations from the French, made by Mrs. Centlivre, were very popular and keep the stage for nearly a century.

COLLIER'S ATTACK ON THE STAGE

Although the Puritans had lost their dominance as a political power, yet they had not lost courage in abusing the stage. The most violent attack was made by the clergyman Jeremy Collier in 1698, in a pamphlet called *A Short View of the Immorality and Profaneness of the English Stage,* in which he denounced not only Congreve and Vanbrugh, but Shakespeare and most of the Elizabethans.

Three points especially drew forth his denunciations: the so-called lewdness of the plays, the frequent references to the Bible and biblical characters, and the criticism, slander and abuse flung from the stage upon the clergy. He would not have any Desdemona, however chaste, show her love before the footlights; he would allow no reference in a comedy to anything connected with the Church or religion; and especially would he prohibit any portrayal of the clergy. Next to the men in holy orders, Collier had a tender heart for the nobility.

He said in effect that if any ridicule or satire were to be indulged in, it should be against persons of low quality. To call a duke a rascal on the stage was far worse than to apply such an epithet to plain Hodge, almost as libellous as to represent a clergyman as a hypocrite.

Collier made the curiously stupid error of accusing the playwrights of glorifying all the sins, passions, or peculiarities which they portrayed in their characters. He had no understanding of the point of view of the literary artist, nor any desire to understand it.

Collier's attack, unjust as it was, and foolish as certain phases of it appear today, yet it made an impression. The king, James II, was so wrought up over it that he issued a solemn proclamation "against vice and profaneness." Congreve and Vanbrugh, together with other writers, were persecuted, and fines were imposed on some of the most popular actors and actresses.

Dryden, Congreve and Vanbrugh made an attempt at a justification of the stage, but it did little good. D'Urfey, Dennis, and others entered the controversy, which raged for many years. The public buzzed with the scandal set forth in *The Short View,* but did not stay away altogether from the playhouses. The poets answered the attack not by reformation, but by new plays in which the laughter, the satire, and the ridicule were turned upon their enemies.

Chapter 3

The Just and the Lively

The title of Michael Werth Gelber's book is drawn from John Dryden's working definition of a play in An Essay of Dramatick Poesie, published in 1667, in which he describes a play as ideally encompassing "A just and lively Image of Humane Nature, representing its Passions and Humours, and the Changes of Fortune to which it is subject; for the Delight and Instruction of Mankind" (Works of John Dryden, 17:15).

Gelber traces this critical formula through John Dryden's dramatic criticism, focusing on "Dryden's abiding attempt to reconcile opposing strains in literature (the just and the lively), along with the mental faculties (judgment and imagination) in which they originate".

The "just" and the "lively" soon double for a variety of competing aesthetic claims and literary traditions. At different points in Gelber's study, the "just" and the "lively" embody the rival claims of (Jonsonian) critical judgment and (Shakespearean) imagination, Jonsonian humours comedy and Shakespearean romance, continental French classicism and native English tragicomedy, the classical unities and the centrifugal romance plot, reason and passion, plot and character, among others.

It bears recalling that Lisideius volunteers his "rude Notion" (Works, 17: 14) of a play in Dramatick Poesie only after some prompting by the other speakers and that he emphasizes that his definition is being offered in the spirit of intellectual inquiry that governs their debate. The "just" and the "lively" are understood by the company to be provisional terms, just as the quickly-limned definition of a play is itself, as Crites is quick to point out, "a genere & fine, and so not altogether perfect" (Works, 17:15). In proposing this single pair of terms as the foundation for his reading of Dryden's extensive and wide-ranging body of criticism, Michael Gelber may assign them more freight than they can reasonably bear.

Gelber argues that Dryden's criticism is a coherent body of work written in three distinct periods, each correlating not only to a stable, if ultimately provisional, authorial identity but to a different stage in Dryden's thinking about the competing claims of judgment and imagination.

Dryden thus begins as a courtier, ingratiating himself with the aristocratic dedicatees of his works, before the appointment as Poet Laureate in 1668 allows him to re-present himself as a professional writer; in the final transformation of the chrysalis, after 1680, "he assumes the mantle of an authoritative teacher of literary subjects,... above and beyond all controversy: he has become a man of letters".

This approach usefully challenges the view that the value of Dryden's criticism is compromised by his partisan investments in the controversies of the moment. However, Gelber's reading fails in many instances to reflect the tonal complexities of Dryden's voice in his essays or the fluctuations in his critical stances, in part because Gelber applies his chronological schema to Dryden's career as a writer between 1664 and 1700 too dogmatically.

Stephen N. Zwicker's convincing account in Politics and Language in Dryden's Poetry: The Arts of Disguise (1984) of John Dryden's keen awareness of his embattled circumstances in the 1690s, after his ouster in the wake of the Glorious Revolution from the offices of historiographer royal and the laureateship he had held in pre-Williamite England, runs counter to Gelber's emphasis on Dryden's serene confidence in his final years.

The centerpiece of Gelber's book is his revisionist interpretation of Dramatick Poesie. Gelber argues that readers have been misled into thinking the dialogic structure of Dryden's essay mirrors—and subtly advocates—its humanist investments in the ideal of "Gentlemen, [disputing] with candour and civility" (Works, 17:6) literary topics of shared interest. In his view, only Neander's perspective is convincing; the other speakers "argue, by inadvertence, against [themselves]", since Dryden's strategy is to advance a "manifesto" under the guise of a dialogue.

One wonders, in the light of Gelber's insistence that the first three speakers are "forced to espouse arguments that, in the end, destroy their respective positions and pave the way, inexorably, for the victory of Neander", why he is not troubled by the apparent inconsistency of predicating his own study on Lisideius's definition of a play.

Gelber underscores an insight that has long been recognized in Dryden studies—that Neander most closely approximates Dryden's perspective in the essay and may be given the superior arguments—but he overstates the case.

Ultimately, Dryden is exposed as an antitheatricalist on the basis of Neander's lengthy discourses, which parody the declamatory style of continental drama, making Dryden's elected spokesperson the object of the author's covert ridicule: "The Essay carries distaste for dramatic representation as far as it can go. Dryden's dialogue is a French play reduced to absurdity", Gelber writes.

The credibility of many of Gelber's claims is vitiated by this kind of overstatement, which often reworks a truism—"John Dryden is the father of English literary criticism" —into a farfetched claim: "Like many fathers, even the best of them, either he suffers neglect or he is misunderstood and severely condemned".

The quality of critical analysis in The Just and the Lively is, unfortunately, uneven. In responding to a complex passage on translation in the 1685 Preface to Sylvae, for example, Gelber points out that Dryden "writes (and translates) as if he were the dead poet's alter-ego or reincarnated other self". This is a penetrating insight that could be developed into a discussion of the uncanny intertextuality Dryden celebrated in theorizing the reception of one poet's creative work by another.

Even when as a translator he expands on his original source, Dryden asserts in the Preface to Sylvae, "I desire the false Criticks wou'd not always think that those thoughts are wholly mine, but that either they are secretly in the Poet, or may be fairly deduc'd from him: or at least, if both those considerations should fail, that my own is of a piece with his, and that if he were living, and an Englishman, they are such, as he wou'd probably have written" (Works, 3:4).

Gelber quotes this seminal formulation of Dryden's theory of translation and reception, and then adds this reductive gloss: "He adds as and where he likes. He includes any paraphrase that will make the ancient poem a thoroughly modern one". Literary historians, classicists, and other scholars invested in understanding Dryden's theories of translation may discover their critical flash point at such junctures in Gelber's book. Robert D. Hume's classic, Dryden's Criticism, was published some thirty years ago, in 1970.

While Dryden scholars, among them James Anderson Winn, Edward Pechter, and Cedric Reverand II have explored aspects of Dryden's literary criticism in the intervening decades in important books and essays, Gelber's project identifies an area in Dryden studies that needs revisiting, and his approach, both chronological and systematic, seems in theory a promising one. If The lust and the Lively is not the book it might have been, but an opportunity lost, it is owing to Michael Gelber's repudiation of most prior scholarship in the field.

His bibliography is thorough and comprehensive, and his notes run to 47 densely-argued pages; but the rhetorical stance Gelber takes toward other Dryden scholars is so combative and dismissive that his work seems unlikely to win many converts.

In his extraordinary Introduction, Gelber explains his rationale for relegating to the endnotes his "disputation with those other scholars whose views would in advance prove me wrong and with whom I disagree categorically... Upon my coadjutors, both those with whom I agree (more or less) and those with whom I clearly disagree, I have chosen on the whole to avoid direct comment in the text.... It would have been, I believe, an act of violent and tedious supererogation".

At the risk of being brusque, enough said. The community of scholars who have elucidated John Dryden's work in recent decades will hardly warm to Gelber's fighting words.

As to the unities, Dryden has merely laid down "some opinions of the ancients and moderns," together with some of his own. The argument is rather conventional, based, with frequent invocations of the goddess of Reason, on the law of imitation.

The chief significance of this essay lies in the fact that it places Dryden definitely before us as the defender of the reigning modes. Sir Robert Howard, a champion of the old English dramatic traditions, has defended blank verse and utmost liberty in the structure of plots; Dryden exerts all his skill in the defense of rime and the unities.

His authorities are Virgil (mentioned as the only perfect poet), Jonson ("in judgment above all other poets"), the ancients, especially Aristotle and Horace (whom he" will still think as wise as those who so confidently correct them"), and Corneille.

This array of authorities alone, taken in connection with the apparent humility with which Dryden is willing to submit to them, would be sufficient to show how complete has been his change of heart since the writing of the Essay itself. It is especially noticeable that the thoro-going good-sense which gave tone to the dedication of Annus Iirabilis has already been perverted. Dryden is here using the logical methods of the rationalist to defend a sort of play as irrational as can be imagined.

The preface to An Evening's Love, or the Mock Astrologer Q (1668) shows how Dryden's conformity and his resulting popularity even thus early began to colour his opinion of the Elizabethans. According to his opening statement he originally intended to discuss in this preface the difference between the plays of his age and those of his predecessors on the English stage, and also the improvement of the language since Fletcher's and Jonson's day: intentions which he is to carry out in The Defense of the Epilog.

But eventhough he has given over for the present the idea

of treating systematically the superiority of his own time, the feeling of this superiority is so strong upon him that it will not be smothered. Ben Jonson comes off pretty well: "But Ben Jonson is to be admired for his many excellencies; and can be taxed with fewer failings than any English poet. I know I have been accused as an enemy of his writings; but without any other reason than that I do not admire him blindly, and without looking into his imperfections.

For why should he alone be exempted from those frailties, from which Homer and Virgil are not free? Or why should there be any Ipse dixit in our poetry, any more than in our philosophy? I admire and applaud him where I ought: those who do more, do but value themselves in their admiration of him; and, by telling you they extol Ben Jonson's way, will insinuate to you that they can practise it. For my part, I declare that I want judgment to imitate him; and should think it a great impudence in myself to attempt it.

To make men appear pleasantly ridiculous on the stage, was, as I have said, his talent; and in this he needed not the acumen of wit but that of judgment. For the characters and representations of folly are only the effects of observation; and observation is an effect of judgment."

This is merely patronizing, but when he comes to Shakespe are and Fletcher our author assumes quite a different tone: " I think there is no folly so great in any poet of our age, as the superfluity and waste of wit was in some of our predecessors: particularly we may say of Fletcher and of Shakespeare, what was said of Ovid, in omni ejus ingenio facilius quod rejici, quam quod adjioi potest, invenies.

The contrary of which was true in Virgil and our incomparable Jonson."In answer to the charge of plagiarism Dryden modestly refers to King Charles, who has lately remarked that he wishes others would steal him such plays as Dryden's: but his real defense is an analysis of the poet's work, in which he proves that the mere outline which an author can steal is but a small part of a play.

This analysis is very like the one which we examined in the preface to Annus Mirabilis, but its conclusion seems worth quoting: "But in general, the employment of a poet is like that of a curious gunsmith, or watchmaker; the iron or silver is not his own; but they are the least part of that which gives the value: the price lies wholly in the workmanship."

It would hardly be fair to hold Dryden responsible for all the implications of this mechanical figure; but it is surely significant of his general state of mind. This preface distinctly foreshadows the Defense of the Epilog (1672), with its sharp arraignment of the faults of Shakespeare. That is a significant sentence in which Dryden connects philosophy and poetry: "Or why should there be any Ipse dixit in our poetry, any more than in our philosophy?"

He has lost faith in the traditions which called forth the enthusiasm of his youth, but, like the English philosophers of his time, he has abundant confidence in the principles and methods of the present. In the critical works just examined Dryden shows that he has been for some time revolving in his mind the various aspects of the heroic drama, and, as one is thus led to expect, it is in plays of the heroic type that the dramatic activity of the period finally culminates.

The first of these is Tyrannic Love, or the Royal Martyr (1669). Dryden begins his preface to this drama: " I was moved to write this play by many reasons: amongst the others, the commands of some persons of honor, for whom I have a most particular respect, were daily sounding in my ears, that it would be of good example to undertake a poem of this nature. Neither was my own inclination wanting to second their desires."

The drama which was thus written at the suggestion of "some persons of honor" presents most of the features of a typical heroic play: a rather colorless heroine of irreproachable character, a fine code of honor, and a warrior who storms against gods and men. In accordance with Dryden's theories it exhibits, also, miracles, guardian angels, and spirits of divers descriptions.

But Maximin, the fearless warrior, is villain rather than hero, and in the end the play is an apotheosis of Christian faith rather than of romantic courage. It is in the two parts of The

Conquest of Granada (1670) that the English heroic type reaches its culmination. Here we have the all-conquering hero who whistles fortune after him, makes and unmakes kings, single-handed disperses armies, and, quite contrary to Restoration standards, loves with a nice regard for an extremely conventional code of honor. The other chief characters, the villains, merely male and female devils, and the heroine, spotlessly insipid, are mere abstractions.

There are no lights or shades; all the actions are either miraculously heroic or unspeakably heinous. It is really a complete order of things that we have before us here; no one acts or talks like a person in the real world, but, under the conditions of this artificial universe, all is consistent. Every character does what is expected of him, and the whole scheme of things makes it possible to carry out a plot which any relation to reality would render impossible.

The polish versification merely gives a fitting exterior to this material. But what I wish to emphasize is the fact that this whole make-believe universe is a glorification of royalty and nobility. At this time the king and his court are attempting to maintain their position, especially to assert their supremacy over "the town."

Thus it may readily be understood how a stage world in which their superiority over the common herd is a fundamental principle, and throughout which is maintained the elevation of thought and conduct to which they lay claim, is as incense in their nostrils. Nothing else could have been so suitable for the entertaining of "a noble audience." This period reached its dramatic and critical climaxes in the same volume: with the two parts of The Conquest of Granada were published in 1672 an essay Of Heroic Plays and the Defense of the Epilog.

The first of these, Dry den's chief apology for a type of literature to which he devoted some of his most ambitious efforts and for which he was the accepted sponsor, begins in a tone of triumph: "Whether heroic verse ought to be admitted into serious plays, is not now to be disputed: it is already in possession of the stage; and I dare confidently affirm that very few tragedies, in this age, shall be received without it.

Then, after repeating an argument for rime which we have already heard in the Defense of an Essay of Dramatic Poesy, he goes on to relate the history of the heroic play: during the time when plays were prohibited in England Sir William Davenant introduced from Italy " examples of moral virtue, writ in verse and performed in recitative music; "after the Restoration these entertainments developed into heroic plays.

But, according to Dry den, Davenant's plays lacked fulness of plot and variety of characters, and something might have been added to the beauty of the style. Here Dry den begins with becoming modesty, to give an account of what he himself has performed. Whereas Davenant took his image of a heroic poem from the drama, Dryden derived his ideal of a heroic drama from the heroic poem. Therefore, it seemed to our author, he was the first to give epic dignity to the heroic play.

The inspiration of our author's innovations, he tells us, came from a passage of Ariosto's: "*Le donne, i cavalier, l'arme, gli amori, Le cortesie, l'audaci imprese io canto.*" The ministry of gods as well as of disembodied spirits and the performance of deeds of valor by heroes has always been allowed in heroic poetry, and is, therefore, essential to the heroic play. A detailed account of this essay is unnecessary: it exhibits an exceptional unity of principle.

The heroic play in all its attributes is defended on the basis of the theory of idealization: everything is to be heightened; or, to use Dryden's own figure, we are to fly rather than walk. At first thought this essay may seem to stand in direct contradiction to the preface of An Evening's Love. In the preface of 1671 we saw Dryden the cool champion of moderation; and now, in 1672, he is defending excesses which seemed ridiculous even to many of his contemporaries.

The apparent anomaly becomes intelligible if we remember that in both, as also in the Defense of an Essay of Dramatic Poesy, Dryden is defending at once himself and the literary fashions of the day. There is a tone almost domineering in the concluding sentence of the essay Of Heroic Plays: " But I have already swept the stakes; and, with the good fortune of prosperous gamesters, can be, content to sit quietly; to hear my fortune cursed by some, and my faults arraigned by others, and to suffer both without reply."

In the Defense of the Epilog 2 Dryden avowedly sets out to examine the works of his predecessors on the English stage. A passage from the opening paragraph will serve to show the temper of the entire essay. After explaining that he feels obliged to defend the epilog in which he has taxed " the former writing " Dryden fortifies himself against misinterpretation:

"Yet I would so maintain my opinion of the present age, as not to be wanting in my veneration for the past: I would ascribe to dead authors their just praises in those things wherein they have excelled us; and in those wherein we contend with them for the preeminence, I would acknowledge our advantage to the age, and claim

Following are the essential parts of this epilog:

"They, who have best succeeded on the stage,
Have still conformed their genius to the age.
Thus Jonson did mechanic humor show,
When men were dull, and conversation low.
Then, Comedy was faultless, but 'twas coarse:
Cobb's tankard was a jest, and Otter's horse.
And, as their Comedy, their love was mean;
Except, by chance, in some one labored scene,
Which must atone for an ill-written play:
They rose, but at their height could seldom stay.
Fame then was cheap, and the first comer sped;
And they have kept it since by being dead.
If Love and Honor now are higher rais'd
'Tis not the poet but the age is prais'd.
Wit's now arrived to a more high degree;
Our native language more refined and free.
Our ladies and our men now speak more wit
In conversation, than those poets writ."
no victory from our wit.

This being what I have proposed to myself, I hope I shall not be thought arrogant when I inquire into their errors. For we live in an age so sceptical, that as it determines little, so it takes nothing from antiquity on trust; and I confess to have no other ambition in this essay, than that poetry may not go backward, when all other arts and sciences are advancing." And a little later Dryden adds, on the authority of Horace, "that antiquity alone is no plea for the excellency of a poem."

Here again our author brings together philosophy and poetry; the literature of the former age is to be examined sceptically, coldly, in the manner of contemporaneous English philosophy; there are to be no fond enthusiasms here.

Very methodically Dryden goes about his exposition: first he will show that since the age of Shakespeare and Fletcher there has been "an improvement of our wit, language and conversation; or an alteration in them for the better." Improper words and phrases have been dropped. There is to be found some solecism of speech or notorious flaw in sense in every page of Shakespeare or Fletcher.

The times were ignorant wherein they wrote; witness the lameness of their plots; Fletcher understood not correct plotting or the decorum of the stage. "But these absurdities, which those poets committed, may more properly be called the age's faults than theirs; for, besides the want of education and learning (which was their particular unhappiness), they wanted the benefit of converse."

Poor Ben Jonson's linguistic sins are dragged to light till our author grows weary of his task: "And what correctness, after this, can be expected from Shakespeare or from Fletcher, who wanted that learning and care which Jonson had?" Besides rejecting improper words and phrases, continues Dryden, it is obvious that we have admitted many good ones, some of which we wanted, others of which are rather ornamental than necessary.

Our tongue has been beautified by Shakespeare, Fletcher, Jonson, Suckling, and Waller. In addition to refinement of speech there has been a refinement of wit: "The wit of the last age was yet more incorrect than their language. Shakespeare, who many times has written better than any poet, in any language, is yet so far from writing wit always, or expressing that wit according to the dignity of the subject, that he writes, in many places, below the dullest writer of ours, or any precedent age. Never did any author precipitate himself from such a height of thought to so low expressions, as he often does. He is the very Janus of poets; he wears almost everywhere two faces; you have scarce begun to admire the one, ere you despise the other."

After stating that even Ben Jonson descended to the "most grovelling kind of wit, which we call clenches," Dryden goes on to say: " But, to conclude with what brevity I can, I will only add this, in defence of our present writers, that, if they reach not the excellencies of Ben Jonson (which no age, I am confident, ever shall), yet, at least, they are above that meanness of thought which I have taxed, and which is frequent in him. "That the wit of this age is courtlier may easily be proved, by viewing the characters of gentlemen which were written in the last."

And then, after some remarks on Truewit, Mercutio, and Don John: "I have always acknowledged the wit of our predecessors, with all the veneration which becomes me; but, I am sure, their wit was not that of gentlemen; there was ever something that was ill-bred and clownish in it, and which confessed the conversation of the authors." And this leads Dryden to the last and greatest advantage of the Restoration literature, which proceeds from conversation: through the influence of the court there has been added to the drama a touch of gallantry which was quit impossible to the plain-bred Elizabethans.

The essay closes as it began: "To conclude all, let us render to our predecessors what was their due, without confining ourselves to servile imitation of all they writ; and, without assuming to ourselves the title of better poets, let us ascribe to the gallantry and civility of our age the advantage which we have above them, and to our knowledge of the customs and manner of it the happiness we have to please beyond them." As Professor Hamelius has said, this essay marks Dryden as class-conscious.

He has married into a noble family and is on familiar terms with the great; and therefore he represents the tastes of the governing classes. The stage has learned its fine manners from the court, and must be defended against the lower strata of society: "Gentlemen will now be entertained with the follies of each other; and though they allow Cobb and Tib to speak properly, yet they are not much pleased with their tankard or with their rags.

"In the age wherein those poets lived, there was less of gallantry than in ours; neither did they keep the best company of theirs. Their fortune has been much like that of Epicurus, in the retirement of his gardens; to live almost unknown, and to be celebrated after their decease. I cannot find that any of them had been conversant in courts, except Ben Jonson; and his genius lay not so much that way, as to make an improvement by it.

Greatness was not then so easy of access, nor conversation so free as it now is. I cannot, therefore, conceive it any insolence to affirm, that, by the knowledge and pattern of their wit who writ before us, and by the advantage of our own conversation, the discourse and raillery of our comedies excel what has been written by them.

And this will be denied by none, but some few old fellows who value themselves on their acquaintance with the Black Friars; who, because they saw their plays, would pretend to the right to judge ours." And surely their conversation can be no jest to them on the theater, when they could avoid it in the streets."

And just as this courtly literature is to be defended "against the lower classes of the present, so it is to be defended against the sturdy, human, romantic English literature of the past. It is noticeable that the Ipse dixit that Dryden opposes is not that of the ancients: the theories of Aristotle and Horace crop out on nearly every page. "Some few old fellows who value themselves on their acquaintance with the Black Friars" — that is, the champions of the Elizabethans — are his real opponents.

He has the spirit of English science and philosophy, he delights in breaking from the past; but it is from the past of Shakespeare and Fletcher that he is taking leave. The magisterial tone of the introduction is in itself extremely significant: in the Essay of Dramatic Poesy Dryden loved Shakespeare: here there is no talk of love; instead we are to have a scientific impartiality. But even this profession is hardly justified by what follows. With the exception of a patronizing apology here and there, the entire essay is a piece of fault-finding.

Taking for granted, even, that the criticism is just, for us the important thing is that in 1672 Dryden is disposed to pass the virtues of the great Elizabethans without more than a perfunctory acknowledgment. His praise is for Virgil, Jonson, and, above all, for the playwrights of the Restoration. The present is to Dryden a golden age: The heroic play, the polisht versification, the gay and courtly manners mark for him the height of culture and of art.

The Defense of the Epilog marks the end of the critical activity of Dryden's second period. It remains only to make brief mention of two non-critical works which show the transition to the third period. The State of Innocence and the Fall of Man (1674) gives evidence of a decided change in our author's artistic purposes.

Scott is no doubt correct in supposing that this piece, an opera, could never have been seriously intended for the stage; there could, then, have been very little financial motive for the writing of it. Here we have, it thus appears, an author who has been adapting his work to the taste of king and court following for once the promptings of his own judgment. In taking his material from the still obscure Paradise Lost Dryden gives incontrovertible evidence of literary judgment far above contemporary modes.

The result of his effort is what we should expect: tho tinged with courtly smartness and adorned with turns of thought and polisht riming verse, The State of Innocence contains passages of rare dignity and beauty. Aureng-Zebe, a Tragedy (1675) is the last and best of Dryden's heroic plays — best because it is least heroic. It is in the prolog to this play that our author makes the profession of a change of taste which marks the beginning of the third critical period. "Agreeably to what might be expected from this declaration," says Scott, "the verse used in Aureng-Zebe is of that kind which may be most easily applied to the purposes of ordinary dialog.

There is much less of ornate structure and emphatic swell, than occurs in the speeches of Almanzor and Maximin; and Dryden, though late, seems to have at length discovered, that the language of true passion is inconsistent with that regular modulation, to maintain which the actor must mouth each couplet in a sort of recitative."

It may be added that in the more vital features of the play, in the characters and action, Aureng- Zebe comes nearer to life than any of our author's preceding tragedies. This play, then, like the State of Innocence, fore- shadows a change in the direction of romanticism.

This period as a whole is best described as one of perfect conformity. We have found in it, especially at first, some of the doctrine and a good deal of the pose of neoclassicism; and in a sense these persist throughout. Nevertheless neoclassicism does not give the key-note to this period.

When Dryden had carefully worked up an epic poem in praise of the king he was under the necessity of explaining and defending his method, and, since the poem had been wrought with infinite pains, it was truly represented as a work of the judgment.

But once started on the really characteristic work of the period, our author threw his judgment to the winds. It was all to the glory of the king, as had been the poem referred to above, but now the king required extravagance rather than reason, and extravagance was supplied.

To be sure it was put into a highly polisht and conventional form, but this only served the more to cut it of from life and from the ideals of Dryden's earlier period. And in his criticism our author set himself to justify the form and content of this literature, and to denounce the older English drama, which, of course, stood in direct contrast to it.

Considered from a purely formal point of view, it is true, his critical methods remained those of a neoclassicist, but the plays which he wrote and defended were such as would have put to the blush any French classicist or any good- sense author of eighteenth century England. The English heroic play was, to be sure, related to the French classic drama: its versification, its conventionality of plot and character, etc., was neoclassic traits. In its general spirit, moreover, it was no doubt related to the contemporary baroque architecture and painting of the continent.

But it cannot be too strongly insisted upon that the form of play of which we are talking was peculiar to England: the exuberant complexity of many of its plots, the extravagance of its characters, its negligence of the probabilities of the real world were not in the least classical, but, on the contrary, thoroly, unmistakably English.

So it is necessary to insist upon the fact that also the forms of Dry den's theory were, at this time, the same, in large measure, as those of the real neoclassicists, the inner, organizing force of his activity was not the classicist creed — in fact was not a creed at all.

His use of the classicist doctrines merely resulted in a sort of pseudo-neoclassicism. So when I say that this critical period was one of conformity I mean to imply that during this time Dryden' s work — poems, plays, and criticism alike — was but a phase of the life of the court.

The court, not rigidly classical in its life or tastes, demanded a characteristic literature; and Dryden, perfectly adapted to his surroundings, quick to respond to every demand made upon him, was the one best fitted to produce that literature, and to explain and defend it. If the criticism which grew out of these circumstances, while preserving much of the outward form of neoclassicism, is not true to its inner spirit, this fact hardly gives occasion for surprise.

THE THIRD PERIOD

One cannot read far into the criticism which Dryden produced between 1G75 and 1679 without discovering that both in substance and spirit it divides itself sharply from that of the period which immediately preceded it. There is here a return to the feeling which inspired the best passages of the

Essay of Dramatic Poesy. The love for Shakespeare and his contemporaries which was so strong upon our author during his first period, has returned with redoubled force.

And with this change there is noticeable a remarkable increase in sincerity. Here, as never before, we feel that we are getting at Dryden's inmost convictions. I shall attempt to show that the new spirit which has come over on author's criticism connects itself with a change in his literary and financial relations — especially his relations with the court.

In his second period we have seen Dryden loaded with such favors as had fallen to the lot of no English poet before him. But sooner than one might expect thorns began to appear among his laurels.

As early as 1671 was produced upon the stage The Rehearsal, by the Duke of Buckingham and others, in which our author's plays were made a public laughing stock. In 1672 Dryden was violently attacked, again on the score of his plays, by Mathew Clifford in his Four Letters.

In 1673 came the famous controversy with Elkanah Settle, which showed Dryden's hold upon the public to be astonishingly precarious. This quarrel was connected with our author's much more important relations with John Wilmot, Earl of Rochester. This brilliant young nobleman, an active, though capricious, patron of letters, had bestowed his favor very liberally upon Dryden.

But unfortunately the latter formed a connection with the Earl of Mulgrave, an enemy of Rochester's. Rochester, without any better reason than this, introduced Elkanah Settle to the royal favor. Settle's Empress of Morocco (1673) was first acted at Whitehall by the Lords and Ladies of the court, an honor which had never been paid to any of Dryden's compositions. On the stage it had an exceptionally long run, and, according to Dennis, it was the first play to be published with cuts and sold for two shillings.

After Settle Rochester took up first Crowne and then Otway, each of whom seems to have occupied for a time the position at court which rightfully belonged to the laureate. Not content with these slights put upon Dryden, Rochester attacked him in an anonymous imitation of Horace, An Allusion to the Tenth Satire. Of more importance was Mulgrave's Essay on Satire, a piece of sarcasm, frank to the point of brutality, directed against both Rochester and the King. Scott supposes that this was merely revised by Dryden, perhaps about 1675.

But when it was anonymously made public in 1(379, it was Dryden who was held responsible for it. In consequence, upon the night of the eighteenth of December, 1679, he was waylaid and beaten by ruffians in the hire of Rochester. The fact that in 1679 Dryden was readily believed to be the author of a satire on the King suggests a decline of royal favor.

In the dedication of Aureng-Zebe, addressing Lord Mulgrave, Dryden wrote: "As I am no successor to Homer in his wit, so neither do I desire to be in his poverty. I can make no rhapsodies, nor go abegging at the Grecian doors, while I sing the praises of their ancestors.

The times of Virgil please me better, because he had an Augustus for his patron; and, to draw the allegory nearer you, I am sure I shall not want a Maecenas with him. It is for your lordship to stir up that remembrance in his Majesty, which his many avocations of business have caused him, I fear, to lay aside."

About the time of the appearance of the Essay on Satire, says Scott, "Mulgrave seems to have fallen into disgrace, and was considered as in opposition to the court. Dryden was deprived of his intercession and appears in some degree to have shared his disgrace. 2 As to the results of this loss of favor he adds: "It is said distinctly by one libeller, that his pension was for a time interrupted.

This does not seem likely: it is more probable, that Dry den sliared the general fate of the household of Charles II, whose appointments were but irregularly paid; but perhaps his supposed delinquency made it more difficult for him than others to obtain redress." It remains only to add to this recital the evidence from Dryden's works.

In his dedication of Aureng-Zebe (1679) he complained bitterly against the court. In the preface to All for Love 2 (1678), and the dedication of The Kind Keeper 3 (1678) he returned to the attack with even greater poet laureate to Shaftesbury, imagined to have been elected king of Poland."

The satire referred to is given in a note as "A modest Vindication of the Earl of Shaftesbury, in a Letter to a Friend, concerning his being elected King of Poland."Poetical Worts, xlvi." And is not this a wretched affectation, not to be contented with what fortune has done for them, and sit down quietly with their estates, but they must call their wits in question, and needlessly expose their nakedness to public view ?

Not considering that they are not to expect the same approbation from sobre men, which they found from their flatterers after the third bottle. If a little glittering in discourse has passed them on us for witty men, where was the necessity of undeceiving the world? Would a man who has an ill title to an estate, but yet is in possession of it; would he bring it of his own accord, to be tried at Westminster?

We, who write, if we want the talent, yet have the excuse that we do it for a poor subsistence; but what can be urged in their defense, who, not having the vocation of poverty to scribble, out of mere wantonness take pains to make themselves ridiculous?

Horace was certainly in the right when he said that no man is satisfied with his own condition. A poet is not pleased, because he is not rich; and the rich are discontented, because the poets will not admit them of their number." Practically all of the essays of this time breathe a hatred against those in high places which is absolutely out of keeping with the position which Dryden occupied during his earlier period.

In accordance with what one is led to expect from our author's changed position is the discovery that the two plays of the period now under discussion were not written with a view to supplying the demands of the market.

In 1695 Dryden wrote with regard to the first of these: "I never writ anything for myself but Antony and Cleopatra " (All for Love). The Kind Keeper or Mr. Limberham (1678), a comedy, he professed to have written as "an honest satire against our crying sin of keeping." It was a complete failure — being acted but three nights. "The crime," says Dryden in his dedication, "for which it suffered, was that which is objected against the satires of Juvenal, that it expressed too much of the vice which it decried." But he will not remonstrate, "for," he continues, "their authority is, and shall be, ever sacred to me, as much absent as present, and in all alterations of their fortunes, who for these reasons have stop its further appearance on the theater."

Christy, in his memoir of Dryden, suggests: "It is to be inferred from Dryden's language that strong remonstrances from powerful friends of his own, probably from the highest placed in the land, led him to withdraw this piece. Since keeping was the vice made popular by the court, this play is first-rate evidence but as the world goes now, 'tis very hard to predicate one upon the other; and 'tis yet more difficult to prove, that a nobleman can be a friend to poetry.

Were it not for two or three instances in "Whitehall and in the town, the poets of this age would find so little encouragement of their labors, and so few understanders, that they might have leisure to turn pamphleteers, and augment the number of those abominable scribblers, who, in this time of license, abuse the press, almost every day, with nonsense, and railing against the government."

It is significant that it was acted at the Duke's theater, which was patronized chiefly by the citizen class. During our author's second period his plays and criticism "were given over to the exemplification and defense of the tastes to which the court had given popularity.

Now that "'his relations with the court had altered he returned both in his plays and in his criticism, to greater sanity, genuineness, and real poetic spirit. It was in the prolog to Aureng-Zebe, or the Great Mogul (1675) that Dryden first proclaimed his new faith; the theory of the heroic play, the admiration for rime had gone, and love of Shakespeare had returned. Two years later, in the Apology for Heroic Poetry, came an elaborate prose statement of the new doctrines, which, after all, turn out to be but those of the first period clarified and reinforced.

One who comes to this Apology fresh from the Defense

of the Epilog may be pardoned for wondering if the two works are from the same hand. In the Defense Dryden taxed all his ingenuity to pick flaws in the works of the Elizabethan masters; now, bolstering himself up with numerous quotations from Longinus, he remonstrates with all his force against carping criticism.

The critic, so he maintains, should pass his judgment in favor of the sublime genius that sometimes errs rather than prefer the indifferent author who "makes few faults, but seldom or never rises to any excellence." And then follows the beautiful passage, loosely quoted from Longinus, in which the great genius is likened to a man of large possessions who "will not debase himself to the management of every trifle," and the correct author, to a person of mean fortune, "who manages his store with extreme frugality, or rather parsimony."

The description of the "correct" author is the classic denunciation of the entire tribe: "This kind of genius writes indeed correctly. A wary man he is in grammar, very nice as to solecism or barbarism, judges to a hair of little decencies, knows better than any man what is not to be written, and never hazards himself so far as to fall, but plods on deliberately, and, as a grave man ought, is sure to put his staff before him; in short, he sets his heart upon it, and with wonderful care makes his business sure; that is, in plain English, neither to be blamed or praised."

'Having, in the first paragraph of the essay, paid a generous tribute to Paradise Lost, "undoubtedly one of the greatest, most noble, and most sublime poems which either this age or nation has produced," Dryden goes on to make a general plea for the freedom of the poetic imagination.

His opponents, interpreting the Aristotelian doctrine of imitation to suit their taste, would keep poetry near to the actualities of life. Dryden holds that poetry which has pleased all ages must be an imitation of nature, and therefore we are justified in giving the principle the most liberal interpretation. That is, he is practically throwing the principle of imitation overboard, and working out new rules on the basis of art history.

Relying on these he defends bold figures of speech and the use of fairies and other supernatural agencies in particular he defends Milton, Cowley, and himself against their detractors. And with full assurance of victory he concludes: " but all reasonable men will conclude it necessary, that sublime subjects ought to be adorned with the sublimest, and consequently with the most figurative expressions."

This essay reminds one strongly of the Essay of Heroic Plays (1672), but in reality it is very different. In the essay of 1672 Dry den defended the heroic play with all its extravagances; but now, in 1677, he is defending the great epic poets, Homer, Virgil, and Milton.

Ker describes the situation exactly: "Drydeu, like Tasso before him, is compelled to stand up against the scholars who have learned their lesson too well; it is as if he foresaw the sterilizing influence of the prose-understanding, and the harm that might be done by correctness if the principles of correctness were vulgarized."

The fact that here for the first time Dryden draws upon Longinus is sufficient to show that a new spirit has come over him. The Heads of an Answer to Rymer, a rough outline of an intended answer to Thomas Rymer's Tragedies of the Last Age, was not designed for publication. Written) like the Essay of Dramaiie Poesy, without any possible selfish motive, we are justified in supposing that in it we have an especially sincere expression of opinion.

From the point of view of the similarity of the circumstances under which the two works were composed, it is interesting to notice that in the Heads of an Answer Dryden returns very definitely to the doctrines of·the earlier essay. Rymer, a rigid scholastic, has ruthlessly examined the plays of Shakespeare and Fletcher in the light furnished by the strictest pseudo-classic rules. And Dryden, who, in 1672, was himself inclined to carp at these two, now takes up the cudgels in their defense.

His argument as a whole is based on the theory of the historical development of the drama: Aristotle's experience was necessarily limited to the Greek theater; hence his definition of a play is too narrow; if English plays have not the beauties of those of Greece, and they have others—perhaps greater.

Referring to the success of the English drama, Dryden says: "And one reason for that success is, in my opinion, this, that Shakespeare and Fletcher have written to the genius of the age and nation in which they lived; for the nature, as he objects, is the same in all places, and reason too the same, yet the climate, the age, the disposition of the people, to whom a poet writes, may be so different, that what pleased the Greeks would not satisfy an English audience."

In the Essay of Dramatic Poesy, it will be remembered, in attempting to define the quality which distinguished English poetry from French, Dryden hit upon the terms, "masculine fancy " and "spirit in the writing." Here in the Heads of an Answer, he is laboring to make clear the nature of the same quality; and the terms which now serve his purpose, e. g. "the genius of poetry in the writing," carry back over the intervening thirteen years to the earlier work.

Notice, in this connection, the spirit and terminology of the following passage: "Rapin attributes more to the dictio, that is, to the words and discourse of a tragedy, than Aristotle has done, who places them in the last rank of beauties; perhaps only last in order, because they are the last product of the design. Rapin's words are remarkable: It is not the admirable intrigue, the surprising events, and the extraordinary incidents that make the beauty of a tragedy; it is the discourses, when they are natural and passionate."

Within the year of the writing of the Heads of an Answer to Rymer came also the production of All for Love, or the World Well Lost, a tragedy on the subject of Antony and Cleopatra, avowedly written in imitation of Shakespeare. Dryden's characters and plot are not up to the Shakespearean standard; neither can his blank verse, as a whole, be pronounced equal to that of his great original. But it must be acknowledged that this is the best of all his plays; it is full of noble scenes and of poetical passages which do not suffer by comparison with the best in English literature.

Here, in the play which Dry den professedly wrote for himself, the genuinely romantic spirit has replaced the mock heroic. The preface which introduced this play is chiefly remarkable for a spirited attack on the conventionality of French literature; all the feeling which in the two preceding essays was directed against pedants in general is here turned against the poets of France and their English imitators.

In this period, then, during which Dryden is not writing as the favorite of town and court, during which, it appears, he is even cut off from many of his old associations and put under suspicion, his literary productions show him in a state of revolt. The life of the court nauseates him; the degenerate heroic drama, as it is carried on in the hands of succeeding favorites, he can not endure; and no more can he tolerate the clean-cut and heartless neoclassic criticism as he sees it in the works of Rymer.

The three pieces of criticism which mark the culmination of the period exhibit a singular unity of feeling. In all of them Dryden strikes out squarely counter to the current of contemporary opinion. In all of them he warmly upbraids merely rational criticism; he maintains that literary types should be left free to develop, that the critic should draw his rules from literature rather than prescribe laws to literature; he contends most of all for the spirit of poetry, for genius in literary material as against all the conventions of form. These three essays are, perhaps, the most remarkable of all Dryden's prose works.

Lacking, often, the refined spirit and elegant form of the Essay of Dramatic Poesy, for courage, for refreshing sincerity, for unconventional originality, they can hardly be matched from Dryden's other critical works, or from the works of any other critic of Dryden's time. The criticism produced by Dryden during the decade between 1680 and 1689 is best characterized as rationalistic.

Here we find well formulated, probably for the first time in England, that common-sense system of literary production and evaluation which had been so well organized by Boileau and was to be further developed by Pope. A reading of this criticism in connection with Dry den's biography immediately suggests the thought that his theory was, during this period, very definitely related to the literary occupations to which, thro the pressure of economic circumstances, he was forced to surrender himself.

During Dryden' s second period we have seen him the servant of a court which demanded amusement; during his third period we have seen him cast upon his own resources; but during the period under consideration we find him in a new role; as during the second period, he is the servant of a court, but of a court which demands — not amusement — but defense against its enemies.

Dryden entered upon his fourth period rather poorer than usual. The King's Theater, in the profits of which he had had a share, had burnt down in 1672, and his income had suffered in consequence. After the production of All for Love (1677—8) he quarreled with the King's Company and the contract in accordance with which he had shared in its profits was abrogated.

The complaint in the dedication of Aureng-Zebe and the belief that his pension had been cut off, show at least that it was irregularly paid. One is somewhat surprised, therefore, to learn that as early as 1679 our author was granted by the king a special annual pension of one hundred pounds, and that in 1683 he was appointed collector of customs for the p ort of London.

The Whigs, representing Protestantism, were/becoming more and more of a menace to the royal faction; and in his hour of need Charles did not disdain to assure himself of Dryden's support. And Dryden, as we have seen, was in no position to refuse to give his services.

In 1681 our author produced upon the stage The Spanish Friar, his "Protestant play" — surely no evidence of loyalty. But later in the same year he published Absalom and Aehitophel and from that time to the death of Charles II, in 1G85, there was no interruption in Dryden's devoted service; the king was defended against all his enemies, the Church of England against all the sectaries. But during this time important changes were taking place in the life of the court. The Catholic Duke of York was the heir apparent, and the Duchess of York shared his religious faith.

Charles himself was under suspicion of a leaning in the direction of Catholicism. The tide was unmistakably setting in the direction of the Church of Rome, and the author of the "Protestant Play" could hardly be expected to remain independent of its influence. The fact that Dryden turned Catholic about the time of the succession of James II, when a change in religion was patently advantageous to him, has been interpreted by more than one of his biographers as evidence of rank turn coatism.

The answer to these has been found in the fact that as early as 1682, in the Religio Laid, Dryden gave unmistakable evidence of a genuine leaning in the direction of Catholicism. It seems to me that we have here merely another case to show Dryden's sensitiveness to his environment. No one who sympathetically reads the Religio Laid or Dryden's later religious poems can doubt the sincerity of his conversion: neither can anyone who has taken into account the changing atmosphere of the court imagine that this conversion was quite independent of our author's milieu.

Dryden's world gradually changed, and he himself, with perfect sincerity, gradually changed with it. As one result of Dry den's religious conversion he was continued in office as the chief literary representative of the court, his pension of one hundred pounds being guaranteed him by a royal patent. In 1686 he published his Defense of Papers written by the late King and the Duchess of York — which papers seemed to indicate (a fact now much to the purpose) that Charles II had been at heart a Catholic.

And from this time down to the dethronement of James II in 1688-89 Dry den served his second master as faithfully as he had served his first. The mere labor demanded by Dryden's new position of chief apologist for the crown, was tremendous. In Ker's list of his publications there are to be found within the limits of this period the titles of fourteen works which formed part of his public service. Among these are registered, first of all, works like the translation of Maimburg's History of the League and the Defense of Papers written by the late King and the Duchess of York, long and dreary pieces of prose which must have meant to their author weary months of drudgery.

But the chief works of the list are the satirical and didactic masterpieces: Absalom and Achitophel (1681), The Medal (1682), MacFlecknoe (1682), Absalom and Achitophel, Part II (1682), Beligio Laid (1682), and The Hind and the Panther (1687). For us it is merely necessary to notice two things with regard to these supreme works.

In the first place not a single one of them was introduced with a critical dissertation of great importance. The production of this form of literature was not calculated to keep alive in our author's mind his former interest in the vital problems of esthetics.

Even the mere quantity of his criticism was cut down; we have only four slender pieces to represent what was Dryden's most productive literary period. The other point which demands our attention is the fact that satire belongs distinctly to the rationalistic, rather than to the romantic, consciousness; to the period of Pope, rather than to the period of Shakespeare.

Since, then, the characteristic poetic production of this period links Dryden to the eighteenth century, rather than to the sixteenth, one is prepared to expect in the critical essays a predominantly rationalistic tone.

Before entering upon a discussion of the characteristic criticism of the fourth period it is necessary to notice an essay which is clearly transitional. In 1679 Dryden published Troilus and Cressida, rather an "improvement" of Shakespeare's play of the same name than a noble imitation like Ail for Love. And with this play, which in itself seemed to indicate a dying down of poetical fervor, he published his Preface containing the Grounds of Criticism in Tragedy — a most interesting composite of the antagonistic spirits of the third and fourth periods.

In the introduction, although a high regard for Shakespeare is expressed, the chief emphasis is laid upon his petty faults;

his phrases are, some of them, "scarce intelligible," others, "ungrammatical and coarse; "his style is" so pestered with figurative expressions, that it is as affected as it is obscure."

The essay on The Grounds of Criticism in Tragedy is introduced with a formal outline: our author thinks it would be neither unprofitable nor unpleasant to inquire" how far we ought to imitate our poets, Shakespeare and Fletcher, in their tragedies; and this will occasion another inquiry, how those two writers differ among themselves."

But in order to prosecute these investigations he will first attempt "to discover the grounds and reasons of all criticism, applying them in this place only to tragedy. "Then there follows one of the most carefully reasoned of all Dryden's essays. Beginning with Aristotle's definition of a play our author proceeds in an abstract, formal manner to discuss the action, the manners, the characters, and the passions.

After the, regular discussion of each heading Shakespeare and Fletcher "are brought up for comparison, and one who has recently read the Heads of an Answer may well be surprised to discover that they are often measured by the classical standard as ruthlessly as Rymer himself could have wished. But, happily, this essay is one of those which are remarkable for their "purple patches."

It is evident from one of these that the Dryden's new formalism can make no room for Shakespeare; the old love of him still survives. In the preface to Dryden's translation of Ovid's epistles (1680) we have the first piece of criticism perfectly representative of the fourth period; it is representative both in its brevity and in its thoroly prosaic tone.

The only really significant passage in it is one in which Ovid is guardedly praised for the vivacity of his poetry, but roundly scored for not having been a better master of his wit. "Nothing too much," is our author's law, and it is applied especially to wit, to eloquence, to the inward fire that may now and then strain a conventionality.

In the dedication of The Spanish Friar (1681) we might expect a different feeling. The play which it introduced was written, not to support the king, but to catch the public ear; l and, despite its faults, one must confess that it has in it some of the life of real comedy.

Here, then, if anywhere, we might expect a return to the standards of 1678. But what do we find? First of all, a criticism, searching and just, of our author's own heroic plays: they cry vengeance upon him for their extravagance, and he wishes them heartily in the fire.

His only excuse for them is that they were bad enough to please; but for the future he is resolved to settle himself no reputation "by the applause of fools." The effect of the "prose-understanding" is not entirely evil; if it condemns the romantic by judicious strictures and faint praise, it damns the heroic utterly.

Dryden was too philosophical to rest content with individual literary judgments; he must give his theory abstract statement. It is significant that when he comes to do this Y he takes his figure from architecture, of all the arts the one, perhaps, in which a riotous fancy can have least place:

"But as in a room contrived for state, the height of the roof should bear a proportion to the area; so, in the heightenings of poetry, the strength and vehemence of the figures should be suited to the occasion, the subject, and the persons."Propriety of thoughts and words is the chief virtue of a play.

Here, it thus appears, even in the dedication of a popular play, Dryden's new deity, good sense, is the supreme god. In the preface to Sylvae (1685) we find that after a lapse of four years our author's esthetic creed has remained unchanged. With great show of erudition, but without touching upon a single vital literary problem, he discusses the four authors he has been translating. In the one passage which has real significance he treats Cowley as he treated Ovid in the preface of 1680.

It is true that Cowley had the soul of poetry, the "warmth and vigor of fancy," "but he lacked somewhat of equal thoughts," and "somewhat of the purity of English." And after he has applied his unvarying measure, Dryden peevishly demands what rules of morality or respect he has broken:

"There are few poets who deserve to be models in all they write." Horace himself could hardly have excelled this for classic coolness; one is instantly reminded of nodding Homer. There is nothing here, except, of course, the over-sensitive apology for irreverence, which, so far as theory is concerned, might not have been written by Pope. But it is in the preface to Albion and Albanius (1685) that Dryden undertakes the formal exposition of his doctrine.

The essay begins with a highly significant definition of wit. It will be remembered that in the Essay of Dramatic Poesy (1665) Dryden wrote, referring to Jonson: "I must acknowledge him the more correct poet, but Shakespeare the greater wit." Wit, in this connection, was evidently used to signify the possession of a prolific poetic genius, or an abundance of poetic material.

In the preface to Annus Mirabilis (1666) this notion was decidedly modified: " wit-writing " was there defined as a nimble spaniel, which "beats over and ranges through the field of memory, till it springs the quarry it hunted after;" and "wit-written" was described as that which is "well defined, the happy result of thought, or product of imagination."

This confusing division is evidently a compromise; wit is thought of as being at once the creative quality of the imagination and the well-defined product of the judgment. In 1677, in the Apology for Heroic Poetry, Dryden formally defined wit as "a propriety of thoughts and words," 3 but used this two-edged definition to show that in the treatment of great subjects the poetic imagination should be allowed free rein.

But now, in the preface to Albion and Albanius, he develops this definition and attempts to show on the strength of it that all poetic beauty depends upon the exercise of the judgment. Thus in the course of twenty years one of the most important terms of seventeenth century criticism, following the evolution of our author's mind, has exactly reversed its meaning. With its new definition it is made to cover a complete system of poetic theory.

The thoughts are to be proper to the subject, the words, to the thoughts, "and from both of these, if they be judiciously performed, the delight of poetry results."Pope, in the Essay on Criticism, seems merely to return an echo: "Expression is the dress of thought, and still appears more decent as more suitable." The criticism of this period, it thus appears, is rationalistic. In its general spirit it bears some resemblance to that of the second period, nevertheless the two should be sharply distinguished.

The critical theory of the second period, it will be remembered, was characterized as pseudo neoclassic; that of the period now under consideration is best defined as English rationalistic. The English heroic play which furnished the occasion for the characteristic criticism of the second period was a natural outgrowth of the life of the Restoration, and with the passing of that life, it, too, past away with all its related theory.

Even before it had reached its zenith there had appeared in England the beginnings of a school of critics, best represented by Hobbes, who introduced into their thinking about literature the spirit and doctrines of English sensationalistic philosophy. The French neoclassicists, we have seen, made literature rational and intelligible by working it out in accordance with an a priori scheme attributed to the ancients. The English rationalists, thorogoing sensationalists in philosophy, achieved practically the same result by bringing art down to the actualities of life.

To them prose furnished an ideal form and, in the eighteenth century, the realistic novel, an ideal content: even in Dryden's day they were dubbed "prose-critics." Under the predominance of these prose- critics the heroic play fell under constantly increasing condemnation.

Dryden's unequivocal denunciation of it in the dedication of The Spanish Friar, furnishes a measure of his evolution: during his fourth period he was, at least in his general spirit, a rationalist. The worship of good sense had become his controlling motive.

This rationalism is precisely what an examination of Dryden's life during this period would lead one to expect. We have seen him constrained by circumstances to throw the chief energy saved from uninspiring hack-work into a "series of poetical satires. The first result of this new direction of his activity was naturally a diminution of his interest in critical problems. But the second result was more important. A man like Dryden, versatile, easily adapting himself to new conditions, could hardly be imagined dividing his mental life; doing his daily stint of toil for the royal cause and then taking up the consideration of literary problems with his old romantic fervor.

On the contrary, he gave himself up wholly to the required labor. So thoroly did he fuse his personality with the cause of his party that in MacFlecknoe, passages of Absalom and Achitophel, and in other poems, he paid at once his own scores and those of the king. Satire had become his natural mode of expression. But satire is itself but a sort of criticism it has always been the form assumed by the highly trained, versifying prose-understanding.

If, then, while satire was Dryden's natural mode of expression his critical essays are almost equally judges when we are concerned in the representation of them." And a little later he criticizes Ovid for leaving "the imitation of nature, and the cooler dictates of his judgment, for the false applause of fancy became eminently rationalistic, it is merely because they were of a piece with his whole mental life.

The fifth period of Dryden's critical development includes, approximately, the last decade of his life. With the revolution of 1688-9 our author lost at once his offices and his pension; but what was apparently a crushing reverse proved o to be a boon — at once to Dryden and to English literature. His position now became practically that of a free man of letters. And in this character he was left at liberty to give himself up to literary labors of his own choice. Under these circumstances his critical faculty naturally regained free play. The result is noticeable, first of all, in the imposing amount of criticism written during this period.

But the quality is more remarkable than the quantity; beginning the period as a rationalist, Dryden gradually developed in the direction of the theory and feeling of the first and third periods. The old love for the spirit of great literature returned, and more and more dominated the good-sense mood and method. The criticism is distinguished from that of the first and third periods by a broader, steadier grasp of esthetic problems and by a beautiful evenness of feeling.

It is, to be sure, a sort Perhaps the reader does not need to be again reminded that I do not pretend to have accounted completely for all the differences between the various periods of Dryden's critical development. The causes for the transition from the third to the fourth period seem to have been especially complex.

I have my attention drawn to the fact that during the third period Dryden leaned pretty heavily on Rapin and that, although he was using his contemporary French critic in the support of romanticism, Rapin may have influenced him in the direction of rationalism.

Rapin had after all more affinity to Rymer than to Dryden. It is not impossible that our author's very attacks on Rymer may have reacted in favor of Rymer's own doctrines of classicism which we have here, but a deep and humanized classicism. 'After the downfall of James II our author, now nearly sixty years old, was cast out to write for a living. During the first years of the period he was still partially dependent, but his dependence was of a kind which did not entail actual servitude.

Don Sebastian (1690) he dedicated to the Earl of Leicester, a supporter of the new government. In the dedication of Amphitrion (1690) to Sir William Leveson Gower, also a revolutionist, he wrote: " And as, since this wonderful revolution, I have begun with the best pattern of humanity, the Earl of Leicester, I shall continue to follow the same method, in all to whom I shall address; and endeavor to pitch on such only as have been pleased to own me in this ruin of my small fortune; who, though they are of a contrary opinion themselves, yet blame not me for adhering to a lost cause, and judging for myself,

What I cannot choose but judge, so long as I am a patient sufferer, and no disturber of the government." 1 One of

Dryden's most generous friends was Charles, Earl of Dorset and Middlesex, after the revolution appointed to the post of Lord Chamberlain.

Addressing to this nobleman his Discourse concerning the Original and Progress of Satire (1693), Dryden wrote: " I must ever acknowledge, to the honor of your lordship, and the eternal memory of your charity, that, since this revolution, wherein I have patiently suffered the ruin of my small fortune, and the loss of that poor subsistence which I had from two kings, whom I had served more faithfully than profitably to myself; then your.

Lordship was pleased, out of no other motive than your nobleness, without any desert of mine, or the least solicitation from me, to make me a most bountiful present, which at that time, when I was most in want of it, came most seasonably and unexpectedly to my relief.

I must not presume to defend the cause for which I suffer, because your Lordship is engaged against it; but the more you are so, the greater is my obligation to you, for your laying aside all the considerations of factions and parties, to do an action of pure disinterested charity." Dryden's patrons were, it thus appears, persons who were drawn to him either out of personal regard or because of an interest in letters: being, most of them, at least, opposed to our author in politics, they could not ask political services.

Dryden's relations with them were always dignified and honorable. The same can be said of his attitude toward the government. In his dedication of the Aeneis (1697), about to discuss Virgil's relations with Augustus, he remarked by way of introduction: " I shall continue to speak my thoughts like a free- born subject, as I am; though such things, perhaps, as no Dutch commentator could, and I am sure no Frenchman durst."

This honorable attitude toward patrons and government is at least partially to be explained from the fact that Dryden had now thrown himself chiefly upon the support of the rapidly increasing reading public. It is true that in 1691 he w r rote a panegyric, Eleanora, on the deceased Countess of

Abdingdon, a person whom he acknowledges never to have seen, and that he received for the performance of this task a fee of five hundred pounds. But the translations were the characteristic works of this period, and it is evident that they became more and more remunerative.

The translation of Virgil (1697), as appears from a letter to William Walsh, 3 was published by subscription: a hundred and two copies, "having an hundred and two brass cuts, with the coat of arms of the subscriber to each cut," were subscribed for at five guineas apiece; another lot were taken at two guineas the copy.

In a letter to Jacob Tonson, Dryden stated that he had just finished the seventh Aeneid and expected soon to start the eighth, and continued: "when that is finished, I expect fifty pounds in good silver." The number of books for which this sum was to be received is not clear.

A little later in the same letter Dryden added: "but the thirty shillings upon every book remains with me." Pope had heard that the Virgil translation as a whole brought Dryden the sum of 1,200 pounds. For the Fables (1700), according to a signed agreement still extaut, Dryden was to receive from Tonson the sum of three hundred pounds.

In connection with our author's changed position there is noticeable a general elevation of his moral standards. This is to be remarked, first of all, in his attitude toward his art. In his dedication of the Examen Poeticum (1693), after a discussion of the corruption of governments, he continued: "These considerations have given me a kind of contempt for those who have risen by unworthy ways.

I am not ashamed to be little, when I see them so infamously great; neither do I know why the name of poet should be dishonorable to me, if I am truly one, as I hope I am; for I will never do anything that will dishonor it." In Dryden's view of the moral aspects of literature, also, there took place a notable alteration.

In the last paragraph of his last critical work, the preface to the Fables, he replied to Jeremy Collier's attack on him: " I shall say the less of Mr. Collier, because in many things he has taxed me justly; and I have pleaded guilty to all thoughts and expressions of mine, which can be truly argued of obscenity, profaneness, or immorality, and retract them. If he be my enemy, let him triumph; if he be my friend, as I have given him no personal reason to be otherwise, he will be glad of my repentance."

As to our author's literary activity under the new circumstances, the first thing to demand notice is a decline in his dramatic production and a consequent falling off of interest in the problems of the stage. The five plays which came from his pen between 1690 and 1694 attained dramatic and literary merit to a rapidly diminishing degree.

At the beginning of this, his last period of play writing, Dryden wrote: "Having been longer acquainted with the stage than any other poet now living, and having observed how difficult it was to please; that the humors of comedy were almost spent; that love and honor (the mistaken topics of tragedy) were quite worn out; that the theaters could not support their charges;

That the audience forsook them; that young men, without learning, set up for judges, and that they talked loudest who understood the least; all these discouragements had not only weaned me from the stage, but had also given me a loathing for it. But enough of this: the difficulties continue; they increase; and I am still condemned to dig in those exhausted mines."

And in 1692 he protested; "Nobody can imagine that, in my declining age, I write willingly, or that I am desirous of exposing, at this time of day, the small reputation which I have gotten on the theater.

The subsistence which I had from the former government is lost; and the reward I have from the stage is so little, that it is not worth my labor." The story of Dryden's dramatic degeneration, then, may be summed up as follows. In 1690, having been cast upon the resources of his pen, he turned to the public, especially to the citizen class, which, with the coming of William and Mary, had gained a decided ascendency.

The public was most easily reached thro the theater; hence Don Sebastian (1690), worked out with extraordinary care. But Dryden soon discovered that times were changed. Citizen morality was more and more making itself felt, and plays were more and more subjected to sharpest criticism.

In fact the theater seemed to be sinking into a certain decline. Thus dramatic work, never to Dry- den's taste, grew constantly more irksome; and at last, according to his own statement, the economic motive for '" continuing it well nigh disappeared. But for us the important thing to notice is, that Dryden lost interest in dramatic problems. Not one of the five plays of this period is preceded by a critical dissertation of any importance.

The change which began in 1684 with the publication of Miscellany Poems is now complete, and it is chiefly in connection with his translations that we must henceforth follow the development of Dryden's critical theory. The translations of this period include selections from Juvenal, Persius, and Ovid, the works of Virgil, and the so-called fables from Homer, Boccacio, and Chaucer. Four of the five volumes in which these translations appeared Dryden introduced with critical prefaces.

Occasionally, notably in the dedication of the Examen Poetieum (1693), he wandered back into the discussion of the drama, but for the most part his attention was given up to the poetic forms, especially to the epic. A chronological list of the translations of the last seven years of Dryden's life shows that his interest developed steadily in the direction of really poetic appreciation.

After his long period of satire writing Juvenal may naturally have interested him; but, left free to follow his literary impulse, he translated Virgil, whose formal virtues few have been able to appreciate more sincerely, and during his last years worked over with amazing freedom and spirit selections from Homer, Boccacio, and Chaucer.

Thus the development of his criticism during this period seems to correspond to a development in his poetical activity. The first important critical work of this period is, naturally enough, on satire. A Discourse concerning the Original and Progress of Satire, published in 1693 with a translation of the satires of Juvenal, is a long and formal treatise liberally padded with borrowed learning.

Dryden carefully announces his purpose to give, " from the best authors, the origin, the antiquity, the growth, the change, and the completement of satire among the Romans; to describe, if not define, the nature of that poem, with its several qualifications and virtues, together with the several sorts of it; to compare the excellencies of Horace, Persius, and Juvenal, and show the particular manner of their satires; and, lastly, to give an account of this new way of version, which is attempted in our performance."

Fortified with an imposing list of authorities, Dryden executes his plan with more than customary method and care. Only in the wanderings of his introduction does he express

1 It is to be regretted that studies of Dryden's translations do not furnish sufficient material to warrant a generalization as to his tendency as translator. It seems extremely probable that he allowed himself constantly in- creasing liberties with his originals.

As to the war between ancients and moderns, he maintains that in drama and satire the moderns have excelled; Milton is searchingly criticized, but admired for his elevated thoughts and sounding words. It must be confessed, however, that this essay as a whole exhibits more keen discrimination than real literary enthusiasm.

In the epistle dedicatory of the Examen Poeticum (1693) we recognize again the Dryden of the first and third periods. It is significant that the immediate occasion for the greater part of this essay is identical with that which we noticed in connection with the Defense of the Epilog. In 1672, being attacked by the old-fashioned devotees of the Elizabethans, Dryden replied by belittling Shakespeare's virtues and enlarging upon his faults: in 1693, under exactly the same circumstances, our author gracefully acknowledges the superiority of his great predecessors and challenges the sincerity of his critics.

But, recalling in this the spirit of the Essay of Dramatic Poesy, he will defend the English Drama against all comers: again the English genius comes to its own; again Dryden searches for words with which to characterize that vital thing which is the heart of English poetry. The passages in question are distinguished from "Tis not with an ultimate intention to pay reverence to the Manes of Shakespeare, Fletcher, and Ben Jonson that they commend their writings, hut to throw dirt on the writers of this age.

Peace be to the venerable shades of Shakespeare and Ben Jonson none of the living will presume to have any competition with them; as they were our predecessors, so they were our masters." "As little can I grant, that the French dramatic writers excel the English. Our authors as far surpass them in genius, as our soldiers excel theirs in courage. 'Tis true, in conduct they surpass us either way; yet that proceeds not so much from their greater knowledge, as from the difference in tastes in the two nations. They content themselves with a thin design, without episodes, and managed by few persons.

Our audience will not be pleased, but with variety of accidents, an under plot, and many actors our author's previous expressions on the same subject only by an evident desire to do justice both to the faults of the English and the virtues of the French.

A denunciation of Homer's "ungodly man-killers" (heroes) and a tacit commendation of a "more moderate heroism" seem to indicate a temperate, Virgilian state of mind. But if this essay is milder than the great documents of our author's third period, it is filled with the same fine independence. Dryden's next piece of criticism, the famous Parallel between Poetry and Painting, prefixed to a translation of Du Fresnoy, De Arte Graphica (1695), is unique among his works in its purpose and scope.

It resembles most the preface to Troilus and Cressida (1679), but in the actual nature of its material it is much more abstract. Here Dryden starts out with the set purpose of laying down the rules of art which belong to poetry and painting in common. In no other work has he undertaken a task so entirely formal; here, then, if anywhere, one might expect a cold outline of the artist's activities approximating, perhaps, the good-sense doctrine of the fourth period. And it must be confessed that in its general tone this esssay is far more rationalistic than the one which preceded it. But, nevertheless, a close reading reveals something like an attempt to harmonize the formal conception of literature with the intuitions of a genuinely poetic consciousness.

Naturally our author begins the systematic part of his treatise with a statement of rules: this is in the very nature of the case; if there are no accepted laws applying to the artist's methods, then no such treatise as this can be written at all.

They follow the ancients too servilely in the mechanic rules, and we assume too much licence to ourselves, in keeping them only in view at too great a distance. But if our audience had their tastes, our poets could more easily comply with them, than the French writers could come up to the sublimity of our thoughts, or to the difficult variety of our designs." From the practise, then, of "the poets and painters in ancient times and the best ages" rules have been drawn, and these are to furnish the basis of our discussion.

Treating the steps of a poet's or painter's work in order, Dryden begins with a discussion of invention, and we are relieved to read: "Invention is the first part, and absolutely necessary to them both; yet no rule ever was or ever can be given, how to compass it."

But the disposition, or arrangement, of the work is to be according to law. Coming to the description of the passions, Dryden again admits the inadequacy of rules: " This, says my author, is the gift of Jupiter; and to speak in the same heathen language, we call it the gift of our Apollo — not to be obtained by pains or study, if we are not born to it; for the motions which are studied are never so natural as those which break out in the height of a real passion."

When he comes to the principles of ornamentation Dryden finds the abstract rule too much for him and, with evident compunction, admits the formal indefensibility of the English tragi-comedy.

One remark on the cromatic, or coloring, the last step in the production of an art work, shows again that Dryden is attempting to maintain an esthetic balance: "A work may be overwrought as well as underwrought; too much labor often takes away the spirit by adding to the polishing, so that there remains nothing but a dull correctness, a piece without any considerable faults, but with few beauties; for when the spirits are drawn off, there is nothing but a caput mortuwm."

Taking into account such passages as these it seems to me that whereas we found in the preface to Troilus and Cressida a formal treatment of the rules of the drama with here and there an outbreak of romantic feeling, we are justified in describing the Parallel as a studied attempt to harmonize the formal, practical, working conception of an artist's labors with the intuitions of a poetic appreciator of the finished art-product.

Dry den's theory, it is true, is inadequate to his purpose; he is still bound by the principle of imitation and the allegorical conception of art. But the attempt is none the less evident: an inexplicable genius produces the material, and the judgment disposes it; genius describes the passions, while study and care polish the language. The dedication with which Dryden introduced his translation of the Aeneid (1697) naturally concerns itself with the old question of the relative advantages of drama and epic and the defense and praise of the poetry of Virgil.

So v it happens, as has been the case with more than one of Dryden's essays that the really significant passages of this work are in the nature of digressions. In general these "significant passages are pretty much of a piece with those which we examined in the dedicatory epistle of the Examen Poeticum. Their chief value lies in the fact that, like the v epistle of 1693, they exhibit Dryden expressing with his old-time freedom the doctrines of his earliest period.

The figure once before used to define his feeling as to the nature of the English poetic spirit is further developed: "For, impartially speaking, the French are as much better critics than the English, as they are worse poets. Thus we generally allow that they better understand the management of a war than our islanders; but we know we are superior to them in the day of battle.

They value themselves on their generals, we on our soldiers." In another spirited passage on the same subject he characterizes the informing spirit of English poetry as "a masculine vigor," recalling forcibly his earlier expressions, "masculine fancy" (1665), and "genius of poetry in the writing" (1678). Our author has consistently maintained, especially in the Parallel, that the epic is farther from life than the drama, and thus better adapted to ornamentation; but now he demands, even in the epic, something of genuine virility and passion.

It is in the preface to the Fables (1700), Dryden's last essay that the criticism of this period culminates. Here, more than in any other work of the period, we get warm, spontaneous appreciation unmixed with empty formulas. Homer, Chaucer, Ovid, and Boccaccio are the natural subjects of the essay; but it is the first two that call forth the best passages. Here concludes, so far as Dryden is concerned, that long conflict between Homer and Virgil.

The result is, first of all, an attempt to estimate the virtues of each without injustice to the other. But one cannot help feeling that, as Homer was Dryden's favorite in youth, so he is at the last. In fact our author states specifically that he has found Homer more according to his genius than the Latin poet.

And in passages like the following the nature of his feeling can hardly be mistaken: "The action of Homer, being more full of vigor than that of Virgil, according to the temper of the writer, is of a consequence more pleasing to the reader. One warms you by degrees; the other sets you on fire all at once, and never intermits his heat. 'Tis the same difference which Longinus makes betwixt the effects of eloquence in Demosthenes or Tully; one persuades, the other commands."

"Let the French and Italians value themselves on their regularity; strength and elevation are our standard. I said before, and I repeat it, that the affected purity of the French has unsinewed their heroic verse. The language of an epic poem is almost wholly figurative: yet they are so fearful of a metaphor, that no example of Virgil can encourage them to be bold with safety.

Sure they might warm themselves by that sprightly blaze, without approaching it so close as to singe their wings; they may come as near it as their master" with Ovid, Dryden conies upon the subject of the much admired " turn of words; " as the poet of Charles II he had much admired this taking ornament, but in his present mood he sees that in strong passions it is always to be shunned.

As to Chaucer he speaks praise which can only be compared with his eulogy of Shakespeare: " He must have been a man of most wonderful comprehensive nature, because, as has been truly observed of him, he has taken into the compass of his Canterbury Tales the various manners and humors (as we now call them) of the whole English nation, in his age." "He is a perpetual fountain of good sense; learn'd in all sciences; and, therefore, speaks properly on all subjects."

Even the verse of Chaucer, the meter of which, because of changes in pronunciation, Dryden was quite unable to appreciate, seemed to him to have the "rude sweetness of a Scotch tune in it." Coming at a time when Chaucer was considered "a dry old-fashioned wit," the exclusive property of "some old Saxon friends," this frank and hearty appreciation has an astonishingly modern ring.

Here is a poet who seems to lack most of the qualities of form which have sometimes appeared to Dryden as the essentials of poetry: and yet he is praised and loved for the truth of nature in him and for his abundance of wit.

This preface, written only a few months before Dryden's death, is, from nearly every point of view, one of his best critical works. There is little theorizing here, to be sure, but there is an abundance of original comparison and sincere appreciation. And the favorites of our author's last days are Homer and Chaucer.

It is the inner spirit of poetry i which seems now to attract him, rather than niceties of versification. It is noteworthy that the material which he " is treating here is all of the epic kind;

and it has been for the epic that he has heretofore so steadily insisted on formal virtues.

During his fifth period Dryden has, more than at any other time of his life, been left free to develop his personality. Except for the pressure exerted by the necessity of writing for the public, he has been at liberty to choose his form of activity and to express with perfect sincerity the literary tastes which, in a man of his type, naturally developed under favorable influences.

Besides being free from any sort of restraint Dryden has been writing during his last years as the recognized master of English poetry; this, joined perhaps, with the fact that he has dealt chiefly with classical material, has given him a fine dignity of manner and catholic breadth of feeling.

This, then, is the Dryden of the last phase; and the criticism we have examined is just what one would expect from such a man. Of the five critical documents of the period, the first, we have seen, was transitional: the other four, it seems to me, are related in spirit and material to the essays of the first and third periods.

In one respect they indicate a distinct advance over all their predecessors: Dryden has gained in judicial poise, and logicality of thought; he is trying to bring together his instinctive feelings for literature and his reasoned theory. This very effort, to be sure, savors of the eighteenth century, but Dryden has not again struck the dead-level of the "prose-critics."

He has still, especially during the latter part of the period, the fine, free spirit of the Essay of Dramatic Poesy and the preface to All for Love. It is mellowed a bit by age, and there is not now so much of the fire of conflict in it, but it is still the same in its nature. The results of this investigation may be summed up in the statement that Dryden's critical activity was an organic part of his life. And it follows as a corollary of this statement that, since his life, because of its intimate connection with the vicissitudes of the age, divides itself into periods, his criticism, together with his entire literary activity, falls into approximately corresponding periods.

During the first John Stuart Collins, in his extremely valuable work, Diyden's Dramatic Theory and Praxis, makes an elaborate comparison of Dryden's critical theory as set forth in the prefaces and his practise in the plays.

The prefaces, especially the passages dealing with rime, the unities, the decorum of the stage, and the like, he examines in order, and in connection with each tries to make out whether the theory enunciated is developed in the accompanying play or in other plays of the same period. His general conclusion is as follows: "On the whole, I fail to discover any such intimate connection between theory and praxis in Dry- den's dramatic authorship as might reasonably be expected.

Nowhere does he say: 'thus and thus shall be written' and then follow up these exact lines." After recognizing a distinct connection between Dryden's theory and practise during the heroic period, Mr. Collins proceeds. "

A comparison of such statements of individual opinion as are to be found in Dryden's essays, prefaces, and dedications regarding points of dramatic technic, with his practise in dramatic composition, leads to the discovery of the lack of any exact organic connection in every particular between the two: an attempt to show either a complete reconciliation between theory and praxis or a complete divergence of each from the other leads to no precise results."

The obvious comment on this is that the connection which was sought in certain details of dramatic theory and practise might have been found in the general spirit of the two. Dryden was far too careless a playwright to work out every detail according to theory: but the essays and plays of any particular period were acted upon by the same general influences, were expressions of the same personality at a particular stage of its development, and one would expect to find in them substantial agreement as to mood and purpose of these Dryden, with the fine enthusiasm of a young poet still upon him, has not yet settled upon a literary ideal, has not yet submitted himself to the dominance of a formal scheme of theory; and the criticism of this time is full of genuine appreciations of literature and remarkably modern discussions of literary problems.

The second period exhibits a striking unity of development: Dryden becomes the great literary favorite of the court; in his serious plays he furnishes precisely the heroic literature which the court demands; and in his criticism, being obliged to defend this literature, he stretches the doctrines of neoclassicism to include the theory of it, and, in self-defense, attacks the rival drama of the great Elizabethans.

During the third period our author's central motive is rebellion against all that he has lately believed in and supported: attacked by numberless foes, he is neglected, if not actually discountenanced by the king; in his serious plays he discontinues the heroic manner for imitation of Shakespeare, while in his comedy he attacks a notorious court vice; in his criticism he returns to the enthusiasms of his first period, making it his special concern to defend real poetry, above all that of the Elizabethans, against carping fault-finders.

At the beginning of the fourth period Dryden is called back, in time of need, to the service of the court; but now, instead of being expected to write plays for the royal amusement, he is set to produce in rapid succession, pamphlets and satires in defense of his master's cause: and the criticism produced during this period is, as one might expect, meager in quantity, and as to its spirit, coldly rationalistic, approximating the character of eighteenth century English rationalism.

During his fifth period our author gains his livelihood chiefly by catering to the constantly growing literary public, and thus gains moral and intellectual independence; after having failed at play- writing he gives almost undivided attention to his translations: his time and energy being now entirely taken up by purely literary labors, his critical dissertations, some of them long and carefully worked out, gradually increase in spirit and originality till they resemble those of the first and third periods; they differentiate themselves from these by an evenness of tone and a certainty of grasp, and, more especially, by an evident attempt on Dry den's part to harmonize his instinctive feelings toward literature with his reasoned judgments.

I have not been able to discover a clean-cut, logical development either in Dryden's critical methods or in his formal literary creed. In 1665, when he wrote the Essay v of Dramatic Poesy, he seems to have been master of all the critical tools which he was to use during his long and active career. He never formally adopted and defended the doctrines of any critical school.

The periods in his critical evolution which I have attempted to define are, at least in chief part, the results of his adaptation to changing conditions. But these changing conditions did not impose upon him a profession of faith in abstract principles. Each new environment called for defense of, or opposition to, certain literary men or literary types; and though the development of critical theory is of the utmost importance to the student of esthetics, it made little difference to Dryden, or to those whom he tried to please, just how he went about his task.

Therefore 4t —is- his literary allegiances, rather than his " literary methods or theories, which divide our author's criticism into periods. In stating that abstract theories did not furnish the points of departure for Dryden's critical development I do not wish to imply that the periods of this development are formally indistinguishable.

With our author's changing environment and the consequent variation in his literary motives and purposes there naturally went alterations in it more or less clearly mirrored in his formal critical theory. Before attempting formally to characterize Dryden's critical periods it w.ill, be necessary to make a classification of critical methods.

The history of criticism may be roughly represented as a long conflict between two parties: on the one side are those who insist on understanding what they enjoy, or, as it has often worked out in practice, enjoying only what they understand; on the other are those who allow full play to their instinctive feelings, either making no inquiry for systematic explanations, or, when these are given, attempting to bend them to the task of justifying the pleasurable emotion already experienced.

These parties represent two opposite types of mind —

the rationalistic and the romantic. In Dryden's time the rationalists were, as has been re- marked above, of two sorts: on the one hand were those of the French school, usually called neoclassicists, rationalizing literature by creating it in accordance with logical principles; on the other were the representatives of the English school achieving much the same result by holding literature down to the good-sense standards of ordinary life.

The romanticist, of course, has no critical method; absence of method is the very essence of his way of looking at art. When he begins to account for the charm of romantic literature, as did the critics of the nineteenth century, he develops in the direction of a larger rationalism.

A really romantic critic, in the sense in which I am using the term, is not merely one who defends romantic literature — the most cold- blooded modern rationalist can do that — but one who defends it, as Matthew Arnold so often did, by an immediate appeal to the emotions.

Looking back on the long struggle between romanticism and rationalism, we usually give our sympathy to the former, while we visit with something like scorn the dogmatic blindness of the latter. And it must be confessed that, judged by the standards of our taste, the rationalist of the past has usually been in the wrong: he has habitually supposed his analysis complete when, perhaps, the very heart of the matter has escaped him.

But although the rationalist of outlived periods loses nearly all the cases which he pleads before the jury of modern opinion, it is true, nevertheless, that in one sense the history of criticism exhibits him in the character of victor.

His analyses have never been complete; he has never been able, either to justify the literature which instinct has recognized as great or to outline a successful theory for the production of such literature. But, from age to age, his critical scheme of things has widened tremendously. The very attacks of the romanticists have forced upon him doctrines which have permitted the formal recognition of the romantic types of literature.

The majority of modern critics, pouring out the "vials of their wrath upon seventeenth century rationalists, are merely later rationalists with a widened scheme of esthetic theory. It is true that during the seventeenth century the rationalistic creed seemed to be narrowing itself down, crystalizing itself. Just at this time, nevertheless, men like Dryden, largely romantic in their temperament, were attempting to force upon it the historical manner of looking at literature.

In one sense the historical method combines, and mediates between, rationalism and romanticism: attempts, by historical analysis, to explain all types and view-points. But in another sense it is merely a rationalism made broad enough to include everything else; its attempt is always to make intelligible the creation and character of works of art.

In attempting to give formal characterization to the periods of Dryden's critical development we should bear in mind these four methods of criticism, with the definitions which have been given to them: the romantic, the French rationalistic, or neoclassic, the English rationalistic, and the historical.

One should also remember that Dryden's transitions were not conscious and formal, that he was always bent on vindicating his man, his poem, his type of literature, never on exhibiting a method of criticism. With the reservations which these statements imply the following generalizations are approximately accurate.

During his first period Dryden used practically all four of the methods which have been defined above; but the period is given its prevailing character by the fact that the English rationalistic way of looking at literature played a decidedly subordinate part, and that the romantic method stood out prominently above the others.

Chapter 4

Fables Ancient and Modern

John Dryden's last, and one of his finest, literary achievements was a collection of new translations of classical and medieval poetry, published together with some of his own original poems and a preface considered to be one of his most important critical essays.

This volume, entitled *Fables, Ancient and Modern,* was published in 1700 to the acclaim of Dryden's English contemporaries. Dryden had already translated classical poetry by authors like Ovid and Juvenal in the 1680s, and he turned to translating again in the early 1690s to provide himself with a source of income as his dramatic success declined.

Literary translation from the Greek and Latin poets was a conventional exercise, but Dryden's genius for poetry enabled him to create superlative new editions of the ancient works. In 1697 Dryden published his complete poetic translations of Virgil's *Aeneid, Pastorals,* and *Georgics,* which earned him increasing fame and considerable financial gain. The public's enthusiasm for more translated classics then inspired him to write Fables, Ancient and Modern.

Fables, Ancient and Modern contains ancient, medieval and original poetry: verse translations of the First Book of Homer's Iliad and selected tales from Ovid's Metamorphoses; three stories from the Italian poet Giovanni Boccaccio and five from the English poet Geoffrey Chaucer's Canterbury Tales; and one of Dryden's finest lyrical works, "Alexander's Feast", an ode written for the 1697 musical celebration of St. Cecilia's Day in London. A fable also includes one of Dryden's most influential critical essays, "Preface to the *Fables*".

In translation, the central difficulty is the necessity of reproducing both the meaning and versification of the original poem. The translator's art must approximate the original in its style of diction and verse. Translators prior to Dryden usually succeeded in restating the ideas of the original while too often sacrificing meter.

Dryden thus formulated the new principles of poetic translation: that the closest translations were to be considered the best, but that translators might reshape their materials, seeking an equivalent meaning to preserve meter. "Translation therefore is not so loose as paraphrase, nor so close as metaphrase", stated Dryden. The poetic translations in *Fables, Ancient and Modern* are considered to be some of his finest.

In the course of his career, Dryden had created the first major body of works in English literary criticism. Dryden's principles of composition in poetry and drama influenced writers throughout the eighteenth century, when critic Samuel Johnson designated him as "the Father of English criticism". "Preface to the *Fables*" is arguably Dryden's most important critical work. Here Dryden explains his criteria for selecting the poetry included in the *Fables*, Christianity and Criticism.

Michael Blowhard's recent post on G.K. Chesterton and his previous post on C.S. Lewis provoked me to some thinking about Christianity and its relation to the arts and their criticism. Michael asks why Chesterton eventually embraced Catholicism? Well, part of the impulse towards monotheism is desire for the unification of all life into a coherent whole. Its a kind of way to collect all the scattered parts of ourself and the universe and put them into some relative order. Somebody out there is in charge. Somebody knows the truth. I would guess that is what appealed to Chesterton the quasi-autistic system lover.

But while Chesterton was an intense admirer of reason and system making (one of his best books is on Thomas Aquinas), he also loved to enter into imaginative sympathy with all the great diversity of life. He read and appreciated everything. So, how to pack his genuine appreciation for all the wonderful stuff that's out there into just one system? Well, the Catholic Church, for all its faults, does at least *try* to include everything. If you like a simple, nature loving Christianity there is St. Francis; if you love poetry there is Dante; love art, there is Michelangelo and Bernini; like heavy duty logic, Aquinas; Puritanical rigor, Pascal; tripped out mysticism, there is St. Theresa; or Protestant-like Bible reading, St. John of the Cross. What ultimately brought Chesterton to Catholicism was that it included all that under one roof, that it reconciled his desire to do right by both the one and the many.

Now, perhaps this desire to fit everything into a system was the reason Chesterton was a better critic and essayist than he was a poet. Michael discerns a definite link between Christianity and Western rational thought, and criticism, unlike poetry, does have something of a systemizing element to it. "I will not reason and compare, it is my business to create," wrote William Blake, but while that is all well and good for the poet, the critic's job, or at least part of his job, *is* to reason and compare. Criticism is, at least partially, an attempt to put everything in its rightful place.

Perhaps there is something inherently congenial about this process for devout Christians: if you know the appeal of the imaginative, but at the same time feel the pull of the systematic and logical, then maybe you might be attracted to literary criticism, or to Christianity.

This brings me back to something that has always struck me: why are so many of the great literary critics, at least in English, devout, orthodox Christians? Examples include not only Chesterton, but Dryden, Johnson, Coleridge, Lewis, Eliot, Auden. Compare the rate of devout Christian critics with that of poets and there is just no question the trend is real. Furthermore, is it any co-incidence that that Harold Bloom has (very reluctantly) called the Augustine of *The Confessions* the originator of modern literary criticism?

But if perhaps there is something almost inherently Christian about literary criticism, perhaps there is also something inherently pagan about poetry. Harold Bloom remarks of Portuguese poet Camoes that a return of great poetry is almost always a return of the gods. Zeus, Apollo,

Venus, Ares and the rest of the Greco-Roman pantheon are ready made metaphors. They are a constant stimulus to the imagination. Poets too need an unconventional atmosphere, they are always looking to shake things loose in hope of new images. Unlike the critic, they need not concern themselve overly much with the truth or with consistency, theological or otherwise.

"If I contradict myself, I contradict myself; I contain multitudes." If the critic in someway needs know what is true, the poet need only know what is pleasing. I should note that it is not that monotheism is wholly antithetical to poetry. Steve Sailer rightly responds to Michael on C.S. Lewis:

Surely, the Christian psychological emphasis on the need for greatness is one of the reasons that Christendom has produced more individual greatness in the arts and sciences than other civilizations.

The problem is that while monotheism is long on inspiration, it is short on images. Perhaps the example of the Koran is instructive. No one is more stridently monotheistic, or more eloquent, than the voice of God in the Koran. It is one of the most awesome poetic performances ever. (Technically, it is in what is called rhymed prose.) Yet many readers have found the book rather monotonous and repetitive. The same message is driven home with the same images over and over again, with indeniable power but with little variation.

I would note that perhaps the only truly successful reconciliation of monotheism and poetry, outside the Bible at least, is Dante's *Commedia,* and he, like Chesterton, was a Catholic. The *Commedia*'s saints and sinners, its monsters and madonnas are indeed an endless variety, but, in the end, they all rest in the one. It is an amazing performance, but perhaps unique. Only a Dante could pull it off. Only the greatest of poets could clothe the old truths in new images. I'm afraid we should expect no great return to God among the poets. But that is okay.

It no knock against monotheism to say that the poets will always err on the side of the many, the various, the new. But if poetry will always remain half-pagan, yet there is much to be said for Christianity's attempt to heal the divide between it and the rational.

We cannot live all our lives in the numinous. I for one would not want to. I do not doubt poetry's link to the divine, but I also do not doubt its link to madness. It is perhaps no co-incidence that Augustine the great literary critic was also the author of the great rationalist tract *The City of God* (a book more accurately represented by its subtitle *Against the Pagans*) where he subjects Greco-Roman paganism to such withering analysis that no one in the West has been able to take polytheism really seriously since.

Though its undoubted heir, I myself actually find *The City of God* to be a rather boring book. (Been there, done that.) Those however who would return us to the gods, great poets or not, would still be well advised to seek it out.

Chapter 5

The Origins of Criticism: From Dryden to Manley

The theatrical and literary writings of John Dryden, his influence as a pivotal figure during the emergence of literary criticism and his reputation in subsequent centuries stand at the centre of Marcie Frank's book. Dealing with the interrelated fields of gender, theatre and literary criticism, the introduction and first three chapters of the book weave a careful argument for Dryden's rehabilitation as a pre-eminent and originary critic.

The remaining two chapters are used to assess the criticism of Aphra Behn, Catherine Trotter, and Delarivier Manley who, Frank argues, were permitted access to such writings partly through Dryden's own gendering of the discourse of criticism and those subjects which it addressed. One aim of the book is to show that, 'in the later seventeenth and early eighteenth centuries, criticism was not a male genre'.

Invoking Samuel Johnson's description of Dryden as 'the "father" of criticism in English', Frank argues for a consideration of dramatic prologues, prose and verse justifications, introductory and theatrical companion pieces such as were often appended to Dryden's theatrical publications, as an early form of literary criticism. The texts under consideration include Dryden's *Essay of Dramatick Poesy* (1668), the epilogue to the second part of *The Conquest of Granada* (1672),

'The Defense of the Epilogue', his prologue to his rewriting of Shakespeare's *Troilus and Cressida*, and among those texts which have traditionally garnered more critical attention, *All For Love* and *Oedipus* (1679), which he wrote in collaboration with Nathaniel Lee. Frank's initial approach is to unpick the generational or genealogical concepts within Dryden's criticism, particularly in his treatment of his theatrical predecessors – Fletcher, Jonson and Shakespeare – to reveal the central role which theatre played in the germination of literary criticism prior to its flowering in the prose of Addison and Steele.

In doing so, the book outlines the national and gendered discourses which flow through Dryden's work and which, Frank claims, profoundly impact upon later responses to and considerations of these earlier playwrights. However, it should be said that this is not a book which centres on theatre itself, but which rather approaches it obliquely through an analysis of materials written in proximity to the early modern stage.

Those looking for a close consideration of the theatre of Dryden, Behn or Trotter will not find it here, since Frank is more interested in the idea of theatre and theatricality as a general, authorizing trope for criticism than in the practicalities or details of the late seventeenth-century stage.

Among the other theatrical texts mentioned above, Frank does turn her attention to Dryden's *The State of Innocence and the Fall of Man* (1677), his critically neglected (not to say derided) theatrical adaptation of Milton's *Paradise Lost*, but she prefers to use the idea of the stage rather loosely in order to explore the role of the genre at the root of the discourse of criticism. If occasionally the book could go further in its analysis of criticism as 'theatricalised' and 'performative' this is perhaps a question of emphasis and scholarly interest rather than a real flaw in Frank's work.

Gender, Theatre, and the Origins of Criticism is an avowedly historicist book. Finding the roots of writing practice in its cultural and social moment, Frank employs this method of reading to illuminate knotty and occasionally opaque texts and to open them out to wider meanings. Among other critics with whom the author wrestles, she takes issue with what she sees as Harold Bloom's elision of the Augustans from his study of poetic influence and with those critics she describes as 'feminist Bloomians' such as Sandra Gilbert, Susan Gubar and Dale Spender and their search for 'strictly female genealogy'. A great deal of the opening chapters are spent outlining the significance for Dryden's writing of the image of paternity, inheritance and disinheritance in the wake of the social upheaval of the mid-seventeenth century.

Her reading of Dryden's critique of his own *All For Love,* in which he voices his concern over his deployment of Octavia and the potential negative effects her presence might have upon audience sympathy for his Anthony and Cleopatra, allow Frank to bring into focus the extent to which such late seventeenth-century aesthetic debates were carried out through the discourse of gender, here specifically through the feminisation and domestication of Shakespeare's protagonists.

Having established the significance of gender as an underlying metaphor for literary criticism, Frank moves on in her final chapters to discuss the ramifications of the availability of this metaphor, one of which is the literary and critical engagement of Behn, Trotter and Manley.

In her consideration of the three women writers under scrutiny in the final two chapters of the book, Frank helpfully invokes the idea of influence, describing these writers as claiming access, through Dryden, to a national 'literary tradition and to the critical discourse whose subsequent histories have written them out'.

Frank is a careful polemicist, who develops her arguments from the work of critics such as Catherine Gallagher and Rosalind Ballaster and is subtle in the realignments which she suggests. In her reshaping of literary and critical history through the reconsideration of the relationship of male and female writers, Frank's book stands well alongside such recent work as Jennifer Summit's *Lost Property: The Women Writer and English Literary History 1380-1589* (Chicago University Press, 2000).

That said, there are a couple of odd moments in the book. For instance, Frank does not explain, and it is not clear, why Sir Charles Sedley having Edward Kynaston (the former boy actor and player of female roles) beaten up for his mockery of the peer might be 'an early instance of 'gay-bashing''. If Frank considers the actor as 'gay' (a term she always uses within scare-quotes and never simplistically) because of his previous career as a performer of female roles, this is a slip of some significance.

More importantly, perhaps, some definition of what constitutes criticism and what its aims might be would be helpful: Frank could occasionally do more to bring the contexts for her broader claims into view and to make the impact of those claims more strongly felt.

However, this is a book which is worthy of interest and which makes significant claims about the history and the gendering of literary criticism. Frank comes closest to a full articulation of those claims in the final pages of the book, when, at the end of a chapter on Delarivier Manley's *The New Atalantis* and other critical writings, she expresses the hope that her book will allow the reclamation of 'a venerable history for the scandals of criticism' (p. 138).

Chapter 6

John Dryden 1631-1700

John Dryden, the jewel of Restoration letters, was born on the 9th of August 1631, in the old calendar. His parents, Mary and Erasmus, were both members of prominent Northamptonshire puritan families, the Drydens holding land in Canons Ashby, the Pickerings, in Titchmarsh. Dryden passed his youth in the latter, until sent to Westminster School. The exact date of his entry is unknown, although it was probably around 1644. He was, therefore, in London during the height of the Civil War.

Here he would have encountered a counter-influence to his puritan upbringing, since the school had as its head Richard Busby. Besides being one of the country's most distinguished intellectual establishments (producing Sir Christopher Wren, Robert Hooke, and Dryden's contemporary, John Locke), under Busby the institution had strong leanings towards Royalism and High Church Anglicanism. This is evident in the style of Dryden's first published poem, the elegy 'Upon the Death of the Lord Hastings', composed in 1649.

In May 1650, Dryden went up as a scholar to Trinity College, Cambridge. After the Royalism of Westminster, this was a return to the culture of his family. Thomas Hill, the Master of Trinity, committed to the Parliamentary side in the recent Civil Wars, was also a proponent of godly reform in the Universities.

We know little of Dryden's life in these years: there are references to punishment for 'disobediency' and 'contumacy'; three decades later, his enemy Thomas Shadwell suggests Dryden 'traduc'd a nobleman' during this period. Detail and further evidence, as so often in Dryden's life, are wanting. He took his Bachelor's Degree in 1654, and, rather than staying to continue his education, moved to London. Presumably through the influence of his cousin, Sir Gilbert Pickering, Cromwell's Lord Chamberlain, Dryden seems to have worked as a secretary, translator, and clerk for the Commonwealth. Precise detail is again absent, but at the very least he would have been acquainted with John Milton and Andrew Marvell, employed in the same department. The three marched together in Cromwell's state funeral.

Dryden's first significant poem took as its occasion the death of Cromwell. The 'Heroic Stanzas' of 1659 break a decade-long silence (interrupted only by some minor undergraduate pieces), and show an enormous advance in the poet's work. There is a complex technical and political understanding of the possibilities of language and imagery. This poem also marks the beginning of his association with Henry Herringman, his publisher until 1678, when Dryden's relationship with Jacob Tonson begins.

With the fall of the Protectorate, and the subsequent Restoration of the Monarchy in 1660, Dryden moved, with the country, towards an endorsement of Royalism. His prolific production of significant works began here. There are the Restoration panegyrics, *Astraea Redux* and *To His Sacred Majesty*, emphatically celebrating the return of monarchy, and the Stuart Dynasty to which he would remain loyal throughout his life.

There are also the complementary addresses, early demonstrations of the astute sense for patronage and advancement through judicious dedication that can be observed throughout his career. Those praised in this period include the Chancellor, Lord Clarendon; the King's Sister-in-law, the Duchess of York; his Mistress, Lady Castlemaine; and Sir Robert Howard.

This Howard was Dryden's most significant connection in the early years of his career. The poet lodged with him for a while; they collaborated on *The Indian Queen* in 1664; fell out over the role of rhyme in Drama; and, on December 1, 1663, became Brothers-in-law, when Dryden married Elizabeth Howard. The match holds a number of mysteries: there is the problem of class difference in the marriage between a poet from the gentry and this aristocrat; the faintly disreputable past of Elizabeth, which may explain why the wedding was allowed; and religious issues, Dryden's own puritan background clashing with the Catholic leanings of the Howards. The poet had little good to say of marriage, and around 1670 took Anne Reeves, an actress, as his mistress.

In these early years of London life, there was other activity. Dryden subscribed to the Royal Society in 1662 (four years later he was ejected for non-payment of dues), and he had already begun to take his place in coffee-house society. He was, until his death, to be closely associated with Will's, in Covent-Garden, where a distinct circle of authors formed around him, including, over the years, William Congreve, John Dennis, and Samuel Garth.

There was also, in 1663, the beginning of Dryden's theatrical career. While *The Wild Gallant*, derived from a lost original of the 1630s by Richard Brome, is inadequate journeyman work, and failed commercially, it is first in the long sequence of plays that provided Dryden's main source of literary income through the next two decades.

In Summer 1665, the Theatres closed, due to the plague. Dryden retreated, with his wife, to her Father's seat in Charlton, Wiltshire. The next year was spent there, and over that time, he produced (besides a son, Charles), the first of three works that would, upon his return to London, firmly establish his reputation as dramatist, poet, and theorist.

The play was *Secret Love*, of which the King was especially fond; the poem was *Annus Mirabilis*, an 'epic in small' that combined classicism and contemporary events to create a piece of timely propaganda for an ailing government; the critical work was *Of Dramatic Poesy*, published in 1668.

The latter is particularly important. Though Dryden had written brief critical pieces before, generally as prefatory material to publications, the sustained dialogue and arguments of this piece establish him as a major poet-critic, arguably first in an important line. While his criticism may not be consistent across his career, and sometimes has a difficult relationship to practice in the works, it is an important body of thought on literature, casting light on Restoration aesthetics, and the concerns of a major artist.

Following these successes, in 1668 Dryden was appointed Poet Laureate. In 1669 the post of Historiographer Royal was also conferred. He left the Duke's theatre company for the better terms its rival, the King's, now offered, becoming a shareholder in exchange for three plays a year. June 1668 also marks the beginning of his quarrel with Howard. This was the first of many such disputes, usually much uglier, with rival poets and playwrights.

The 1670s were years largely devoted to the Drama. He wrote a large number of plays, with numerous successes soured by some failures. This body of work contains a wide range of styles: there are adaptations (1678's *Oedipus,* cowritten with Nathaniel Lee), comedies (*Marriage A-la-Mode* of 1671), tragedies (*All for Love,* 1677), and peculiar white elephants (the unperformed adaptation of John Milton's *Paradise Lost,* called *The State of Innocence* and published in 1677).

There are also the heroic dramas, a form which Dryden was instrumental in establishing. Though little read today, they retain substantial historical and cultural interest, and Restoration theatre is misunderstood without some grasp of this genre. Many of these plays also propose suprisingly radical intellectual positions, and have their share of powerful verse. They run from *The Indian Queen,* co-authored with Howard in 1664, to the best example, *Aureng-Zebe,* of 1675.

Dryden writes the first of his major satires in the middle of this decade. *Mac Flecknoe* is, particularly, an attack on the rival dramatist Thomas Shadwell. More broadly, it is an important exercise in mock-heroic verse, where classical allusion and political rhetoric are pressed into a squalid mix of literary and literal ordure:

From dusty shops neglected Authors come
Martyrs of Pies, and relics of the Bum.
Much Heywood, Shirley, Ogleby there lay,

But loads of Sh— — almost choked the way.

Composed in 1676, it remained unpublished until a pirated edition of 1682. Dryden did not acknowledge it as his own for another decade.

On the 18th of December, 1679, the poet was ambushed and brutally beaten by hired thugs in Rose Alley, near his London home. Despite the offer of a fifty pound reward, no culprit was found. Later scholarship can add little. There are suspects: the Earl of Rochester, insulted in the Earl of Mulgrave's *Essay on Satire,* with which Dryden helped; Louise Kerouaille, Duchess of Portsmouth, another of the King's mistresses, like Rochester abused in Mulgrave's work; or possibly members of the Whig party, already attacked by the Tory Dryden. There is evidence against each hypothesis, and the incident remains mysterious.

Dryden's true return to verse followed almost immediately, along with full engagement in partisan political conflict. This was the period of the 'Popish Plot' and 'Exclusion Crisis'. In short, Titus Oates, a clergyman with an extraordinarily shady and disreputable history, made a sequence of depositions, claiming a Jesuit plot to assassinate the King and take over the country. After a murder which seemed to endorse this story, public hysteria rose, leading to a parliamentary movement to exclude the King's heir, his Catholic brother the Duke of York (later James II) from the throne. In his place, they demanded that the King legitimise his bastard son, the Duke of Monmouth.

This movement was led by the First Earl of Shaftesbury, and was known as the Whig party. Those loyal to the King and Duke were Tories. Thanks in part to a lapse in the laws to license printing, both sides produced an enormous amount of pamphlets and propaganda.

Dryden's first real contribution to the debate was 1680's *The Spanish Friar,* a tragicomedy concerned with problems of succession, and mob rule. He then most probably wrote the pamphlet *His Majesties Declaration Defended,* again following the anti-whig, anti-exclusion line. This was followed in 1681 by Dryden's satirical masterpiece, *Absalom and Achitophel*. This takes the biblical story of David and Absalom, from II Samuel, and applies it to the contemporary political scene: David is Charles II; Absalom is Monmouth; and Achitophel is Shaftesbury. It is a remarkable piece of propaganda and poetry, an exercise in pretended moderation, allusive satire, and a control of register, figure and metre that overshoots its particular political purpose:

But wild Ambition loves to slide, not stand,
And Fortune's ice prefers to Virtue's land.

The Medal followed in 1682, an impressive, if less orderly attack on Shaftesbury.

1682 was also the year of *Religio Laici,* a profession of faith that defended an apparently moderate Anglicanism against the arguments of dissenters, deists and Catholics. It is another demonstration of Dryden's gift for argument in verse, and its fluid rhetoric manages to distract, for the most part, from the ambiguities and heresies that are under its surface.

More Exclusion propaganda followed, but as the crisis drew to a close in 1683, other projects and pieces emerge. Dryden's interest in translation, evident from his important theoretical statement in the 1679 preface to a rendering of Ovid's Epistles by various hands, produced important versions of works by Lucretius and Horace. Much of his most engaging poetry also comes from the middle years of the decade: the Oldham elegy of 1684, the Killigrew ode in 1685, and the Song for St. Cecilia's day in 1687.

Charles II died in 1685, and was succeeded by his brother, James II. The event sent Dryden back to the voice of the Restoration panegyrics, with the elegy *Threnodia Augustalis,* and, later, *Britannia Rediviva,* on the birth of an heir to James. These are mature public poems, encompassing sophisticated poetic experiment, and complex ironies.

Dryden converted to Catholicism at around the time of Charles' death. There seem to be a number of reasons: perhaps advancement at the court of a monarch committed to that faith, and perhaps the influence of his wife's family. In the end, however, the evidence suggests the turn was sincere. He never recanted his faith under later pressures, and one of his sons went on to become a priest. The move to Catholicism also produced his longest, and most difficult, original poem *The Hind and the Panther*. It is a beast fable, opposing the claims of the Catholic (represented by the Hind) and Anglican (the Panther) churches, that contains more fables, inset, and a defence of King James' unpopular policies. Its virtues went unrecognised, and both poem and poet were attacked from all quarters.

In 1688, after James had pushed Royal prerogative too far, too often, a small group of noblemen invited Mary, James' daughter, and her Husband William of Orange, the Dutch stadtholder, to take the throne of England, in order to save the country from its Catholic monarch. On William's arrival, James panicked and fled to France, leaving the nation to the couple.

This sequence of events was the beginning of a difficult last decade for Dryden. He remained loyal to James II, his line, and Catholicism, despite this leading to punitive taxation, and the loss of his posts as Laureate and Historiographer Royal.

These late years were spent still arguing politically, but in a more covert fashion. Beneath the surface of the late plays and translations, there is a thorough criticism and interrogation of the principles and nature of the 'Glorious Revolution' which had taken place.

There are four last plays, including one of the strongest of his tragedies, *Don Sebastian*. The majority of his later poems are translations, of which the most significant is his Virgil. Half again as long as the original, the *Aeneid* is as much a creation of Dryden as a simple translation, and stands in for the epic that he had wanted, but failed, to write throughout his career.

Like the other translations of the 1690s - Juvenal, Persius, Ovid, Chaucer, and Boccaccio - the processes of selection and expansion work to create a poetry complementing the themes of Dryden's original works: history, power, succession, love, piety, and art. Dryden's last volume of verse, *Fables, Ancient and Modern* was published in 1700. He died on May the first of the same year.

Much of Dryden's best writing has been omitted in this

sketch. There are the prefaces and dedications that make up the first major body of criticism in English; there are the prologues and epilogues to the plays, which constitute a sequence of demotic, allusive, and witty poems, containing all the energy and precision wanting in the weaker dramas.

There are also missing oddities, such as *Eleanora*, the lengthy, Donne-influenced elegy for a Woman Dryden had never met, and *The Secular Masque*, his late review of the century. The variety, quality, mass and sense of Dryden's verse still have the power to astonish.

In the years immediately following his death, Dryden was recognised as one of the greatest literary innovators and refiners that the nation had produced. While some were still determined to attack the author, for the most part even enemies were swilling to acknowledge his stature.

His reputation remained high throughout the eighteenth century. Alexander Pope's respect is evident, and Samuel Johnson, despite his reservations, and acute criticisms, still recognises the nature and extent of Dryden's achievement, observing particularly the embellishment of English verse by the poet: 'he found it brick, and left it marble.'

It is with the Romantics that Dryden's reputation truly begins to take a turn downwards. Wordsworth had little time for the author, claiming 'his is not a poetical genius', while Coleridge expresses only a qualified admiration. There are still defenders, however. Most importantly Sir Walter Scott, produced, in 1808, an important edition of the works.

It is with the Victorians that Dryden's standing truly plummets. There is little sustained criticism from the period, and the most significant statements are T.B. Macaulay's *ad hominem* attack, and Matthew Arnold's demotion of both Dryden and Pope: rather than 'classics of our poetry, they are classics of our prose.'

Revival came in the twentieth century. Critical works, such as Mark Van Doren's 1920 *Poetry of John Dryden*, and Louis I. Bredvold's *Intellectual Milieu of John Dryden* (1934) contributed to the construction of an academic industry in studies of the poet, while the sponsorship of T.S. Eliot was still more important, leading to a practical re-evaluation of the poetic virtues present in the works. Since then, the major current in Dryden studies has been a largely historicised approach, concentrating on context and political rhetoric.

The monuments to this reconstruction of Restoration literary culture are the California Edition of the works, and James A. Winn's *John Dryden and his World*, the standard biography. Judith Sloman and William Frost led a revival of interest in the translations, while the poetry has been persuasively interpreted by Earl Miner, James Garrison, and Paul Hammond. More recently, there have been still closer readings of context and convention, notably in the work of Steven Zwicker.

His first important literary effort, *Heroic Stanzas* to the memory of Cromwell, was published in 1659. This was followed the next year by verses on the return of Charles. In order to add to his slender income, he turned to the stage, and after two unsuccessful attempts he produced his first play, *The Wild Gallant*, in 1663. This comedy was not well received, and Dryden confesses that his forte was not comedy.

The same year he produced *The Rival Ladies*, and married Lady Elizabeth Howard. *The Indian Queen* (1664), written in collaboration with Sir Robert Howard, his wife's brother, enjoyed considerable success. Dryden followed this with *The Indian Emperor* (1665). During the Plague Dryden lived with his father-in-law in Wiltshire, where he wrote his *Essay of Dramatick Poesie* (1668). Howard's preface to his *Four New Playes* (1665) called forth a reply from Dryden: *A Defence of an Essay of Dramatique Poesie* (1668). From the re-opening of the theaters in 1666, to 1681, Dryden wrote little except his plays.

The production of Buckingham's satirical play *The Rehearsal* in 1671, in which Dryden was the chief personage, called forth the preface *Of Heroic Plays* and *Defence of the Epilogue* (1672). *All for Love*, in all probability the poet's greatest play, was performed in 1678. He continued to produce plays to the end of his career. In 1681 he turned to satire and wrote *Absalom and Achitophel*, which achieved instant and widespread popularity.

This was followed by other satires. In 1687, after his conversion to the Catholic Church, he wrote *The Hind and the Panther*, a plea for Catholicism. His Catholic leanings lost for him the laureateship and other offices when the Revolution came. During his last ten years he translated many of the Latin classics: Virgil, Ovid, Lucretius, Horace, Theocritus, and others, and modernized Chaucer. He died in 1700, and was buried in Westminster Abbey.

Dryden's contribution to English literature, besides his poems and plays, was the invention of a direct and simple style for literary criticism. He improved upon the prose of the Elizabethan writers in the matter of ridding English of its involved forms, even if through that process he lost some of its gorgeous ornament and rugged strength. Jonson's method in criticism was after all not much more than the note-book method of jotting down stray thoughts and opinions and reactions.

Dryden elaborated his ideas, sought the weight of authority, argued both sides of the question, and adduced proofs. Dryden performed an inestimable service to his countrymen in applying true standards of criticism to the Elizabethans and in showing them a genuine and sympathetic if occasionally misguided love for Shakespeare. Dryden also enjoyed the advantage of being able to bring his knowledge of the drama of Spain and France to bear on his criticism of English dramatists.

John Dryden, an English poet and dramatist who would dominate literary efforts of The Restoration, was born on August 19, 1631, in Aldwinkle, Northamptonshire, England. He received a classical education at Westminster School and Trinity College, Cambridge, then moved to London in 1657 to commence his career as a professional writer. His first play, *The Wild Gallant* (1663), was a failure when first presented, but Dryden soon found more success with *The Indian Queen* (1664) which he co-authored with Sir Robert Howard and which served as his initial attempt to found a new theatrical genre, the heroic tragedy.

Although George Villiers' *The Rehearsal*, a vicious satire

of heroic tragedy, brought a quick end to the form, Dryden still managed to produce a number of successful works in this genre including *The Indian Emperor* (1665) and *Secret Love* (1667) which mixed heroic tragedy with contemporary comedy.

The young playwright's reputation grew quickly, and in 1668, only ten years after his move to London, Dryden was appointed Poet Laureate of England. (He was later stripped of the title because of religious differences when William and Mary came into power.)

That same year, he agreed to write exclusively for Thomas Killigrew's theatrical company and became a shareholder. Both his first offering, *Tyrannick Love* (1669), and his successful follow-up, *The Conquest of Granada by the Spaniards* (1670), are examples of heroic tragedy. In 1672, however, perhaps sensing the demise of his short-lived genre, Dryden turned his hand to comedy and produced *Marriage A-la-Mode*, a brilliant battle of the sexes. Dryden's relationship with Killigrew's company continued until 1678 at which point he broke with the theatre (which was floundering in debt) and offered his latest play, *Oedipus*, a drama he had co-authored with Nathaniel Lee, to another company.

In his later years, Dryden turned to poetry and solidified his reputation as the leading writer of the day with such masterpieces as *Absalom and Achitophel*. However, he continued to write for the theatre, producing such plays as *Don Sebastian* (1689), the story of a king who abdicates his throne after discovering that he has committed incest, and *Amphitryon* (1690), a brilliant retelling of the classic myth.

He also adapted a number of Shakespeare's plays icluding *The Tempest* and *All for Love* (1677), a retelling of *Antony and Cleopatra*. In addition, he wrote the libretto for several operas including *The State of Innocence* (1677) (an adaptation of Milton's *Paradise Lost*) and *King Arthur* (1691) with music by Purcell. John Dryden died in London on May 12, 1700, and was buried in Westminster Abbey next to Chaucer. He left behind almost 30 works for the stage as well as a major critical study (*An Essay on Dramatic Poesy*) and a number of translations including the works of Virgil.

Chapter 7

John Dryden's Translation of Ovid's Metamorphoses

The Latin poet Ovid composed his renowned *Metamorphoses* during the reign of the emperor Augustus. The poem is perhaps best described as in a genre of its own - a super-epic. Constructed of approximately 250 epylia interwoven into one continuous narrative, it is still debated whether or not this has the technical and narrative qualifications for an ancient epic. It is definable as a super-epic, though, as it best formulates what Ovid himself was striving to create; a 'carmen perpetuum' [everlasting song], as he vows in his opening in Book I.

It could be said that it is a work fuelled by egocentricity. He mocks the epic tradition and its hyperbolic gravity and pushes the limits of the epic genre to the full. His frequent bathos and comic attempts in serious moments can however make him seem more of a Puck, not the intended Oberon. But the key to Ovid's trickery is his beautiful and emotional retelling of the myths.

This rich anthology of myth embedded in the poem (varnished with Ovid's fertile imagination) is undeniably what is plundered most from Ovid's work; Chaucer and Shakespeare were frequenters of his poetry.

In *A Midsummer Night's Dream* the Mechanicals' play-within-the-play (the myth of *Pyramus and Thisbe*) has been plucked from *Metamorphoses*. Yet these aspects are all but the tip of the aesthetic iceberg. Ovid's genius lies beneath: His technical mastery and his manipulation of the contents. What comprises *Metamorphoses'* three-dimensional essence is active and sharp imagery, varying narrative perspectives, emotional drama and diversity in mood, pace, tone and subject matter. Though perhaps inappropriate to become engrossed in any allegorical philosophy woven into *Metamorphoses'*, theological threads (i.e. the transmigration of souls) must nonetheless be considered in the poem's meaning. It is Ovid's skill of narrative which turns a set of carved reliefs into a Technicolor film.

Besides imitation and allusion to *Metamorphoses,* perhaps the greatest task is to translate effectively. John Dryden (1631 - 1700) translated approximately forty-thousand lines of ancient language into Jacobean verse; among them, several of Ovid's epylia. Concentrating on his translation of Ovid's story of Ceyx and Alcyone, I wish to discern whether or not Dryden has captured this three-dimensional aspect of *Metamorphoses;* whether or not he has translated the components of both the vivid story and the masterful technique of Ovid.

Dryden himself follows in the tradition of Jacobean modernism after Ben Jonson. Though using the classics as a template for all of his work, he nonetheless pioneered in all major literary fields; literary criticism, poetry, drama, translation and satire. In 1666 he published his modern epic Annus Mirabilis charting the heroic reconstruction of the post-Cromwellian state.

Months later however, this triumph was somewhat overshadowed by Milton's *Paradise Lost,* touching on the deep religious unrest. This suggested that Dryden had not written so pertinently. Owing to religious issues, Dryden became reclusive in retirement and chose to write translation as a social shield. The object of his art was to capture beauty, poetic beauty. His writing is based more around this aesthetic than any other.

The episode that Dryden has translated in *Ceyx and Alcyone* follows Ceyx, the Trachinian king. He is resolved, after certain omens, to go by sea to the oracle at Claros. Alcyone, his beloved queen, begs him in vain not to leave. Ceyx's ship is wrecked in a storm and he dies. The ignorant Alcyone, at home, prays for his return; she angers Juno who orders a dream to be sent to her reporting Ceyx's death. Iris, Juno's messenger, reports this to the god of Sleep. Sleep sends his most capable son, Morpheus, to Alcyone in her sleep. Morpheus imitates Ceyx's ghost and tells her that he is dead. Alcyone, grief-stricken, goes onto the shore where she and Ceyx parted; Ceyx's body returns in the waves to her. She is transformed into a Halcyon bird by Apollo. She kisses Ceyx, who is revived and also transforms into a bird.

Most immediately striking about Dryden's translation is the directness of his writing. It is economical, succinct and full of vitality. It many ways it mirrors Ovid's economy and precision. Both the original and the translation have their virtues and their vices.

But a naked and literal comparison of Dryden to Ovid, using a checklist as it were, would be a biased approach. Dryden's literary intentions for his translation are tantamount to Ovid's. "I have not tied myself to a literal translation; but I have often admitted what I have judged necessary or not of dignity to appear in the company of better thoughts".

Dryden aims to use Ovid's work as a potentially beautiful sculpture, not yet finished; to then chip away at the jagged and incongruous edges, refining every curve and line to maximise the beauty of the original masonry. Dryden's 'Essay on Dramatic Poesy' gives a more specific glimpse of his approach to Ovid, "who wrote things so near the drama". Dryden, like countless others, recognised the sublime dramatic, even theatrical potential within *Metamorphoses*. His translation is very active in exposing capacity for drama within a piece of action.

Early in the passage, Ceyx has left and Alcyone returns to their bed:

Alcyonae lacrimas et, quae pars, admonet, absit.

Lit: '[the bed and surroundings renew] tears in Alcyone, and they remind her of that part which is absent'.

Yet Dryden's adds:

Her husband's pillow, the widowed part
Which once he pressed.

Dryden's detailed observation of the bed is indicative of

his attempts to rouse sympathy for the abandoned Alcyone and increase the drama. He also draws attention to the bed, a recurrent motif in the passage.

Moreover, it is an indication of his liberal use of the text and his licence to modify it to his tastes. On translation, Dryden writes: "But though I grant that here and there we may miss the application of a proverb or custom, yet a thing well said will be writ in all languages, and though it may lose something in translation, yet, to him who reads it in the original, 'tis still the same".

Further, he claims that the elegance of the original words cannot be captured, only the impression of the word upon the line and soul. Dryden's approach is ambitious; in aiming to convey the essence of the piece, he recognises the deeper aspect of the Latin which his work must nurture. The above example immediately suggests that Dryden is trying to recreate this core of intensity and emotion.

There is no doubt that Dryden has the technical skill to match Ovid in ensnaring a feeling. During the shipwreck, Ovid captures the immense force of the waves compressing the sailors into the sea by using phonetically weighty words, such as 'gurgite pressa gravi' [lit: crushed down by the force of the water]. Dryden writes:

Down sinks the ship within the abyss below;
Down with the vessel sinks the main.

Repetition of the plosive 'down' placed emphatically at the beginning of the line resound the impact of the wave, while 'below' is placed just as importantly at the end of the line, trapping the sailors within the line (sea). 'Abyss' is apt word selection by Dryden to heighten the sense of doom for the sailors.

The technical aspects of Dryden's translation are, like Ovid's original, governed by meter and rhythm. Dryden, said to have perfected the use of heroic couplets, uses his forte. Bound by couplet rhyme and iambic pentameter, the form is strict with an ambivalent effect. It can, on the one hand, make his word selection and order more precise, or it can have the opposite effect, filling the line with monosyllabic words and pronouns. Heroic couplets are perhaps limiting, pushing much of the emphasis on rhyme which can often only account for half the beauty of the line. The iambics can result in the reader trundling along to the unchanging rhythm.

Ted Hughes, in his modern translation of some of the *Tales from Ovid*, takes word selection and placement to be paramount to portraying an emotion. He is similar to Ovid in this respect. Dactyllic hexameter, the stock Latin epic meter, was used by Ovid for his poem to be regarded as within the said genre. It permits six metrons, four of which can vary as either a dactyl [thesis/ arsis] or a spondee [thesis/ thesis].

This gives the opportunity to vary the pace of the piece, to add gravity or levity when required; both giving the writer greater control of the reader's emotions and creating a more lucid image through sound and length: (When describing Sleep's palace)

Ianua nec verso stridores cardine reddit

[Lit: No door gives a creak with the turning of its hinges]

The two out-bursts of shorter syllables (the creaking) break the predominant silence and calmness of the longer syllables in the line. Or both mood and action can be affected: (When Alcyone discovers her dead Ceyx):

*"Nulla est Alcyone, nulla est!" ait. "Occidit una"**

[Lit: "Alcyone is nothing, nothing!" She said. "She died as one..."] a = elided vowel.

The two elisions at the beginning of the line reflect Alcyone's utter choking with grief, intermittent with sobbing. In a direct comparison, Dryden's initially seems flat:

No more Alcyone, she suffered death

But instead it captures the resoluteness of later in the speech. This is due to Dryden subtly tempering his translation. He does not leap at every opportunity for tragedy, and has "admitted what I judged necessary". Though in the last example Dryden failed to process the emotion which Ovid enhances, he incorporates this technique at a later point, though Ovid this time does not: (When Alcyone realises that the dead sailor is her Ceyx):

"Tis he, 'tis he," she cries, and tears her cheeks

If an apostrophe is a close relation to the elision, Dryden has succeeded in intensifying Alcyone's tears in the disjointed effect which it brings upon the sentence. Though the flowing iambics do not permit the control of pace, Dryden uses punctuation to good effect. By his sensitive placement of punctuation and aided by language, he can influence the mood. Here, with up-beat, energetic language: (As Iris enters the palace of Sleep)

The Virgin, entering bright, indulged the day
To the brown cave, and brushed the dreams away;

The two commas in the first line serve to speed the pace, aided by the enjambment into the next line. This acceleration is timely by Dryden. He uses pace to create an entirely fresh mood from the previous line and passage, in which the reader has been introduced to the land of Sleep. (Describing the river running from a rock)

An arm of Lethe, with a gentle flow

By placing a comma in the middle of several lines, having more or less the same number of syllables either side, he gives the passage a balanced, rocking, soporific quality - in a different method from Ovid.

The passage ends with a deliberately long thirteen-syllable line, placed by Dryden to again draw out the languid feel of the passage, and at the same time indicate the number of dreams in the place. Again, it has that balanced quality: (In comparison to the number of dreams, there are not as many leaves in a wood)

Nor bearded ears in fields, nor sands upon the shore.

Just as the reader is being drawn into the slow rhythm, Dryden injects pace with the new passage of "The virgin, entering bright...", more so than is notable with Ovid, who at this point chooses to highlight a different matter; Iris's hand physically pushing through these empty dreams through word order. The strength of the hand in the middle of the line (emphasised by a dactyl) parts the dreams:

Quo simul intravit, manibusque obstantia virgo

[Lit: As soon as the virgin entered, she brushed aside the dreams with her hand.]

In comparing many of the more common techniques of Ovid and Dryden (pace, enjambment, alliteration polyptoton, juxtaposition etc.) it is similar to watching a game of chess; the same pieces either side, but moves at different intervals. Dryden is being innovative in this aspect, judging for himself where the minor technicalities help to vitalise the poem. In alliteration, for example:

The winds augment the winter of the sky
And wage intestine wars.

The pounding of 'w' resounds the futility of the tempest. In another area, Ovid chooses to recreate the trickling waters of the river Lethe:

invitat somnos crepitantibus unda lapillis.

[Lit: The water, moaning, invites sleep, drifting with the pattering pebbles].

Repetition is likewise. Though perhaps commonly used by both poets for metrical means, they are placed appropriately, and serve often to alert the reader to emotional intensity. In Dryden, Ceyx's demand for the attention and co-operation of the sailors has a similar effect in gaining the reader's attention:

Strike, strike the top of the sail; let the main sheet fly.

Dryden has also captured Ovid's frequent use of juxtaposition: Used so often in *Ceyx and Alcyone* to suggest an imbalance in the relationship of things so close - namely the king and queen. In an Ovidian example, when Alcyone is begging Ceyx not to leave:

Nec nisi quae patiar metuam: pariterque feremus
Quidquid erit, pariter super aequora lata feremur.

[Lit: I shall not fear, except for what I am suffering. We shall carry equally

And we shall be carried equally by the sea, what ever it will be.]

The polyptoton of 'pariterque...pariter' and 'feremus...feremur' is used in a microcosmic sense by Ovid to foreshadow inequality; an upset in the loving harmony of the relationship of Ceyx and Alcoyne - indeed, Ceyx will die. Here polyptoton is used, in the extreme sense, to represent the harmony of life being disrupted to lead to death. Dryden, in a characteristically perceptive and direct manner, translates:

Then o'er the bounding billows shall we fly,
Secure to live together, or to die.

The clear juxtaposition of life and death between Alcyone and Ceyx, as a means of exciting pity in the reader, is a recurring motif used by both poets, often with Dryden mirroring Ovid's placement. Despite being used to highlight a particular point, juxtaposition is also more concerned with the structure of the poem, in which Dryden rarely differs from Ovid. He is committed to "not meddling with the design [myth elements] or the disposition of it". Moreover, he acts more as the editor of appropriate material and moods, rather than taking a designer's role.

Cohesion was one of Ovid's secondary objectives in *Metamorphoses*. It was the key to his making the work appear continuous and vital in creating an epic. Ovid works tirelessly to link the epylia together. Also, in a story such as Ceyx and Alcyone where propheticism and the completion of fate play so large a part, he must make each individual story coherent and whole.

The more the fate element is highlighted, the more harrowing it is for the reader. Dryden saves himself half the onus by translating only three-quarters of this single epylion; (Ceyx and Alcyone were introduced two stories earlier).

Ring composition is used by Ovid to realise the cyclic cruelty of fate, while also to create a continuity of character. Since Alcyone parted from her husband on the shores of Trachinia, she is compelled by grief (after Morpheus' dream) to return to there. Dryden chooses to augment the sense of Alcyone's grief, by making her destination utterly precise:

That place, that very spot she sought,
Or thither where her destiny was brought.

Dryden observes that Alcyone is caught in a 'sliding doors' complex. He makes her relive exactly the events of before, again highlighting fatalism. Once more, he elucidates the catastrophic outcome of life and death separating the two lovers. The ring composition is echoed when Alcyone "embraced the dead", where formerly she had embraced her husband as he departed. Though first initiated by Ovid, they are clearly also a vital structure of Dryden's work. Dryden is also avid in bringing the reader's attention (more so than Ovid) to the recurring motif of the bed; both Alcyone and the god of Sleep centre around them. He makes it a symbol of where the absent or dead Ceyx and the living Alcyone are joined in dreams, and where the suffering Alcyone endures without Ceyx physically beside her.

The neo-classicist enters whole-heartedly into both aping and embellishing Ovid's structural techniques which are concerned with the narrative. In the similes which Ovid uses, predominantly during the shipwreck scene, Dryden is only too keen to follow suit:

Ovid:
Dat quoque ima saltus intra cava texta carinae
Fluctus; et ut milites, numero praestantior omni,
Cum saepe adsilarit defensae moenibus urbis...
Dryden:
Now all the waves their scattered force unite;
And as a soldier, foremost in the fight,
Makes way for the others, and, a host alone,
Still presses on, and, urging, gains the town.

The simile continues with the soldiers (waves) attacking the beleaguered town (ship). The simile serves to paint a more vivid picture of the nature of the shipwreck, while relating the experience to the reader through human action. The suspense of the action (which Ovid builds) in waiting for the ship to be inevitably destroyed is increased by Dryden, who, of his own accord, incorporates the same soldier simile:

The sea grew white, with rolling waves from far,
Like heralds, first denounce the watery war.

The final line is a preparatory line of Dryden's, used cleverly at the end of the passage to build up the suspense of the next passage and the shipwreck as a whole. His awareness to relate the shipwreck to human experience using personification is furthered by a metaphor he adds, again of his own doing. The victimised ship is diseased in the water:

The frothy white appear the flatted seas,
And change their colour, changing their disease.
Like various fits the Trachin vessel finds,

This very apt and vivid metaphor adds another aspect of the pain and suffering of those in the shipwreck, inducing a further element of pity. The storm scene is intended by Ovid to be deliberately hyperbolic, and Dryden achieves the same effect:

Seas dash on seas, and clouds encounter clouds;
At once from east to west, from pole to pole.

These two lines capture the repeated alliterative sounds of the war of the elements. But Dryden again exceeds Ovid, whose hyperbole is restricted vertically to the "pontus" [sea] and "nubes" [clouds]. Dryden is geographical; his entire world is shaken by the tempest.

Dryden relishes these dramatic moments, frequently commenting upon *Metamorphoses*'s theatrical potential: "Yet he of them who had a genius most proper for the stage was Ovid". But further than dramatic is Ovid's profound cinematic (by 20th Century standards) sense in his writing. This is imitated closely by Dryden to fulfil its potential to captivate the reader. From the panoramic view to the action-packed view, Ovid again adjusts the camera to zoom in on the suffering individuals:

Ovid:

Non tenet hic lacrimas, stupet hic, vocat ille beatos,
Funera quos maneant: Hic votis numen adorat
Bracchiaque ad caelum...

Dryden:

One weeps, and yet despairs of late relief;
One cannot weep, his fears congeal his grief;
But stupid, with dry eyes, expects his fate.
One with loud shrieks laments his lost estate,
And calls those happy whom their funerals await.
This wretch with prayers and vows the god implores...

It is not only Ovid's individual focus which is cinematic, but switching from person to person, giving in snap-shots a popular account of the suffering of the sailors. Dryden is only too ready to imitate. Ovid's narrative diversity is further exemplified in speech. The classical epic poems such as Virgil's *Aeneid* were all told from the third-person. Yet Ovid mocks this tradition and intensifies feeling when he moves from third-person to first-person in character speech.

The lens moves into the eye of the character as Ovid combines the form of elegiac poetry with epic poetry, never previously done in the epic tradition before him. Dryden follows suit, besides which he adds something to the translation to increase the drama.

The final key structural matter is dividing elements of comedy and tragedy. Ovid's comedy is made most commonly through (besides those already mentioned) bathos, asides to the reader and anachronism. Perhaps from a narrative perspective; the sense of a looming figure behind the scenes, manipulating the action, adds a hidden depth to the poem. But on the comedy issue, Dryden is apprehensive: "On these [emotional] occasions the poet should endeavour to raise pity; but instead of this, Ovid is tickling you to laugh".

Dryden is not opposed to comedy, having written much himself, such as the mock epic *MacFlecknoe*. He dislikes the notion of tragicomedy–or at least mixing the two emotions; in his eyes, it is fundamental that the more appropriate of the two must prevail. *Ceyx and Alcyone* is a love story; a tragedy. Still, Ovid's purpose is to mock its form and coax the reader to laugh at what Dryden considers to be inappropriate times.

Some of the supposed comedy in Ovid is so subtle that the tone of the piece is entirely subjective, according to the reader's immediate attitude. It can be considered as either poking frequent fun at the traditional love story, or dividing into two halves a predominant emotional love story with a quite independent comic interlude. Dryden certainly tries to mould it into the latter. In doing so, he makes a bold attempt to keep to his philosophy on comedy, and treats the 'Sleep episode' as a near separate story.

Ovid's text allows for that. After Iris takes off to fly to Sleep's palace, having received her orders from Juno, Ovid switches the scene. New characters are introduced (Sleep,

Morpheus, Icelus and Phantasus). Ovid's switch from the love story is definite, and the Sleep episode is unmistakably a more comic piece; Sleep himself is a satirical portrayal of an omnipotent deity. Dryden recognises this switch, increasing its potential. After the eerie, atmospheric introduction to the land of Sleep, Dryden, as mentioned before, injects sudden pace with Iris' entrance:

The virgin, entering, bright, indulged the day
To the brown cave, and brushed the dreams away.

He successfully undermines the gloomy blackness and ghostly dreams and the "quiet next to death". There is clear bathos in Iris entering with a multicoloured cloak and committing, through light, something near sacrilege. The looming dreams with haunting potential are simply "brushed" aside. The colour black has been mentioned by Dryden thrice in the last seven lines; deliberately to be undermined by the cave now being a normal brown.

From here on Dryden, following Ovid, enters precipitously into a new comic style. When Sleep finally awakes, he is comically overcome by his own powers:

Ovid: Excussit tandem sibi se...
Dryden: At length shook off himself...

In the next line, Dryden adds some comedy of his own accord, in the form of an aside:

...he asked the dame
(And asking yawned), for what intent she came?

The power of Sleep is contagious. After Iris has delivered her message, she herself is "unable to support the fumes of sleep".

Then, while discussing what Icelus (Morpheus' brother) can conjure up, Dryden lets his imagination run into the preternatural:

Beasts...dragons...dreadful images...monster shapes
Ovid states he merely
fit fera, fit volucres, fit longo corpore serpens

[Lit: becomes animals, becomes birds, becomes a snake with a long body"].

Dryden's deliberately grotesque and hellish version could

be perceived as entering further into the spirit of comedy; but it is not without its Christian undertones.

With further bathos, there is perhaps an aristocratic snigger intended, when Dryden has just described what the three dream-creating brothers can display:

These three to kings and chiefs their scenes display,
The rest before the ignoble commons play;

The idea of artificial theatricality (perhaps connected to what Dryden thought of as *Metamorphoses*' potential for the stage) in which these dreams are performed is highlighted singularly by Dryden. In particular, it is prominent in Morpheus' performance as Ceyx. First, Morpheus is "prepared for flight". Then there is a comic undermining of this "demon" creature having to do a quick change of costume:

Then lays aside the steerage of his wings
...[then] Assumes the king's;

Having delivered his monologue as Ceyx:

Thus said the player god; and adding art
Of voice and gesture, so performed his part.

There is a certain mockery to the whole 'dream-business' of Sleep and Morpheus, which is subtle comedy by Dryden. The joke is perhaps realised with Dryden imitating the comically harsh tone which Ovid gives to Morpheus (as Ceyx):

Rise, wretched widow, rise, nor undeplored...

Full of harsh imperatives, it is perhaps comic that Morpheus is unskilled and insensitive in his art. But at this point the Sleep episode begins to merge back into *Ceyx and Alcyone*. Where Ovid quite easily and inconspicuously blends his comic tone back into the tragicomic tone, Dryden becomes ambiguous. The analogy of theatre could be either subtle comedy or just imaginative writing.

After a somewhat 'iffy' changeover, Dryden realigns himself back to the tragic love story, with not a whiff of comedy throughout the remaining events. So Dryden's structure of comedy and tragedy does not differ greatly from Ovid's, but is certainly more categorised into tragedy, separate comedy, then tragedy.

Dryden's inclusion of this comedy may also serve to

increase the pity for Ceyx and Alcyone - that there are comic, insensitive gods behind the scenes controlling their two fated lives. Anachronisms are a common feature of *Metamorphoses*: This is again Ovid poking fun at the epic tradition by including Roman habit into ancient mythical times. In the previous story of *Daedalion and Chione*, Ovid mentions that the beautiful Chione's face was 'snow-white'; it was a feature of aristocratic Roman women to wear white make-up. Likewise, in *Ceyx and Alcyone*, when she finds out that her husband is to leave,

Alcyone tore apart her
totos capillos nondum ornata
[Lit: whole hair, not yet decorated].

It was also a feature of Roman women to decorate and style their hair. While Dryden includes these anachronisms he makes a point of including his own. But they are not intended for comic value. They are more connected with elements of romantic poetry, using modern versions of English myth.

"Maid" and "court" and "mansion" seem to be used for aiding the English reader to enter into the spirit of myth. However, the ghoulish anachronisms used when describing what Icelus can imitate - "dragons...monster shapes" - are also associated with English myth. Dryden is perhaps not mocking the epic tradition, but the concept of such things being able to exist in unreal dreams.

The theatricality which Dryden draws upon is one of the many aspects of his own which he mixes into the story. Dryden intends to make this a grave and emotional love story, adhering to the love story tradition rather than mocking it. This is initially indicated by the point at which he starts his translation.

After a brief prologue explaining the background of events, Dryden launches straight into Ovid's 'serious bit'. Ceyx has been portrayed by Ovid as a wimpish, neurotic king. Dryden does not give this background, but immediately creates Ceyx as a "pious prince" who is "more perplexed" by the portents, rather than Ovid's "anxia" [lit: fearful] Ceyx. For Dryden, piety and love are the virtues of Ceyx. During the shipwreck, when Ovid highlights the comic helplessness and non-heroic nature of Ceyx, the Dryden reader is more compelled to regard Ceyx as a pious victim of the gods' will.

"I comprehend the passions and, in a larger sense, the descriptions of persons and their very habits", Dryden immodestly writes. But by no means does Ovid leave Dryden with much to create with the characters, who are perfectly apt and two-dimensional for a love story. Dryden does observe characters appropriately and does not add independent actions or speeches to what Ovid has already written.

Moreover, the neo-classicist increases some of the detail with which things are done, whilst always ready to highlight issues surrounding the separation of the two, as exemplified when Alcyone returns to the shore. This is a successful technique to further excite pity for Ceyx, but predominantly distressed Alcyone (whom most of the story observes).

The only other minor difference here between the original and the translation is that Dryden's Alcyone seems to have extra elements of strength and resoluteness, as mentioned before. This idea of endurance of the human soul links well with Ceyx's piety.

Dryden is also keen to emphasise the situation in which Ovid places his characters - two inferior human lovers versus the immensity of nature and the fate of the gods. This very Hardy-esque idea emerges from Dryden's frequent reference to propheticism. Where it is implied by Ovid, Dryden prefers to state it. When Alcyone begs Ceyx not to leave, having seen visions of tombs without names on the shore:

And fears are oft prophetic of the event.

Then, when she sees the dead Ceyx in Morpheus' dream:

And my prophetic fear presaged too true.

The semi-conscious sense which Alcyone has of being aware of her own tragedy adds a further emotional element to the story. It also intensifies the theme of fate running through Ceyx and Alcyone.

Both poets' attention to the descriptive lighting elements of the story are vital in creating fuller images. But another continuous theme which Dryden includes, this time of his own accord, is the opposition of vision and blindness. During the shipwreck, he not only paints an appropriately black, Acherontic picture (as Ovid does) but he further mentions:

So swirl the seas, such darkness blinds the sky.

There is also the conflict of Alcyone's foresight and then its cyclic fulfilment in the dream. She is adamant that she saw the real Ceyx:

I saw, I saw him manifest in view.

Then there is a further sight element when Alcyone, mourning, stands on the shore and sees a dead sailor float towards her; her eyes cannot make out who it is; "...Who could judge aright?", as Dryden moves Ovid's narrative camera to behind Alcyone's eyes. Then, when the body is closer, she sees truly and realises it is Ceyx. The sight element is closely linked with fate, and again it indicates Alcyone's consciousness of her own fate.

Mistrust and misjudgement of sight is also suggested, and serves to heighten the pathos felt for Alcyone when she so desires Ceyx to be physically with her. Her hopes are betrayed by sight, and she is grappling with what is truth and what is illusion.

There is a slight philosophical element here about perceiving truth, perhaps referring to the empirical theories of contemporary philosophers such as John Locke (1632 - 1704), and the ability to find truth through the five senses. In his poem *Veni, Creator Spiritus*, a prayer to God, Dryden begs for God to "Submit the senses to our soul" and "Make us Eternal Truths receive".

This quest for truth can possibly only be fulfilled by God, and the human senses are unreliable to the eternal soul. This issue of whether man was able to act independently of God was a subject of contemporary philosophical debate, highlighted by Milton's *Paradise Lost*. Dryden's Augustan successor, Pope, discussed this topic in his *Essay on Man*.

However, it is presumptuous to attribute personal truths to Dryden in the translated text. He has written a poem "which I hope I have translated closely enough and given them the same turn of verse which they had in the original". Translating was a means for Dryden to make a living. Having lost his office as poet laureate upon the accession of the Protestant William III in 1689, Dryden, a convert to Roman Catholicism, was urged to become more guarded in his opinions and beliefs. Translating was a way of doing this.

Despite this, there is a clear Christian theme running through *Ceyx and Alcyone* - an extension, perhaps, of the anachronism. The structure of Ovid's story is close to the English romantic structure like that of *Sir Gawain*. In this, for example, the hero leaves the Christian sophistication of Arthur's court, entering into the preternatural heathen world on his quest, until he finds a haven-castle by the will of God. The action then comes in the hunts of his host and the moral is given, somewhat subversively in this case, by the Green Knight at the end of the tale.

In Dryden's translation Ceyx is the "pious prince" who sails off into the shipwreck (the action), then the gloomy world of Sleep (in which Dryden places Christian images concerned with Hell) and then the resolution, with Ceyx coming back to life. "I have endeavoured to choose such fables, both ancient and modern, as contain each of them some instructive moral".

If Dryden does intend to include an *instructive* moral in *Ceyx and Alcyone,* it is difficult to recognise and state precisely without being tenuous. At best, love, Platonic love, is eternal. However, this is perhaps what Ovid himself was trying to say - and thus the reason Dryden translated it. Themes are indeed captured by Dryden. But to be instructive would be rash and anaesthetically blunt:

This is the intelligentsia being written to. It is also worth considering that quite what constituted a moral parameter by which to instruct in late 1600s society was significantly doubtful. I prefer the suggestion that this is a faint moralising stab of an ostracised and ageing conservative Catholic to the emerging sceptical materialists of the cosmopolitan class - the class which Pope was soon to satirise in *The Rape of the Lock.*

"I have but a house where I intended but a lodge", wrote Dryden on his composition of translation poetry. This is indicative of the creative process through which he has gone in translating *Ceyx and Alcyone.* He entered it with strong intentions and has proved an effective judge of appropriate material. If his ultimate objective was to capture "Ovid's beaux", as Dryden puts it, he has succeeded. His ability to imitate Ovid and innovate to equal Ovid's technical brilliance has resulted in Dryden's translation being thorough, full of imagery, diverse and energetic. Moreover, his sensitivity towards the reader's emotions (rather than the egotism engulfing Ovid's work) has created a temperate piece of poetry.

Dryden has overcome the language barrier and captured that all-important three-dimensional effect of Ovid's. The dramatic scenes, the cinematic element, the descriptive vigour and the narrative diversity of both poets bring the work alive. Dryden's translation apes those techniques and descriptions which create the effect, and where the drama can be increased, does so suitably. Though his moral intention is not clear, the work has emotional and some philosophical depth.

On translation, the present-day poet Seamus Heaney writes; "It is one thing to find lexical meaning for the words and to have some feel for how the meter might go, but it is quite another thing to find the tuning fork that will give you the note and pitch of the overall work". In a brief modern comparison with Dryden, Heaney's translation of *Beowulf* also both innovates and imitates.

Heaney does not conform to the strict, alliterative Anglo-Saxon meter, yet his word selection and creation resounds the organic and onomatopoeic feel to every Anglo-Saxon word. For both translators it is fundamental to retain a feeling of the work. For Dryden it is essential to convey this to the soul, and he uses all necessary means to do this. In his own words: "An author is not to write all he can, but all he ought".

WHO ACTUALLY WROTE SHAKESPEARE?

"Things without remedy, should be without regard; what is done, is done"

Over the centuries there has been much debate (which still continues today) on scholars' claims that Shakespeare actually wrote all of the works which have been accredited to him. The idea that Shakespeare's plays and poems were not actually written by William Shakespeare of Stratford has been the subject of many books and is widely regarded as at least an interesting possibility. The source of all doubts about the authorship of the plays lies in the disparity between the greatness of Shakespeare's literary achievement and his comparatively humble origin, the supposed inadequacy of his education and the obscurity of his life.

In Shakespeare's writings, people have claimed to discover a familiarity with languages and literature, with such subjects as law, history, politics and geography, and with the manners and speech of courts, which they regard as inconceivable in a common player, the son of a provincial tradesman. This range of knowledge, it is said, is to be expected at that period only in a man of extensive education, one who was familiar with such royal and noble personages as figure largely in Shakespeare's plays.

And the dearth of contemporary records has been regarded as incompatible with Shakespeare's eminence and as therefore suggestive of mystery. That none of his manuscripts has survived has been taken as evidence that they were destroyed to conceal the identity of their author.

IF SHAKESPEARE DIDN'T WRITE SHAKESPEARE, THEN WHO DID?

Since Shakespeare's four centuries' ago, hypotheses put forward are that: Francis Bacon wrote Shakespeare, Edward de Vere (Earl of Oxford) wrote Shakespeare, William Stanley (Earl of Dérby) wrote Shakespeare, Roger Manners (Earl of Rutland) wrote Shakespeare, Christopher Marlowe wrote Shakespeare, several of these (and others) wrote Shakespeare or that Shakespeare himself stole others' works!

The outward events of Shakespeare's life are ordinary. He was hard-working, sobre, and middle-class in his ways. He steadily gathered wealth and took good care of his family. Many people have found it impossible to believe that such a man could have written the plays. They feel that he could not have known such heights and depths of passion. They believe that the people around Shakespeare expressed little realisation of his greatness. Some say that a man of his little schooling could not have learned about the professions, the aristocratic sports of hawking and hunting, the speech and manners of the upper classes. However, some men around Shakespeare for example, Meres in 1598 and Jonson in 1623 did recognise his worth as a man and as a writer.

To argue that an obscure Stratford boy could not have become the Shakespeare of literature is to ignore the mystery of genius. His knowledge is of the kind that could not be learned in school. It is the kind that only a genius could learn, by applying a keen intelligence to everyday life. Some great writers have had even less schooling than Shakespeare.

The Claims Put Forward for Bacon

The first suggestion that the author of Shakespeare's plays might be Francis Bacon, Viscount St. Albans, seems to have been made in the middle of the 19th century, inquiry at first centring on textual comparison between Bacon's known writings and the plays. A discovery was made that references to the Bible, the law, and the classics were given similar treatment in both canons.

In the later 19th century a search was made for ciphered messages embedded in the dramatic texts. In Love's Labour's Lost, for example, it was found that the Latin word "honorificabilitudinitatibus" is an anagram of Hi ludi F. Baconis nati tuiti orbi ("These plays, the offspring of F. Bacon, are preserved for the world."). Professional cryptographers of the 20th century, however, examining all the Baconian ciphers, have rejected them as invalid, and interest in the Shakespeare-Bacon controversy has diminished.

Other Candidates

A theory that the author of the plays was Edward de Vere, 17th earl of Oxford, receives some circumstantial support from the coincidence that Oxford's known poems apparently ceased just before Shakespeare's work began to appear. It is argued that Oxford assumed a pseudonym in order to protect his family from the social stigma then attached to the stage and also because extravagance had brought him into disrepute at court.

Another candidate is William Stanley, 6th earl of Derby, who was keenly interested in the theatre and was patron of his own company of actors. Several poems, written in the 1580s and exhibiting signs of an immature Shakespearean style, cannot well have been written by Shakespeare himself. One of these is in Derby's handwriting, and three of them are signed "W.S." These initials are thought by some to have been a concealment for Derby's identity (for some such motives as were attributed to Oxford) and to have been later expanded into "William Shakespeare."

Shakespeare has also been identified with Christopher Marlowe, one theory even going so far as to assert that Marlowe was not killed in a tavern brawl in 1593 (the corpse of another being represented as his own) but was smuggled to France and thence to Italy where he continued to write in exile—his plays being fathered on Shakespeare, who was paid to keep silent.

The Case for Shakespeare

In spite of recorded allusions to Shakespeare as the author of many plays in the canon, made by about 50 men during his lifetime, it is arguable that his greatness was not as clearly recognized in his own day as one might expect. But on the other hand, the difficulties are not so great as many disbelievers have held, and their proposals have all too often raised larger problems than they have resolved. Shakespeare's contemporaries, after all, wrote of him unequivocally as the author of the plays.

Ben Jonson, who knew him well, contributed verses to the First Folio of 1623, where (as elsewhere) he criticizes and praises Shakespeare as the author. John Heminge and Henry Condell, fellow actors and theatre owners with Shakespeare, signed the dedication and a foreword to the First Folio and described their methods as editors. In his own day, therefore, he was accepted as the author of the plays.

Throughout his lifetime, and for long after, no person is

known to have questioned his authorship. In an age that loved gossip and mystery as much as any, it seems hardly conceivable that Jonson and Shakespeare's theatrical associates shared the secret of a gigantic literary hoax without a single leak or that they could have been imposed upon without suspicion.

Unsupported assertions that the author of the plays was a man of great learning and that Shakespeare of Stratford was an illiterate rustic no longer carry weight, and only when a believer in Bacon or Oxford or Marlowe produces sound evidence will scholars pay close attention to it and to him.

Linguistic and Historical Problems

Since the days of Shakespeare, the English language has changed, and so have audiences, theatres, actors, and customary patterns of thought and feeling. Time has placed an ever-increasing cloud before the mirror he held up to life, and it is here that scholarship can help.

Problems are most obvious in single words. In the 20th century, "presently," for instance, does not mean "immediately," as it usually did for Shakespeare, or "will" mean "lust" or "rage" mean "folly" or "silly" denote "innocence" and "purity." In Shakespeare's day, words sounded different, too, so that "ably" could rhyme with "eye" or "tomb" with "dumb." Syntax was often different, and, far more difficult to define, so was response to metre and phrase. What sounds formal and stiff to a modern hearer might have sounded fresh and gay to an Elizabethan.

Ideas have changed, too, most obviously political ones. Shakespeare's contemporaries almost unanimously believed in authoritarian monarchy and recognized divine intervention in history. Most of them would have agreed that a man should be burned for ultimate religious heresies. It is the office of linguistic and historical scholarship to aid the understanding of the multitude of factors that have significantly affected the impressions made by Shakespeare's plays.

Textual and Editorial Problems

None of Shakespeare's plays has survived in his

handwritten manuscript, and, in the printed texts of some plays, notably King Lear and Richard III, there are passages manifestly corrupt, with no clue to the words Shakespeare once wrote. Even if the printer received a good manuscript, small errors could still be introduced.

Compositors were less than perfect; they often "regularized" the readings of their copy, altered punctuation because they lacked the necessary pieces of type, or made mistakes because they had to work too hurriedly. Even the correction of proof sheets in the printing house could further corrupt the text, since such correction was usually effected without reference to the author or to the manuscript copy; when both corrected and uncorrected states are still available, it is often the uncorrected version that is preferable. Correctors are undoubtedly responsible for many errors now impossible to right.

OVERCOMING SOME DIFFICULTIES

The Contribution of Textual Criticism

The early editors of Shakespeare saw their task chiefly as one of correction and regularization of the faulty printing and imperfect texts of the original editions or their reprints. Many changes in the text of the quartos and folios that are now accepted derive from Nicholas Rowe (1709) and Alexander Pope (1723-25), but these editors also introduced many thousands of small changes that have since been rejected.

Later in the 18th century, editors compiled collations of alternative and rejected readings. Samuel Johnson (1765), Edward Capell (1767-68), and Edmond Malone (1790) were notable pioneers. Their work reached its most comprehensive form in the Cambridge edition in nine volumes by W.G. Clark, J. Glover, and W.A. Wright, published in 1863-66.

A famous one-volume Globe edition of 1864 was based on this Cambridge text. Each major editor had added to the great number of annotations on textual problems and on linguistic and historical difficulties, and in 1871 was published the first of a series of large volumes, one or two for each play, called "A New Variorum Edition," which aimed at bringing all previous textual scholarship together.

The series remains incomplete, but A.W. Pollard published his Shakespeare Folios and Quartos in 1909 and, together with R.B. McKerrow, Sir Walter Greg, and Charles Sisson, began a concerted study of the manuscript plays surviving from Elizabethan theatres and the practice of Elizabethan printers.

Their work was summed up in Greg's study The Shakespeare First Folio (1955) and Fredson Bowers' On Editing Shakespeare and the Elizabethan Dramatists (1955). By this time a new phase of bibliographic and textual inquiry had begun, and Bowers, with Alice Walker, Charlton Hinman, and others, began studying the minutiae of each substantive early edition. Computers will analyze the huge mass of their detailed information and make available the full results of their investigations.

Also, individual compositors who set in type the early editions are being identified, and already something of their work habits and habitual errors is known. Processes of correction in the Elizabethan printing houses are also being studied more intensively. Before the end of the 20th century, a new edition of Shakespeare may appear in which a multitude of small errors have been removed. But even then, nothing will compensate for the loss of Shakespeare's manuscripts, and numerous important readings and details of presentation will still have to be supplied by educated guesses.

Historical, Linguistic and Dramatic Studies

Since the end of the 19th century, many other problems that hinder the understanding of Shakespeare's texts have been at least partly overcome thanks to extensive investigation into, for example, his syntax, vocabulary, and word usage—especially with regard to other Elizabethan and Jacobean literature.

Such technical works, as well as studies of current theories of composition (the use of rhetoric, metaphor, and simile), have provided material for critical analysis, as have works that examine the ideas and life-style of Shakespeare's contemporaries. An increasingly large proportion of research is devoted to an investigation of contemporary literary and dramatic conventions.

LITERARY CRITICISM

Literary Critics and The Theatre

Shakespeare criticism must take into account the certainty that Shakespeare intended his plays to be acted, that he was the professional playwright of a repertory company, that the success of a play in performance by his company was what determined his income, and that during his lifetime he apparently made no effort (or perhaps was too busy) to gain a "literary" reputation from his plays. Yet, his contemporaries had no doubt about his literary eminence.

Heminge and Condell, his fellow players, and Ben Jonson, his fellow playwright, commended the great Folio of 1623 to "the great variety of readers." The situation has been complicated by the fact that the history of Shakespeare criticism and the stage history of his plays have run parallel but separate courses.

It is fair to say that, from about the mid-18th century onward, there has been a constant tension between the critics and the theatres regarding treatment of Shakespeare. Although Dr. Johnson was the contemporary of David Garrick, Coleridge and Hazlitt the contemporaries of Edmund Kean, Dowden of Sir Henry Irving, and Bradley of Beerbohm Tree, the links between these critics and actors were not notably strong.

Theatregoers were usually impressed by character impersonations rendered by virtuoso actors, while readers became more and more impressed by an awareness and admiration of the special artistic form of the plays. Rather than by stage performances, Shakespeare criticism was influenced by the dominant literary forms of each age: by the self-revelatory poem of the Romantic period, the psychological and ethical novel of the Victorians, the fragmentary revelations of the human condition in 20th-century poetry.

It is a platitude that each age finds what it wants to find in Shakespeare. It will only see what it can. It can only see what it must. But Shakespeare critics, if criticism is to be in a healthy condition, must pay more than lip service to that fact. However deeply embedded in its contemporary situation, good criticism, like all intellectual feats, is a leaping out of the situation. The history of Shakespeare criticism is a subject of more than scholarly interest. It is a cautionary tale. Sometimes it is an awful warning.

The Progress of Shakespeare Criticism

As a basis for the criticism of an author's work, it is reasonable to begin by inquiring how his contemporaries assessed his achievement. But contemporary literary criticism was surprisingly silent about the plays actually being written (though critics were reasonably articulate about the plays they thought ought to be written).

Collections of references made to Shakespeare later, during the 17th century, show that many important writers paid little attention to him. Ben Jonson's reputation was, for a variety of reasons, probably superior for the first half of the century. He was, moreover, the most vocal literary critic of the early 17th century, and he thought of Shakespeare as a naturally gifted writer, who failed to discipline himself.

From his criticism derived the distinction between "nature" and "art" that for long proved to be a pertinacious and unproductive theme of Shakespeare criticism. It was further encouraged by John Milton, when he contrasted Jonson's "learned sock" with Shakespeare's "native wood-notes wild" (which refers to the comedies but came to be treated as a general statement, especially the epithet "wild").

A good deal of the spirit of Ben Jonson's cavillings, rather than his magnificent praise in the poem prefixed to the Folio of 1623, was continued by later 17th-century and 18th-century critics, censuring Shakespeare's carelessness, his artistic "faults." John Dryden (died 1700) was the first great critic of Shakespeare. Much concerned with his own art as a dramatist, he judged Shakespeare in a practical spirit. For 100 years after him, the best literary criticism of Shakespeare was an elaboration and clarification of his opinions. Dryden on some occasions praised Shakespeare in the highest terms and boldly defended the English tradition of the theatre, maintaining that, if it was contrary to the revered classical precepts of Aristotle, it was only because Aristotle had not seen English plays; had he seen them, his precepts would have been different.

Dryden nevertheless at times attributes artistic "faults" to Shakespeare, judging him according to Neoclassical principles of taste that derived from France and soon prevailed throughout Europe.

Shakespeare's dramatic art was so different from that of the admired tragedy of the times (that of Corneille and Racine) that it was difficult for a critic to defend or interpret it in reasonable terms. The gravest charge was the absence of "poetical justice" in Shakespeare's plays.

Although some of the better 18th-century critics, such as Joseph Addison and Dr. Johnson, saw the limitations of "poetical justice" as an artistic theory, they nevertheless generally felt that the ending of King Lear, especially, was intolerable, offending all sense of natural justice by the death of Cordelia.

The play was thus given a "happy ending"—one congruent with "poetical justice"—by the poet and playwright Nahum Tate: Lear was restored to his authority, and Cordelia and Edgar were to be married and could look forward to a prosperous reign over a united Britain. This change was approved by Dr. Johnson, and the revised play held the stage for generations and was the only form of King Lear performed on the stage until the mid-19th century.

In the early 18th century the cumbrous folio editions were replaced by more convenient editions, prepared for the reader. Nicholas Rowe, in a six-volume edition of 1709, tidied up the text of the plays, adding scene divisions, lists of dramatis personae, indications of locality, and so on. Rowe was himself a practicing and successful dramatist, and on the whole he gave a good lead to the dramatic criticism of the plays. The preface to Alexander Pope's edition of 1725, however, had an unhappy influence on criticism. Shakespeare's natural genius, he felt, was hampered by his association with a working theatre. Pope fully accepted the artistic form of Shakespeare's writings as due to their being stage plays.

But he regarded this as a grave disadvantage and the source of their artistic defectiveness. Lewis Theobald took the opposing view to Pope's, claiming that it was an advantage of Shakespeare that he belonged to the theatrical profession. Dr. Johnson similarly realized that methods of producing the plays on the stage influenced the kind of illusion created.

In the splendid preface to his edition (1765), Johnson dismissed, once and for all in English criticism, the Neoclassical theories of "decorum," the "unities," and the mutual exclusiveness of tragedy and comedy—theories now seen as irrelevant to Shakespeare's art and as having confused the discussion of it. In many ways Johnson was the source of the notion of Shakespeare as a realistic dramatist, whose mingling of tragic and comic scenes was justified as "exhibiting the real state of sublunary nature," in which laughter and tears, rejoicing and misery, are found side by side.

Johnson censured Shakespeare as a dramatic artist for his lack of morality. Shakespeare, he wrote, "sacrifices virtue to convenience, and is so much more careful to please than to instruct, that he seems to write without any moral purpose." Later critics have felt compelled to controvert or to circumvent such a judgment. But Johnson's preface, if it did not give the discussion of Shakespeare's artistry a fresh start, cleared away some of the dead or irrelevant doctrines.

During the rest of the 18th century, after Johnson, it was scholarship rather than criticism that advanced in England. The best of literary criticism of the time was in the discovery of new subtleties in Shakespeare, especially in characterization; indeed, the acceptance of Shakespeare as a dramatic artist largely came about through his evident powers of characterization (to which probably the growth of the realistic novel in the 18th century had made readers more sensitive), and inadequate attention was paid to other aspects of his dramatic craftsmanship.

There was nothing in England comparable to the brilliant Shakespeare criticism of Lessing, Goethe, and August von Schlegel in Germany. The latter's essay on Romeo and Juliet of 1797 demonstrated that, apart from a few witticisms, nothing could be taken away from the play, nothing added, nothing rearranged without mutilating the work of art and confusing the author's intentions.

Here modern Shakespeare criticism begins. Indeed, from the time of Lessing, in the 18th century, to the mid-19th century, German critics and scholars made substantial and original contributions to the interpretation of Shakespeare, indicating Shakespeare's superlative artistry, at a time when in England he was admired more as a great poet and a brilliant observer of mankind than as a disciplined artist.

Samuel Taylor Coleridge, the greatest English critic of Shakespeare, vigorously denied that he had been affected by Schlegel (though he acknowledged the influence of Lessing), but there are many similarities between the two. His criticism—which has to be put together from reports of his lectures, from his notebooks, and from memories of his conversation, for he never succeeded in writing an organized book on Shakespeare—at first censured Shakespeare's lack of artistry, but in his lectures, given from 1810 onward, and in his Biographia Literaria (1817), he demonstrated that Shakespeare's "irregularities" were in fact the manifestations of a subtle intelligence.

It was the purpose of criticism to reveal the reasons why the plays are as they are. Shakespeare was a penetrating psychologist and a profound philosopher; but Coleridge claimed that he was an even greater artist, and his artistry was seen to be "unconscious" or "organic," not contrived.

Thus the dominant literary forms of Coleridge's age, which were those of self-revelatory poetry, influenced the criticism of the age: Hamlet was felt to speak with the voice and feeling of Shakespeare, and, as for the sonnets, William Wordsworth, whose greatest achievement was writing a long poem on the growth of his own mind, explained that Shakespeare "unlocked his heart" in his sonnets.

These critical opinions were inclined to degenerate in inferior hands in the course of the 19th century: the belief in Shakespeare's all-pervading artistry led to over-subtle interpretations; the enthusiasm for character analysis led to excessive biography writing outside the strictly dramatic framework; and the acknowledged assessment of Shakespeare's keen intelligence led to his being associated with almost every school of thought in religion, politics, morals, psychology, and metaphysics.

Nevertheless, it was the great achievement of the Romantics to have freed criticism from preoccupation with the "beauties" and "faults" in Shakespeare and to have devoted themselves instead to interpreting the delight that people had always felt in the plays, whether as readers or theatregoers. Shakespeare's "faults" now became "problems," and it was regarded an achievement in literary criticism to have found an explanation for some hitherto difficult or irreconcilable detail in a play. Many of the most brilliant writers of Europe were critics of Shakespeare; and their utterances (whether or not they may be regarded as having correctly interpreted Shakespeare) are notable as recording the impressions he made upon great minds.

Shakespeare's influence

Today Shakespeare's plays are performed throughout the world, and all kinds of new, experimental work finds inspiration in them: "... in the second half of the twentieth century in England," wrote the innovative theatre director Peter Brook, "we are faced with the infuriating fact that Shakespeare is still our model."

Shakespeare's influence on English theatre was evident from the start. John Webster, Philip Massinger, and John Ford are among the better known dramatists who borrowed openly from his plays. His influence is evident on Restoration dramatists, especially Thomas Otway, John Dryden, and William Congreve. John Osborne, Harold Pinter, Samuel Beckett, and George Bernard Shaw are among 20th-century writers in whose works Shakespearean echoes are to be found. Many writers have taken over Shakespeare's plots and characters: Shaw rewrote the last act of Cymbeline, Tom Stoppard invented characters to set against parts of Hamlet in Rosencrantz and Guildenstern Are Dead (1968), and Edward Bond used King Lear as the starting point for his own Lear (1971).

Shakespeare has also influenced dramatists and theatre directors outside his own country. In Germany, English acting troupes were welcomed early in the 17th century, and the German version of Hamlet, Der bestrafte Brudermord ("Fratricide Punished"), testifes to the immediate influence of that play. His influence on later European dramatists ranges from a running allusion to Hamlet in Anton Chekhov's play The Seagull to imitation and parody of Richard III in Bertolt Brecht's Arturo Ui, adaptation of King John by Max Frisch, and André Gide's translation and simplification of Hamlet.

Shakespeare's influence on actors since his own day has been almost as widespread. Many European and American actors have had their greatest successes in Shakespearean roles. In England very few actors or actresses reach pre-eminence without acting in his plays. Each player has the opportunity to make a part his own. This is not because Shakespeare has created only outlines for others to fill but because he left so many and varied invitations for the actor to call upon his deepest, most personal resources.

Theatre directors and designers after Shakespeare's time, with every technical stage resource at their command, have returned repeatedly to his plays, which give opportunity for spectacle and finesse, ritual and realism, music and controlled quietness. Their intrinsic theatricality, too, has led to adaptations into very different media: into opera (as Verdi's Otello) and ballet (as versions of Romeo and Juliet from several nations); into sound recordings, television programs, and films.

Musicals have been made of the comedies (as Kiss Me Kate from The Taming of the Shrew); even a tragedy, Othello, was the inspiration of a "rock" musical in 1971 called Catch My Soul, while Macbeth has yielded a political-satire show called Macbird! (1967).

Shakespeare has Hamlet say that the aim of theatre performance is to "hold the mirror up to nature," and this is what the history of his plays, from their first production to the latest, shows that he has, preeminently, achieved.

Although interesting, the debate cannot be studied in depth here but it would be wise to mention a recent book on the subject written by John Michell: "*Who Wrote Shakespeare?*" (New York: Thames and Hudson, 1996).

Part of the book's review - written by a Bob Grumman - is reproduced here (more can be found at Shakespeare Authorship) and in the links and 'works' sections of this site.

Chapter 8

From John Dryden's of Dramatic Poesy

To begin with Shakespeare; he was the man who of all modern, and perhaps ancient poets, had the largest and most comprehensive soul. All the images of nature were still present to him, and he drew them not laboriously, but luckily: when he describes anything, you more than see it, you feel it too. Those who accuse him to have wanted learning, give him the greater commendation: he was naturally learned; he needed not the spectacles of books to read nature; he looked inwards, and found her there.

I cannot say he is everywhere alike; were he so, I should do him injury to compare him with the greatest of mankind. He is many times flat, insipid; his comic wit degenerating into clenches, his serious swelling into bombast. But he is always great when some great occasion is presented to him: no man can say he ever had a fit subject for his wit and did not then raise himself as high above the rest of poets, Quantum lenta solent inter viburna cupressi.

The consideration of this made Mr. Hales of Eton say that there was no subject of which any poet ever writ, but he would produce it much better done in Shakespeare; and however others are now generally preferred before him, yet the age wherein he lived, which had contemporaries with him, Fletcher and Johnson, never equalled them to him in their esteem. And in the last king's Court, when Ben's reputation was at highest, Sir John Suckling, and with him the greater part of the courtiers, set our Shakespeare far above him.

As for Jonson, to whose character I am now arrived, if we look upon him while he was himself (for his last plays were but his dotages), I think him the most learned and judicious writer which any theatre ever had. He was a most severe judge of himself as well as others.

One cannot say he wanted wit, but rather that he was frugal of it. In his works you find little to retrench or alter. Wit and language, and humour also in some measure we had before him; but something of art was wanting to the drama till he came. He managed his strength to more advantage than any who preceded him.

You seldom find him making love in any of his scenes, or endeavouring to move the passions; his genius was too sullen and saturnine to do it gracefully, especially when he knew he came after those who had performed both to such an height. Humour was his proper sphere, and in that he delighted most to represent mechanic people.

He was deeply conversant in the Ancients, both Greek and Latin, and he borrowed boldly from them. There is scarce a poet or historian among the Roman authors of those times whom he has not translated in Sejanus and Catiline. But he has done his robberies so openly, that one may see he fears not to be taxed by any law.

He invades authors like a monarch, and what would be theft in other poets, is only victory in him. With the spoils of these writers he so represents old Rome to us, in its rites, ceremonies, and customs, that if one of their poets had written either of his tragedies, we had seen less of it than in him.

If there was any fault in his language, 'twas that he weaved it too closely and laboriously, in his comedies especially: perhaps too, he did a little too much romanize our tongue, leaving the words which he translated almost as much Latin as he found them: wherein though he learnedly followed their language, he did not enough comply with the idiom of ours.

If I would compare him with Shakespeare, I must acknowledge him the more correct poet, but Shakespeare the greater wit. Shakespeare was the Homer, or father of our dramatic poets; Jonson was the Virgil, the pattern of elaborate writing. I admire him, but I love Shakespeare.

FROM JOHN DRYDEN'S A DISCOURSE CONCERNING THE ORIGINAL AND PROGRESS OF SATIRE, 1693

Let the chastisements of Juvenal be never so necessary for his new kind of satire; let him declaim as wittily and sharply as he pleases: yet still the nicest and most delicate touches of satire consist in fine raillery....How easy is it to call rogue and villain, and that wittily! But how hard to make a man appear a fool, a blockhead, or a knave, without using any of those opprobrious terms! To spare the grossness of the names, and to do the thing yet more severely, is to draw a full face, and to make the nose and cheeks stand out, and yet not to employ any depth of shadowing.

This is the mystery of that noble trade, which yet no master can teach to his apprentice: he may give the rules, but the scholar is never the nearer in his practice. Neither is it true that this fineness of raillery is offensive. A witty man is tickled while he is hurt in this manner, and a fool feels it not. The occasion of an offence may possibly be given, but he cannot take it.

If it be granted that in effect this way does more mischief; that a man is secretly wounded, and though he be not sensible himself, yet the malicious world will find it for him: yet there is still a vast difference betwixt the slovenly butchering of a man, and the fineness of a stroke that separates the head from the body, and leaves it standing in its place....

It must be granted by the favourers of Juvenal, that Horace is the more copious and profitable in his instructions of human life. But in my particular opinion, which I set not up for a standard to better judgements, Juvenal is the more delightful author. I am profited by both, I am pleased with both; but I owe more to Horace for my instruction, and more to Juvenal, for my pleasure...

...I must confess, that the delight which Horace gives me is but languishing. Be pleased still to understand that I speak of my own taste only. He may ravish other men, but I am too stupid and insensible to be tickled. Where he barely grins himself, and, as Scaliger says, only shows his white teeth, he cannot provoke me to any laughter.

His urbanity, that is, his good manners, are to be commended; but his wit is faint, and his salt, if I may dare to say so, almost insipid. Juvenal is of a more vigorous and masculine wit; he gives me as much pleasure as I can bear.... Add to this, that his thoughts are as just as those of Horace, and much more elevated.

His expressions are sonorous and more noble; his verse more numerous; and his words are suitable to his thoughts, sublime and lofty. All these contribute to the pleasure of the reader, and the greater the soul of him who reads, his transports are the greater. Horace is always on the amble, Juvenal on the gallop, but his way is perpetually on carpet ground. He goes with more impetuosity than Horace, but as securely; and the swiftness adds a more lively agitation to the spirits....

The meat of Horace is more nourishing; but the cookery of Juvenal more exquisite; so that, granting Horace to be the more general philosopher, we cannot deny that Juvenal was the greater poet, I mean in satire. His thoughts are sharper, his indignation against vice is more vehement; his spirit has more of the commonwealth genius; he treats tyranny, and all the vices attending it, as they deserve, with the utmost rigour; and consequently, a noble soul is better pleased with a zealous vindicator of Roman liberty than with a temporizing poet, a well mannered court slave, and a man who is often afraid of laughing in the right place, who is ever decent because he is naturally servile.

After all, Horace had the disadvantage of the times in which he lived; they were better for the man, but worse for the satirist. 'Tis generally said that those enormous vices, which were practised under the reign of Domitian, were unknown in the time of Augustus Caesar, that therefore Juvenal had a larger field than horace. Little follies were out of doors, when oppression was to be scourged instead of avarice. It was no longer time to turn into ridicule the false opinions of philosophers, when the Roman liberty was to be asserted.

FROM DRYDEN'S "AN ACCOUNT OF THE ENSUING POEM" PREFIXED TO ANNUS MIRABILIS, 1666

The composition of all poems is or ought to be of wit, and wit in the poet, or wit writing (if you will give me leave to use a school distinction), is no other than the faculty of imagination in the writer, which, like a nimble spaniel, beats over and ranges through the field of memory, till it springs the quarry it hunted after; or, without metaphor, which searches over all the memory for the species or ideas of those things which it designs to represent.

Wit written, is that which is well defined the happy result of thought, or product of that imagination. But to proceed from wit in the general notion of it to the proper wit of an heroic or historical poem, I judge it chiefly to consist in the delightful imaging of persons, actions, passions, or things.'

T is not the jerk or sting of an epigram, nor the seeming contradiction of a poor antithesis (the delight of an ill-judging audience in a play of rhyme), nor the jingle of a more poor paranomasia: neither is it so much the morality of a grave sentence, affected by Lucan, but more sparingly used by Virgil; but it is some lively and apt description, dressed in such colours of speech, that it sets before youre eyes the absent object as perfectly and more delightfully than nature.

So then, the first happiness of the poet's imagination is properly invention, or finding of the thought; the second is fancy or the variation, driving or moulding of that thought, as the judgement represents it proper to the subject; the third is elocution, or that art of clothing and adorning that thought so found and varied, in apt, significant, and sounding words: the quickness of the imagination is seen in the invention, the fertility in the fancy, and the accuracy in the expression. For the two first of these Ovid is famous amongst the poets, for the latter Virgil.

Ovid images more often the movements and affections of

the mind, either combating between two contrary passions, or extremely discomposed by one: his words therefore are the least part of his care, for he pictures nature in disorder, with which the study and choice of words is inconsistent.

This is the proper wit of dialogue or discourse, and consequently, of the drama, where all that is said is to be supposed the effect of sudden thought; which, though it excludes not the quickness of wit in repartees, yet admits not a too curious election of words, too frequent allusions, or use of tropes, or, in fine, anything that shows remoteness of thought, or labour in the writer.

On the other side, Virgil speaks not so often to us in the person of another, like Ovid, but in his own; he relates almost all things as from himself, and thereby gains more liberty than the other to express his thoughts with all the graces of elocution, to write more figuratively, and to confess as well the labour as the force of his imagination.

FROM A DEFENSE OF AN ESSAY OF DRAMATIC POESY (1668)

Imagination in a man, or reasonable creature, is supposed to participate of reason, and when that governs, as it does in the belief of fiction, reason is not destroyed, but misled, or blinded: that can prescribe tot he reason, during the time of the representation, somewhat like a weak belief of what it sees and hears; and reason suffers itself to be so hoodwinked, that it may better enjoy the pleasures of the fiction: but it is never so wholly made a captive as to be drawn headlong into a persuasion of those things which are most remote from probability: 'tis in that case a free-born subject, not a slave; it will contribute willingly its assent, as far as it sees convenient, but will not be forced....Fancy and reason go hand in hand; the first cannot leave the last behind; and though fancy, when it sees the wide gulf, would venture over, as the nimbler; yet it is withheld by reason, which will refuse to take the leap, when the distance over it appears too large.

Chapter 9

A Study of His Poetry

Ten years later there was enough desire for it in England, and enough difficulty about securing copies, to justify the second edition which Gordon Fraser published at the Minority Press, Cambridge, in 1931. Now, twenty-five years after its original appearance in America, it is published here again. I am grateful to Harcourt, Brace and Company and to the Minority Press for the freedom I enjoy to present the essay a third time for such use as poets, critics, students, and other readers care to make of it.

It is an extended study of one poets art. It stands or falls by the amount of truth about that poet, or about poetry in general, which it contains. For this edition I have made a number of minor revisions, but the essay remains substantially unaltered. My original preface prepared the reader for a more or less enthusiastic treatment of Dryden. I have kept my enthusiasm.

Indeed, the revisions I refer to often consist in efforts to tone up what I once, in an ardor to be judicial, toned down. The essay was a doctoral dissertation at Columbia University, and in writing it I did not take the fullest advantage of a liberty which I still consider myself lucky, not to say unique, for having possessed.

This was the liberty to go ahead and say all I could about animportant writer, in whatever language seemed suitable to my self and him. The suggestion that I do so came from my brother, Carl Van Doren, and was favorably received by W. P, Trent, the professor whom I would have to please. I would have to please him, that is, with a finished essay j meanwhile the vii vili PREFACE risk was altogether mine. The procedure still seems sensible to me, and I have urged it since on many candidates, but none of them has pursued it. If one ever does, I shall recommend that he avoid the cliches of qualification which I seem to have thought it sounded wise to use. I am happy now to have them out of the way.

Dryden is the kind of great poet it is good to know at any time, for he is a great writer. Of some poets, even though they be very fine, we do not say seriously that they are writers. From the way Dryden wrote there is always something to be learned, and in fact it has been said of this essay, by T. S. Eliot and others, that it shows how the learning may be done.

But in twenty-five years I have not seen it being done. I am not saying that it should be done, or that I have succeeded in showing how it could be. I merely observe that contemporary poetry and criticism give no evidence of having benefited by the study of Drydens art.

Clear evidence to the contrary is to be found in the fact that verse is almost everywhere held in contempt. Verse is not every thing, but to assume that it is nothing is to ignore a primary source of pleasure and power, and in the end is to emasculate poetry.

We have cults of sensibility and sincerity 5 we are mar velously responsive to ambiguities 5 we know how to plot the oblique course, to surprise words into revealing threesenses when there was none before we can find politics in metaphor, morality in syntax, and myth in minor parts of speech. But we do not act as if we had ears. Ears are not everything, but the absence of them leaves poetry dangerously dead. Dryden had a great ear...

THOMAS OTWAY'S *VENICE PRESERV'D*

In his article "Political Interpretations of *Venice Preserv'd,*" Philip Harth argues that recent critical attempts to describe Thomas Otway's *Venice Preserv'd* as a "Tory 'political document,' either as allegory or as parallel," have been misguided. Indeed, the presence of so many conflicting opinions about what each component of the play represents might seem to lend support to Harth's argument. The Senate has been seen as the English Court and, conversely, as the English Parliament, while the conspirators have been viewed both as the Popish Plotters and as the Whig exclusionists (Harth 345). But the existence of so many divergent opinions does not mean that *Venice Preserv'd,* as Harth implies, contains no political message beyond its prologue, its epilogue, and its depiction of Antonio.

Harth admits that Otway chose to make a play from Saint-Real's *A Conspiracy of the Spanish against the State of Venice* because of its "unique parallel" to current events, but he argues that Otway is thereby confined merely to "imply[ing] a parallel between Venetian and English history" and that, although he can add a few characters, he can not "invent any vehicle to serve his political tenor".

Yet Otway may have chosen Saint-Real's work precisely because it enabled him, with the addition of just a few characters and no major changes, to present his Tory message. Otway chooses as his source a story in which a conspiracy can be condemned and yet the conspirators can seem sympathetic and their accusations against the Senate can appear credible.

A story line that enables the playwright to express these seeming contradictions is ideal for a Tory who would never condone the Popish Plot to murder his king but who yet despised the way the Whigs manipulated it for their political gain. *Venice Preserv'd* was first performed on February 9, 1682, in the wake of tumultuous political events. Titus Oates had exposed before a magistrate the details of a supposed Popish Plot. A group of Roman Catholics were allegedly planning to murder King Charles II so that his Catholic brother James, the Duke of York, would succeed him to the throne ("Oates" 1).

At this point, the Whigs in Parliament sought to pass a bill (against the opposition of the Tories, who supported Charles) that would have excluded James from the throne (Edie 350). Perhaps the revelation of this supposed Plot genuinely frightened the Whigs and made them fear that Roman Catholicism might be forcibly reinstated in England by James (as "Bloody Mary" had tried to do in 1553).

Or perhaps they merely used the Plot, and the fact of James Catholicism, as a pretense to assert their power over the King, to subject the succession to the prerogative of Parliament. Charles must have thought so, for although he loved his illegitimate son, whom the radical Whig leader Shaftesbury wished to succeed him, more than he did his brother James, Charles nonetheless actively fought the exclusion (Edie 353).

After becoming independent via a subsidy from Louis XIV, he dissolved the Parliament and never summoned it again. The Whigs turned to London as their source of power. And when Charles arrested Shaftesbury for treason, he was acquitted by a London jury packed with Whigs. In response, Charles issued a writ to proceed against London's charter, which had exempted the city from direct royal interference. Just ten days after the proceedings were delayed, and before further action had been taken, *Venice Preserv'd* was performed for the first time (Bywaters 257).

In light of these events, and considering that Otway was a Tory, it might at first seem logical that any rebels he depicted would represent the Whig exclusionists, whose insistence that the crown submit to Parliamentary authority "was barely short of revolution" (Edie 351). In that case, the Senate would have to represent the English Court of the King.

However, such an interpretation is highly unlikely considering that the audience's sympathies naturally rest with Jaffier, a conspirator, and not with the corrupt senators. Priuli cruelly drives out Jaffier and Belvidera, saying, "May the hard hand of a vexatious need / Oppress and grind you" (1.1.56-7).

Although Jaffier had saved his daughter's life, when the two marry, Priuli abuses his power to see to it that a "troop of villains" seizes all of Jaffier's property; indeed, his "cruel hand" signs the commission allowing these "sons of public rapine" to destroy Jaffier's possessions, throwing the very bed in which he consummated his love with Belvidera "amongst the common lumber" (1.1.232-50).

Antonio reveals himself to be a pervert in the scenes with the whore Aquilina (3.1.14-140; 5.1.153-225). Jaffier, on the other hand, though initially motivated by revenge, seeks to fulfill the noble ideals of love and honor, ultimately choosing the latter by dying for his friend Pierre, who says, "This was done nobly" (5.3.101).

The conspirators can not represent the Whig exclusionists, for whom Otway held not a grain of sympathy, but they might represent the Popish Plotters, who fell victim to the Whigs' manipulation. Otway implies in his prologue that "there's not in't [the Plot] one inch-board evidence". Yet the Whigs' frenzy over the Popish Plot lead to the deaths of 35 people, and they used the Plot to consolidate and assert their power ("Oates" 1).

Even Harth admits that the Venetian conspiracy, that "spectacle of a disaffected minority planning to wreak revenge on their countrymen," can resemble "only the Popish Plot". Yet Harth will not concede that the Senate must therefore represent London's corrupt oligarchy of Whigs who sought, like Antonio, to prove the existence of, and cruelly squash, the "bloody, horrid, execrable, damnable, and audacious plot" (5.1.142-43).

Although he writes that in the character of Antonio Otway is "outrageously caricaturing Shaftesbury," the leader of the Whigs, he claims that the Senate is not really corrupt. Harth argues that Otway had no choice but to include the Senate's betrayal of their oath to the conspirators, because the betrayal was in his source.

Yet the presence of this betrayal in the source actually suits Otway's purpose; he wishes to portray the Senate as untrustworthy. In fact, he even adds the characters of Antonio and Priuli (Harth 347). Their decadence confirms the corruption of the Senate.

Harth, however, contends that "the behaviour of Priuli and Antonio" is not "evidence that corruption is rife among the Venetian senators" because we can not "draw generalizations... from a sample of two senators". However, if Otway did not desire his audience to draw such generalizations, surely he would have introduced at least one respectable senator in his play.

It may be true that the conspirators are prejudiced against

the Senate because of their desire for personal revenge (Harth 356). But this does not mean that their accusations must be inaccurate. Not all prejudices are incorrect, and few arise without some motivation. In order for the audience to discredit Pierre's claims, it would have to be presented with some alternative view of the Senate.

But the characters of Priuli and Antonio, as well as the Senate's betrayal of its promise not to kill the conspirators, only reinforce Pierre's accusations. Because Otway gives us no other portrait of the Senate, it is safe to assume that Pierre, despite his suspect motivations, is correct when he asserts that "our senators / Cheat the deluded people with a show / Of liberty" and that in Venice, "innocence / Stoops under vile oppression, and vice lords it".

Indeed, Pierre's desire to "check the growth of these domestic spoilers, / That make us slaves and tell us 'tis our charter" probably resembles Otway's own wish to see London's charter revoked so that the Whigs would not continue to grow in power, exempt from royal influence.

Any confusion as to whom the conspirators and senators represent on the English political scene may stem from the absence of a king in the play.

Since the Popish Plotters were presumably conspiring to kill the King, and not plotting against the Whigs, having the Venetian conspirators conspire against a Senate that represents the Whigs is an imperfect allegory. Obviously, since he is restricted by his source, Otway is not free to "invent a political allegory about England without jettisoning Venetian history" (Harth 348).

But nor does this mean, as Harth assumes, that Otway can not use the play to present a specific, Tory message. The absence of a king, which at first seems to limit Otway's ability to communicate a Tory assessment of current events, actually aids him in that it allows him to express sympathy for the conspirators (i.e. the Popish Plotters) while avoiding any mention of regicide (Bywaters 263).

Because the conspirators plot against the senators instead of a king, Otway can criticize his enemy (the Whigs) and sympathize with their victims (the Popish Plotters) without, at the same time, supporting their conspiracy (to kill the King).

Although the play's absence of a king removes the issue of regicide, Otway must still deal with the wholesale murders allegedly planned by the Popish Plotters. It was rumored that the Roman Catholics were planning to carry out a "general massacre" in the city of London, "which was a notorious Whig strong hold," and that the Plot might include setting a fire like the one the Catholics had allegedly ignited in 1666 (Bywaters 262, 256).

The conspirators may not be planning to kill a king in *Venice Preserv'd,* but they do intend to "[s]hed blood enough, spare; neither sex nor age" in the city of Venice and to "Burn! / First burn, and level Venice to... ruin!" This issue is potentially explosive for Otway, for although he apparently believed the Popish Plot to be fictitious, many Tories did not; they thought it had merely been exaggerated by the Whigs.

Titus Oates was at one time very popular, and had even received a pension. Indeed, it was not until about two years after *Venice Preserv'd* was first performed, in 1684, that Oates was imprisoned, and not until 1685 that he was charged with perjury ("Oates" 1).

David Bywaters (author of "Venice, Its Senate, and Its Plot in Otway's *Venice Preserv'd*") does not perceive this issue to be a problem for Otway, because he believes that the conspiracy represents a mere parody of the Whigs' irrational fear of the Popish Plot. But it is both unconvincing and unnecessary to argue that the play's conspiracy is "hollow and silly" (Bywaters 260).

As Jessica Munns points out in her article, "'Plain as the light in the Cowcumber': A Note on the Conspiracy in Thomas Otway's *Venice Preserv'd,*" Belvidera's "horrified reactions" to the bloody details of the conspiracy would be "absurd if from the first the plot is viewed as ludicrous and impossible".

These details are no parody; they can be found in Otway's source (Harth 352). On the one hand, these details allow him to draw a parallel to the Popish Plot; on the other hand, they require him to condemn it. Because so many people, Whigs and Tories alike, believed the Popish Plot was real, Otway had to be very careful not to appear as though he condoned or excused it.

Fortunately, by adding a single character to his source, Belvidera, Otway can condemn the conspiracy without, at the same time, exonerating the senators who suppress it. Therefore, he can show that although he did not approve of the Popish Plot (assuming it was real), he nonetheless despised the Whigs who sought to expose and crush it.

Through Belvidera, he is able to denounce the conspiracy:

Nay, be a traitor too, and sell thy country?
Can thy great heart descend so vilely low,
Mix with hired slaves, bravoes, and common stabbers,
Nose-slitters, alley-lurking villains? join
With such a crew...
To cut the throats of wretches as they sleep?

Although Belvidera roundly condemns the conspiracy, her condemnation does not imply respect for the Senate. As Otway carefully reminds us, she desires to preserve her father's life despite the fact that he has, in her own words, "persecuted me to my undoing, / Driven me to basest wants". She pleads with Jaffier, "Save thy poor country". But this "certainly does not refer to its political system" (Harth 355). Just because Belvidera wishes Jaffier to "[s]ave the poor, tender lives / Of all those little infants which the swords / Of murderers are whetting for this moment," does not mean she approves of the senate. For, "faced with such a prospect, Abraham pleaded that even Sodom should be spared" (Harth 355).

Likewise, just because Otway would never wish to see London desecrated by Catholics does not mean that he supports the Whigs who exposed, exaggerated, and crushed (if they did not actually fabricate) the Popish Plot.

If Otway criticizes the Popish Plot through Belvidera's words, then he also condemns the Whigs' treatment of the Plot through the Senate's treatment of the conspiracy. Jaffier asks for the Senate's "oaths / And sacred promise" that it will spare the lives of the conspirators he exposes. The entire Senate swears three times, saying, "We all swear," "We swear," and

"Elst be curst forever!" But they renege on their promise, just as the senators did in Saint-Real's work. Not only do they refuse to spare the lives of the conspirators, but they also intend to subject Pierre to "a tormenting and shameful death, / His bleeding bowels, and his broken limbs, / Insulted o'er by a vile, butchering villain". Indeed, it is Belvidera herself who describes this torture, saying that Jaffier's eyes "'twill stream / Like my eyes now".

This is further evidence that Belvidera's opposition to the conspiracy does not imply support of the Senate. Finally, Otway takes a direct shot at the Whigs in Pierre's speech before the Senate:

Curst be your Senate; curst your Constitution.
The curse of growing factions and division
Still vex your councils, shake your public safety,
And make the robes of government you wear
Hateful to you as these base chains to me! (4.2.156-60).

The Whigs had already begun to experience "growing factions." One moderate group had proposed, as a solution to the issue of James's Catholicism, a regency of his Protestant daughters, while a more radical faction, under the leadership of Shaftesbury, had sought to substitute the Duke of Monmouth, and "despite Charles's opposition to either move, controversy had risen and raged" (Edie 355).

In allowing Pierre to curse the Senate and its constitution, Otway is probably cursing the oligarchy of Whigs who ruled London and the charter that freed them from royal interference. Jessica Munns epitomizes the Senate's abuse of the conspiracy:

Venice is preserved by its plots. Nothing else could hold the greedy and self-seeking senators together, but, against the anarchy of rebels who mirror them in corruption, they justify and consolidated their rule. Antonio's ridiculous speech and his anxiety to "prove there's a Plot with a Vengeance" (5.128-29) place Antonio and the senate (but not the conspiracy) in a satiric light.

Rather, the cynical exploitation of an "actual" plot by a frivolous and decadent pervert plays off with bitter irony against Jaffier's agonies of betrayal, his suicide, and the deaths of Belvidera and Pierre.

This "decadent pervert," we should recollect, is a direct caricature of Shaftesbury, who, in the view of the Tories, manipulated the Popish Plot in order to advance his own "frivolous and decadent" views about political order.

The Tories opposed Shaftesbury's attempt to subject succession to the power of Parliament, because with it "crept in the possibility of an elective monarchy," and they believed, as one Tory wrote in *The Original of Kingly and Ecclesiastical Government*, that "[k]ings are not children of the most voices, but children of the most high" (Edie 357).

Otway's choice of source enables him to present a Tory message even in the body of his play. The parallels between the conspiracy and the Popish Plot and between the senators who rule Venice and the Whigs who rule London are too uncanny to be ignored.

It is also the only logical association. As Bywaters argues, "since neither the senate nor the conspiracy against it is politically respectable, neither can be Tory; yet since the two factions are violently opposed, both can not be Whig". The only political groups on the scene at the time were the Tories (who supported the King), the Whigs (who sought exclusion), and the Roman Catholics (who were accused of the Popish Plot). If neither side can be Tory, and only one can be Whig, then there is only one plausible solution: one side (the Senate) must represent the Whigs, and the other (the conspiracy) must represent the Popish Plot.

Yet arguing that *Venice Preserv'd* is indeed a Tory "propaganda piece (which it is)" does not mean that we must exclude thematic interpretations; a historical analysis of *Venice Preserv'd* in no way conflicts with the fact that today the play "is remembered... as a tragedy of pathetic love" (Loftis 18). It is not true, as Harth asserts, that one can present *Venice Preserv'd* as a propaganda piece "only at the cost of contradicting the way most readers and spectators over the years have responded to its plot and characters".

For the sympathies and outrages evoked by the plot and

characters fit ideally with Otway's political message. We can hate the senators as he hates the Whigs. We can disapprove of the conspiracy as he disapproves of the Popish Plot. Yet we can sympathize with the conspirators as he sympathizes with the Popish Plotters, for, in the words of John Dryden, another Tory poet of the age, "that Plot, the Nation's Curse" is "[b]ad in it self, but represented worse".

MOST HIMSELF

Of all the great English poets, Dryden must be the least enjoyed. Once honoured 'rather in the stiffness than in the strength of his eminence', he was soon 'laid carefully away among the heroes', according to Mark Van Doren, the critic who is still, nearly a century on, the most persuasive of his would-be resurrectors.

The same melancholy afflicts his most authoritative modern biographer, James Anderson Winn: 'Any candid teacher of English literature must admit that many students find little pleasure or stimulation in those few selections from Dryden we now ask them to read.'

The difficulty is not confined to students, or to recent times. 'I admire his talents and Genius highly, but his is not a poetical Genius,' Wordsworth said; perhaps predictably, since his notion of poetry differed from Dryden's as much as Romantic 'imagination' differed from Augustan 'wit'.

But here is Dr Johnson: 'to write *con amore*... was... no part of his character.' Verse starved of parental love may well have problems attracting affection later. T.S. Eliot took a charitable interest in the case in 1921, but his contribution is rather reminiscent of Mr Brocklehurst in *Jane Eyre* enjoining the Lowood girls to be glad of their burned breakfast: 'We cannot fully enjoy or rightly estimate a hundred years of English poetry unless we fully enjoy Dryden.'

The need for help in fully enjoying Dryden becomes clear as soon as one looks at a list of the genres in which he excelled. Most of them either need prior contextual knowledge (or annotation) to make them comprehensible, or are some distance from what, for the last couple of hundred years, have been the main concerns of poets; or both. There are the literary and political satires (*Mac Flecknoe, Absalom and Achitophel*). There is panegyric: on Cromwell (*Heroic Stanzas*), on Charles II (*Astraea Redux, To His Sacred Majesty*), on the new baby heir to James II (*Britannia Rediviva*); though never on William and Mary.

Theological disputation, first Anglican in complexion (*Religio Laici*), then Roman Catholic (*The Hind and the Panther*). Historical chronicle (*Annus Mirabilis*). Translation: from Homer, Juvenal, Persius, Ovid, Boccaccio, Chaucer and others; and of the complete works of Virgil.

And then there are the massed and (except *All for Love*) rather mediocre plays which took up most of his time and earned much of his money: heroic tragedies (*The Conquest of Granada, Aureng-Zebe*), tragicomedies (*Marriage à la Mode*) and farce (*An Evening's Love*); and many, many prologues and epilogues to other people's plays as well as his own. Finally, there are the volumes of accompanying criticism (*Of Dramatic Poesy*, 'Discourse Concerning Satire').

This large and not obviously appealing aggregate of writing has not discouraged academic interest; rather the reverse. Drydenian scholarship flourishes, and its crowning glories are the five volumes of the *Poems* edited by Paul Hammond and David Hopkins and published by Longman between 1995 and 2005. But the pleasures of scholarship are not wholly coextensive with those of reading. Students are probably still encouraged to enjoy the measured venom of the satires.

But where to go beyond that? Paul Hammond, in his introduction to the *Poems*, suggests that Dryden's 'translations are far more important, and potentially more attractive to modern readers, than the prevailing consensus would suggest'; this seems plausible, not only because of the translations' inherent qualities but because of the resurgent interest in translation among contemporary poets.

Still, it is an odd and revealing fact about Dryden that his best-liked poems today – 'To the Memory of Mr Oldham' and 'A Song for St Cecilia's Day' – are untypical of him, or at least untypical of his output, and not only because they are short. They are both uncharacteristically open: the one frankly grief-stricken, the other frankly virtuosic.

Dryden has long been dogged by the question of sincerity. In accordance with Fortune's usual bargain, his willingness to please his patrons and audiences has made his work less pleasing in the longer term. One can grant that all published writing, like all public life, requires some accommodation to its readership, and so some liaison with hypocrisy, and yet still be troubled by lines such as these, about Charles II:

Music herself is lost, in vain she brings
Her choicest notes to praise the best of kings.

Dr Johnson was scandalised: 'Of this kind of meanness he never seems to decline the practice, or lament the necessity: he considers the great as entitled to encomiastick homage, and brings praise rather as a tribute than a gift, more delighted with the fertility of his invention than mortified by the prostitution of his judgment.'

Of course there were many strong reasons for approving of Charles, especially in the early years of his reign; and Johnson gives insufficient weight to the fact that panegyric was then a flourishing mode. Still, after the notably measured praise of the *Heroic Stanzas* in memory of Cromwell, Dryden does seem to have given himself over to acclaiming and defending the Stuart monarchs with a readiness that at least challenges the border between loyalty and servility.

One explanation lies in his financial circumstances. He was the eldest son of a not very wealthy family of gentry, obliged to keep up the style of a gentleman without quite having the means, the more so as he had made a grand but not lucrative marriage to the daughter of the Earl of Berkshire.

His salary of £200 a year as poet laureate and historiographer royal was vital to him, as was his income as a shareholder in the king's theatre company. Money was tight after the Theatre Royal burned down in 1672, and again in 1689, when he was sacked from his official posts because he was a Catholic: translating Virgil appealed to him not only for artistic reasons but as a source of cash.

For a taste of the discomforts attaching to his position, sample the brutal class scorn directed against him by the Earl of Rochester after they had fallen out in the mid-1670s: 'He is a Rarity which I cannot but be fond of, as one would be of a Hog that could fiddle, or a singing Owl.'

Various of his relations and acquaintances were much better off: after her apotheosis to intimacy with the king, Dryden's former colleague Nell Gwyn was granted £5000 a year, plus houses, plus land, plus a share of some state revenues. With such associates, and with three sons to put through Westminster and Charterhouse, one can see how the Drydens, like the Blairs, could find it possible to think of themselves as not that rich.

Still, Marvell and Milton got by on much less, their narrower means sufficing to nourish their independent spirits. Dryden's comfortable accommodation with Stuart power must be put down to inclination more than necessity. The developing pressure of his religious feelings has a bearing: he was brought up a puritan, but once you have traced his readings in theology, taken into account the Catholic leanings of his wife and many of his friends, and sampled the relentless doctrinal clarity of *The Hind and the Panther*, little is less persuasive than the claim that his conversion in 1685 after the accession of James II was merely opportunistic.

But there also, simply, seems to have been a peace-loving element to his character: 'common quiet is mankind's concern,' he wrote in *Religio Laici*. In his mild way, he was unprincipled on principle.

Clearly, apologism – in poetry as in life – is less easy to admire than antagonism or independence. But there is a poetry of pliancy which differs from mere propaganda or self-abasement. In this poetry, the words on the page bring with them an awareness that they might have been different: the strain on the bent knee is kept in view.

No one, after all, would take praise in a panegyric as being merely true: the 'judgment' it embodies must therefore concentrate on gauging what will be effective or can be got away with. It follows that one function of panegyric is polite exhortation: when Dryden admires Charles, in *To His Sacred Majesty*, because 'Your love is destined to your country's peace', he also implies – quietly, but nevertheless audibly – that the king should keep looking to his country's peace if he is to continue being worthy of admiration.

This tactical poise is what distinguishes Dryden's panegyric from the wad of similar works by other writers. Waller, for instance, wrote a poem called 'On St James's Park, as lately improved by His Majesty': Dryden steps onto the same ground when he fleetingly praises the new canal dug through the park to the Thames:

Here in a royal bed the waters sleep,
When tired at sea within this bay they creep.

The couplet is absurd, the sort of thing that was to outrage Dr Johnson. In fact, its indulgence of the 'fertility of invention' is so obvious as to be thought-provoking – even, if he ever read it, for Charles.

One can imagine the first flush of pleasure on the royal cheeks evolving into a blush as he registered the triviality of what he was becoming known for. Implicitly, Dryden nudges his attention away from garden design towards what the poem wants to go on to consider: the pressing question of whom to select as his queen.

When he wrote to his friends, Dryden could give his compliments a sharper second edge, as for example in 'To My Honoured Friend Sir Robert Howard, on His Excellent Poems' (Howard later became his brother-in-law). Discussing Howard's translation of Book IV of the *Aeneid*, Dryden says:

Elisa's griefs are so expressed by you,
They are too eloquent to have been true.

'Elisa', as the Longman note reminds us, is Virgil's alternative name for Dido. Dryden's couplet is sarcastic – surely? – and yet this possibility appears to be shut out by the tone of the rest of the poem, no less than by its title. The couplet carries the sort of barb which may be smiled over between friends, but which may also fester. It is perhaps relevant to the intonation of these lines that Dryden and Howard became estranged not many years later (in part because of a dispute over the value of rhyme); as also that at the end of their lives they were reconciled. Dryden's awareness of the prickles within his praises is clear from the shape taken by his first foray into satire. *Mac Flecknoe* is (mostly) a mock encomium spoken by Flecknoe, a prolific poet here figured as 'monarch' of 'nonsense', to Thomas Shadwell, the rival of Dryden who was later to take his place as poet laureate, but who is here represented as Flecknoe's heir:

Shadwell alone, of all my sons, is he
Who stands confirmed in full stupidity.

Just as in the lines to Howard, it is one word, the last of the couplet, that twists the tone from milky encomium to something more acidic: change 'stupidity' to, say, 'celebrity', and 'true' to 'new', and both couplets are rendered equally anodyne. The acid, of course, is much stronger and more consistent in the satire; but the flick of the pen that applies it is the same.

Since the damage is done by a single word, one gets a vivid impression that the word has been chosen; but, because it slots into the space cut out for it by rhyme, one is also made to feel that the choice is inevitable.

This mixture of signals is what gives Dryden's verse its strong, considered quality, so different from the insouciant brilliance of Pope's couplets. The lines may lack the swoon of 'con amore' expressivity (that phrase came into 18th-century English via music) but they are not therefore unemotional. Even when writing with an eye to the main chance, Dryden allows himself a raised eyebrow or a curl of the lip.

Not that he never swoons, but when he does the moment is often placed in a parenthesis or as half of a simile, so as to seem an intermission to the business of the poem in hand. *Annus Mirabilis* (1667) gives a rosy account of naval battles in the Second Dutch War, and of the Fire of London (for a darker view see the 'Advice to a Painter' poems by Marvell). At one point, after much martial talk of 'flagging sails' and 'raking chase-guns', Prince Rupert's ship, its mainmast down, is suddenly transformed into a dog, exhausted from chasing a hare:

With his lolled tongue he faintly licks his prey,
His warm breath blows her flix up as she lies;
She, trembling, creeps upon the ground away,
And looks back to him with beseeching eyes.

'Flix' is surprising: a dialect word for 'fur', it is lifted into prominence by the unexpected rhyme with 'licks'. The word can stand as a reminder that the 'poetic diction' which Dryden was so often praised by later Augustans for having perfected, was not the prissily abstract and monotone vocabulary denounced by Wordsworth but rather a harmonious interlacing of words of different kinds. But what is really startling about this passage is how little it helps us see or understand the naval situation it is presented as an image for.

The modest and (in context) pointed phrase 'upon the ground' tips us the wink that Dryden is, for the time being, not at all interested in boats, but is writing simply for the pleasure of it. It is a telling sign of what sparked his pleasure that this image, which seems so refreshingly oxygenated, has its roots in Ovid (Hammond's note informs us) as much as or more than in outdoor observation.

If the best of Dryden's verse is – as traditionally thought – to be found in the satires, it may be because there, unusually, the surge of con amore writing and the discipline of socio-political appraisal merge. This passage is from *Mac Flecknoe*:

Some beams of wit on other souls may fall,
Strike through and make a lucid interval,
But Shadwell's genuine night admits no ray,
His rising fogs prevail upon the day.
Besides, his goodly fabric fills the eye,
And seems designed for thoughtless majesty:
Thoughtless as monarch oaks that shade the plain,
And, spread in solemn state, supinely reign.

On the one hand, the crescendo of invective: the gathering of sources of darkness and blockage, night, fogs, and the 'goodly fabric' which is a goad at Shadwell's girth. On the other, the growth of the natural image, from 'beams' through many of the words mentioned above on to 'oaks'. The simile makes a vicious point: given that Shadwell is as thoughtless *as* an oak, if only he were thoughtless *like* an oak – i.e. quietly – instead of in the way of jobbing writers who keep on coming out with words. But, equally, the beauty of the imagined scene seems to mitigate the invective, as though Dryden were trying to make even Shadwell smile at the idea of being transformed into an oak, a latter-day English Daphne.

A few years later, Dryden wrote a letter to Richard Busby, his sons' headmaster at Westminster, appealing against the rustication of one of them for some misdemeanour. He sugared the protest like this: 'None complaine, but they desire to be reconcild at the same time: there is no mild Expostulation at least, which does not intimate a kindnesse and respect in him who makes it.' Dryden's satires are often far from kind; but often, too, they keep open the possibility, if not of reconciliation, at least of human warmth.

Since Dryden's writing was so various, the question of what to include in an edition of his poems is vexed. The plays – though largely verse – are excluded from Hammond and Hopkins's volumes, quite justifiably of course (for them, and for all else that is absent from the Longman edition, we must turn to the 20-volume California edition of *The Works of John Dryden*, compiled by generations of editors, and published serially between 1956 and 2000). Likewise, and no less justifiably, the prose is absent; save for the prose passages which prefaced or dedicated poems or volumes of poems, such as the 'Discourse Concerning Satire'.

Happily, all the verse translations are included: all, that is, except *The Works of Virgil*, which, though the editors hope eventually to add it, has been 'excluded from the present scheme because of its bulk' – reasoning which, if generally adopted, will open the way for quite startlingly economical editions of many major poets.

Very much present, on the other hand, are the prologues and epilogues Dryden wrote for his own and other people's plays: though spoken in the theatre, many of them also had semi-independent second lives, being included, for instance, in *Miscellany Poems* (1684). The rationale is unimpeachable, but it makes for an odd reading experience, to be told of the theatre magic one is about to encounter, and then of the theatre magic one has encountered, with only an inch of blank page between the two.

But this feeling of incompleteness is cultivated by the editors, who want to point up the contradiction between the shifting, fragmented existence of Dryden's writing during his lifetime and its re-presentation now in monumental volumes.

Not unusually for his period – but unlike later poets such as Pope or Browning – Dryden seems to have felt 'a reluctance to build a canon over his own name'. Some works were allowed to go out of print; others, including *Absalom and Achitophel,* were published and republished anonymously, even though their authorship was widely known.

This carelessness about the assertion of his identity through publication tallies with another self-effacing aspect of Dryden: his swamp-like openness to influence. Introducing *Annus Mirabilis,* he wrote that Virgil 'has been my master in this poem: I have followed him everywhere. . . my images are many of them copied from him, and the rest are imitations of him'; and he added notes pointing out his greatest debts.

He would, I'm sure, have been glad of Hammond and Hopkins's plenteous annotation, which is both more erudite and better focused than that of the California volumes. Footnotes can look like a pedestal to the column of verse whose canonicity they serve to reinforce; the notes in this edition are more like a root system, leading not only into Dryden's vast classical reading, but towards the ephemeral pamphleteering by which his poems were equally nourished. They are a work of great editorial tact, and they not only satiate, but stimulate, one's curiosity.

Unlike most scholarly editions these days, the Longman series encourages its editors to modernise the spelling and punctuation of poems printed before the advent of modern standard, or nearly standard, English (one can argue about when that was, and as the general editors of the series note, 'the requirements of a particular author take precedence over "principle"': it would be foolish to modernise the spelling of Spenser's *Faerie Queene,* for instance, since it is purposely archaic). One justification for modernisation is that often, and certainly in Dryden's case, the spelling and pointing of the first-printed texts owe more to the compositor than to the poet.

Still, it was in this unreliable and only semi-authorial way that the poems appeared to their first readers and, as Hammond sensibly admits in his introduction, 'some nuances of meaning, rhythm and rhyme are undoubtedly lost through modernisation. For example, in 'To My Dear Friend Mr Congreve', Dryden imagines Congreve inheriting his place as king of poetry:

High on the throne of wit; and seated there
Not mine (that's little) but thy laurel wear.

Turn to the California edition, which retains the original spelling, and Congreve is wearing something slightly different: a 'Lawrel' (this spelling is common in Dryden's printed texts and elsewhere in the period). Does it matter? The capital letter does not, since poems in Dryden's time were liberally and irregularly scattered with them, but the spelling does. You wear a 'Lawrel' on a 'throne'; it 'descends' to you, the poem says, and allows you to 'reign'. This familiar analogy between poetic and political power is energised because the name of the poet's leafy crown includes the word 'Law'.

On the other hand, much that is different in the early texts doesn't carry meaning, and it requires a good deal of mental discipline not to be distracted by the buzz of capitals, italics and surprising semicolons. One can take an antiquarian delight in them; but that is obviously not something Dryden intended to supply.

On the contrary, he felt strongly that old texts needed to be kept readable, hence his translation – or rather his very radical modernisation – of Chaucer, which he justified in terms that harmonise with those used by the Longman editors: 'Something must be lost in all transfusion, that is, in all translations; but the sense will remain, which would otherwise be lost, or at least be maimed, when it is scarce intelligible, and that but to a few.'

One of the great virtues of the Longman series is that it is aimed not at a few professional scholars but, to quote its founder F.W. Bateson's campaigning statement from the 1960s, at 'university students and teachers, and the general reader'. That ambition has had to battle against economic factors (if nothing else): few general readers will wish to fork out for the five hardback volumes of the full edition. The generous paperback selection is therefore particularly welcome.

The 'transfusion' of modernisation suits Dryden's poems because – despite their attachment to contemporary events – they stretch imaginatively through time, both back to the past and on towards the future into which they are set to drift on the current of affairs.

Their persistent classical allusions connect them to antiquity, yet they also give particular attention to what may be about to happen: in *Annus Mirabilis* the first 'scattering sparks' of the Great Fire are already 'big with the flames that to our ruin rose', while children are called 'future people', palimpsests of what is to come.

Dryden's first lines often establish an uneasy relation to the present, seeming somehow both to place the poems in a moment of time and to unseat them from it. *Heroic Stanzas* begins: 'And now 'tis time'.

'Now', of course, hooks into the present; but 'and' pulls the poem back towards things that have gone before ('And' was not unprecedented as a first word, but it is enduringly strange: Blake used it in 'Jerusalem' and Pound in the *Cantos*). The first line of *Astraea Redux* is similarly assertive and uncertain about 'now': 'Now with a general peace the world was blessed.' In this case, the unsettling is done by 'was'.

This interweaving of times shows why translation was so important to Dryden. 'Translation' means a bringing-across, from the Latin; 'metaphor' means the same, but from the Greek. The etymological coincidence is especially suggestive for Dryden because the texts he translated were also sources of metaphor: he saw his own time through them, or gauged it against them. One clear example is the account of 'Nisus and Euryalus' from Virgil, a story of friendship unto death which Dryden draws on for a simile in his poem 'To the Memory of Mr Oldham':

Farewell, too little and too lately known,
Whom I began to think and call my own;
For sure our souls were near allied, and thine
Cast in the same poetic mould with mine.
One common note on either lyre did strike,
And knaves and fools we both abhorred alike:
To the same goal did both our studies drive,
The last set out the soonest did arrive.
Thus Nisus fell upon the slippery place,
While his young friend performed and won the race.

The lines open with Dryden's characteristic attentiveness to time's complexity: 'began', not quite at the beginning of the poem, is ambushed by 'farewell'. But what becomes cumulatively moving is the way the pairing of words which might seem like a laziness of style – 'too little and too lately', 'think and call', 'knaves and fools' – finds its point as an echo of the pairing of souls which the poem celebrates and whose dissolution it mourns.

The Virgilian simile (simile is another kind of pairing) refers to a running race instituted by Aeneas as part of the anniversary games in commemoration of his father. Nisus had been in the lead but slipped, and extended his leg to trip the second-placed runner so that his young friend Euryalus could triumph. The heroes disputed with a toddler's vehemence over who was the true winner; luckily Aeneas had a stash of prizes in reserve.

Dryden does not mention this squabble, but it may nonetheless be present in the imaginative penumbra of his words as a figure for the literary marketplace: Oldham had recently been more successful than most poets in securing patronage. But what is certain is the incongruity of the image. In its new context, that Euryalus 'won the race' takes on the meaning that Oldham died first. The verbal contortion by which Dryden conveys this while also asking us to imagine something quite different is an exquisite example of grief's eloquent inarticulacy.

At about the same time as he wrote 'To the Memory of Mr Oldham', Dryden was translating the Nisus and Euryalus story – not only the race but the later night-time commando mission during which both are killed – for the miscellany *Sylvae*, published by the young entrepreneur Jacob Tonson. As Hammond notes, Dryden's version 'emphasises the bond between the friends': for instance, when Nisus outlines his daring plan but begs Euryalus to stay safely behind, Euryalus protests with a plaintive gulp which is audible in the Latin ('mene igitur socium summis adiungere rebus,/ Nise, fugis?') but louder in Dryden's English: 'All this alone, and leaving me behind!'

In the newish discipline of translation studies, Dryden is known for having introduced a simple technical distinction between 'metaphrase' (word for word translation), 'paraphrase' (freer translation) and 'imitation' (no gloss needed).

As you might guess, these categories begin to melt into one another as soon as they have been erected: what is more persistently thought-provoking is his tendency to see translation in affective terms. This is why he was so responsive to the lineaments of friendship in Virgil: not only because he saw reflected in them friendships of his own, but because, for him, translation was a friendly art.

'A translator is to make his author appear as charming as possibly he can, provided he maintains his character,' he wrote in the preface to *Sylvae*. Sometimes the friendship becomes passionate: translation is a 'disease', like the disease of love; it is 'more pleasing' than 'my ordinary productions'; to translate is to follow 'natural impulses'.

After Dryden's death, William Congreve – himself Dryden's 'dear friend' – paid tribute to his power of friendship, but also remembered that 'he had something in his Nature that abhorr'd Intrusion into any Society whatsoever.' Translation offered him the freedom to pursue imaginative but not merely imaginary friendships without the risk of seeming to intrude.

Repeatedly, he selects passages which have to do with desire, companionship or the dissolution of companionship in death; and he translates them so as to suggest continuities between the relationships that are translated and the relationships established in translation; of English to the other languages of Dryden to the original authors.

Translating Lucretius ('Concerning the Nature of Love'), he achieved a frank sensuality which – as Rochester scoffed – eluded him in his autonomous writing:

They gripe, they squeeze, their humid tongues they dart,
As each would force their way to t'other's heart –
In vain; they only cruise about the coast,
For bodies cannot pierce, nor be in bodies lost:
As sure they strive to be, when both engage
In that tumultuous momentany rage. . .

What is so amusingly right about this is the slackening and resurgence of resolve: 'bodies cannot pierce' – oh yes they can, let's strive again. And what releases Dryden's imagination is the implicit analogy between the lovers' attempt to 'force their way to t'other's heart' and his attempt to get to the heart of Lucretius (that line is tellingly, self-destructively, his interpolation) And when he translates the metamorphosis of Baucis and Philemon from Ovid, he is unusually adventurous in allowing the verse itself to seem to metamorphose:

New roots their fastened feet begin to bind,
Their bodies stiffen in a rising rind;
Then, ere the bark above their shoulders grew,
They give and take at once their last adieu;
At once, 'Farewell, O faithful spouse,' they said;
At once th'encroaching rinds their closing lips invade.

The verbal and phonetic repetitions have a solidifying effect; but it is Dryden's way with tenses that is most brilliantly metamorphic. Ovid does not switch to the present tense until after he has finished narrating the metamorphosis: 'Even to this day the Bithynian peasant in that region points out two trees,' in the Loeb translation. Dryden, often flexible with tenses, shuffles past and present to suggest the creeping finality of the change (and notice the way the 12-syllable last line seems to resist the encroachment of 'invade').

But another imaginative ripple created by this oscillation of tenses is the thought that what has happened to Baucis and Philemon as they are transferred from the unique, historical lifespan of people to the reiterative, natural life-cycle of trees is also what happens in translation. Like the Bithynian peasant, the English reader can (even to this day) point to the result of a Metamorphosis: an Ovid with his roots translated into another language, his feet fastened into different rhythms, and a tight new binding of rhyme.

It is cause for celebration that both 'Baucis and Philemon' and 'Lucretius: Concerning the Nature of Love' are included – along with a good sampling of other translations – in the *Selected Poems.* And it is cause for regret that the editors have been unable to include *The Works of Virgil* even in what ought to be the complete edition. Of course its 'bulk' is not the whole reason for its exclusion: it might well be thought a little odd to place volumes entitled *The Works of Virgil* within an edition of *The Poems of John Dryden.*

This verse is not fully his in the way his autochthonous poems are; and it is not even quite so much his as the other translations are, for at least he has extracted or selected those, adopted them by anthologising as well as by translating. If any poems have to be excluded, it should be these ones.

But to say this is not only to underestimate the imaginative challenge of translation; it is to mistake the character of Dryden as a writer. He is very much himself in the generous, perceptive act of translating another person's words; and most himself when the other person is Virgil.

His account of Virgil's political accommodations, in the 'Dedication of the *Aeneis*', casts fleeting but illuminating reflections on his own sense of himself as a public writer under the Stuarts: 'To infuse an awful Respect into the People, towards such a Prince: By that respect to confirm their obedience to him; and by that Obedience to make them Happy. . . it is possible for a Courtier not to be a Knave.'

And the spin he puts on discussions of kingship in the poem amounts to his most frank statement of opposition to the Williamite regime: for instance, in the opening flash-forward he writes that when Aeneas arrived in Italy: 'His banish'd Gods restor'd to Rites Divine,/And setl'd sure Succession in his Line' (this is the old spelling of the California edition). The poor publisher – still Jacob Tonson – was reduced to adjusting the illustrations so that Aeneas' nose looked a bit like King William's.

But Dryden does not merely use Virgil as a political Trojan horse. When it doesn't concern affairs of state, the translation is an exemplary act of understanding, both honouring the particularity of other characters from other times, and imaginatively reaching out to them. Here, for instance, is Hecuba, Troy collapsing around her, faced with the aged Priam, improbably geared up for combat:

The Queen, when she beheld her trembling Lord,
And hanging by his side a heavy Sword,
What Rage, she cry'd, has seiz'd my Husband's mind;
What Arms are these, and to what use design'd?
These times want other aids: were Hector here,
Ev'n Hector now in vain, like Priam wou'd appear.
With us, one common shelter thou shalt find,
Or in one common Fate with us be join'd.

Dryden slightly exaggerates Virgil's movingly direct language, like an actor sensitively interpreting his lines. He introduces the weak syntactical structure of 'and hanging by his side' – so that the clause itself appears to hang – and the flicker of a pun across 'arms'; the momentary uncertainty after 'were *Hector* here' (you half-expect Hecuba to continue: 'he'd sort things out') is Dryden's touch, as is the repetition of 'one common'.

A forceful appeal to common feeling sounds throughout the scene: it is there in the newly plain words for Priam, 'the poor old Man', and the newly shocked description of his being dragged by Pyrrhus 'slidd'ring through clotter'd Blood, and holy Mire'; there too in the reiteration of the phrase 'one common Fate' when Priam comes to share it.

Oddly, Dryden adds a note to the line describing the body that is no longer Priam ('A headless Carcass, and a nameless thing'): '*This whole line is taken from Sir John Denham.*' It is the only note in the whole translation, and the point of it is to show Dryden not only sharing the words of another English poet, but momentarily snuffing his own light as Priam's is extinguished. Dryden is at his most appealing in the creative fidelity of his translations; and it is here too that he offers the sharpest stimulus to contemporary poets who are so attracted by and yet also (it sometimes seems) a little bit shifty about the partial liberty of the 'version' from another language. Dryden's *Virgil* is a great work – perhaps the great work – of the kind of imagination that is less an originative than a sympathising power.

SWEEPING THE DUST FROM THE BOARDS

The very earliest records of dramatic activity which are held in the Brynmor Jones Library's archives concern the many visits of travelling players to Selby Abbey in the late medieval period. We know that they entertained the monks because the obedientiaries' account rolls intermittently between 1431 and 1532 register payments to various dramatic performers.

The accounts form part of the Earl of Londesborough's archive (DDLO), and are supplemented by further rolls recently transferred from the Westminster Diocesan Record Office (DWE). These are important records precisely because so little material relating to the early English theatre has survived.

The archive of the Hotham family, of South Dalton near Beverley, is a major, if more modern, source. As has been seen in the previous article by Amanda Capern and Ruth Pyle, Sir Charles Hotham, an eighteenth century collector of dramatic and other material, acquired much that is of interest. For example, in 1674

John Crowne, Thomas Shadwell and John Dryden wrote a withering attack on Elkanar Settle's controversial yet successful play *The Empress of Morocco*. This 72-page pamphlet entitled *Notes and Observations on the Empress of Morocco or Some Few Erratas to be printed instead of the Sculptures with the second edition of the play* (1674) is bound into a volume of miscellaneous pamphlets (DDHO/20/154).

Elkanar Settle was one of a band of dramatists encouraged by the restored Charles II to create an English equivalent to French heroic drama. *The Empress of Morocco* was remarkable for being the first Restoration play in which the climax of the drama occurred in a musical scene with its own score. Dryden et al were not impressed. In their pamphlet they reprinted Settle's defence against scurrilous critics only to follow it with a devastating line by line dissection of his play.

Apart from ridiculing Settle's stammer, they abhorred his sense of the dramatic. They argued that his plot did not add up, his dramatic verse was grammatically at fault and his settings were absurd. To make matters worse he made eyes hear and ears see, a particularly heinous crime in an age where the body was a metaphor for the well being of state and nation.

The Empress of Morocco was performed at The Duke's Theatre, Dorset Garden, London in 1673. The published edition of the play included a set of engravings by W. Dolle illustrating scenes from the Dorset Garden production. It is this combined effort which the critical triumvirate target with their withering scorn. Act II for example begins with a description of a great fleet coming up a river and sailing to Morocco. The three authors write:

It is hard to say who has pictured ships worst, the poet Elkanah, or the Sculpture-Maker *Will. Doll.* Of the two I think *Will. Doll* has done the best; for he has scratched out five things which look a little like ships, (which our Poet calls a glorious fleet) but the things which the Poet designs for Ships are Pageants, masques, things with instincts Animal, and no body knows what.

Recourse to Dolle's illustration shows this criticism to be unjust as well as harsh. But, jealous of Settle's popularity as a dramatist (especially with women), Crowne, Sheridan and Dryden put aside their own considerable differences to complete a thorough hatchet job on *The Empress of Morrocco.* At stake of course were their own dramatic careers!

If vicious slander has always been an integral part of the drama critic's armoury so has the tendency to judge the new against the old. *A Short Criticism on the Performance of Hamlet by Mr Kemble* was written in 1789 and is also part of the Hotham Collection (DDHO/20/127). John Philip Kemble, brother of the actress Sarah Siddons, was first engaged by the company at Drury Lane in September 1783. His debut performance was the title role in Hamlet. The author of the pamphlet thinks it unfair that Kemble's performance should be judged in the shadow of another actor's legacy (that of David Garrick). Kemble's more 'majestic form', the 'melancholy visible in his countenance', he argues, 'peculiarly fits him for the filial and grief-worn Hamlet'. Admitting Kemble's occasional 'stiffness of action' the critic nevertheless supports the actor's style of delivery.

In the famous opening scene in which Hamlet sees his father's ghost Garrick had said 'Did you not *speak* to it?' when addressing his friend Horatio. Kemble puts his emphasis in a different place saying, 'Did *you* not speak to it?' Such debate underlines how important good delivery was for a rave review from the eighteenth century critic. Kemble's debut, though less successful than his sister's, put him at the forefront of his profession.

Sir Charles Hotham corresponded with Kemble as well as with actors such as William and Sarah Siddons and Eliza Farren. The Kemble correspondence dates between 1784 and 1791. On 19 September 1787 Kemble wrote excitedly to Hotham about the refurbishment of the Drury Lane Theatre:

... I must think the house ought in justice to be seen, before the smoaky lamps have dull'd the Gold, and darken'd the white, and wither'd the bloom of the rose-coloured Linings in the boxes. (DDHO/4/23) Two years later in 1789 the actor himself became manager of the theatre he admired so much.

Not all managers were as dedicated to the beauty and harmony of their theatre. One of the most peculiar items to be found in the archives is a small notebook which contains the manuscript version of an elaborate criticism of the management of the Bath Theatre Royal (DP/157/1). *The Dangers of a Lee Shore, or an Impartial View of the Bath T- - - -e in the year 1759* is a 48 page pamphlet 'by J Brownsmith Late Prompter to the Said Theatre'.

Part of a small miscellaneous collection, it begins with an allegorical letter 'From a sailor on Board to his friend on Shore'. Evidently the prompter has moved to a new job at Bristol

Theatre and is looking back at Mr John Lee, his old employer. What follows is a long complaint against manager and company. In sum, the notebook is illustrative of some of the many difficulties that could face theatrical companies, engendering backbiting, criticism and jealousy.

Bath was one of the more unusual eighteenth century towns in having a theatre house by 1759. Before 1750, whilst London's theatrical venues were established, the provinces had little such provision.

Additionally, actors and actresses were positively discouraged from seeking work by the licensing acts of 1713 and 1731 which had the power to deprive players of acting for monetary reward. After 1750 more major provincial towns got their own theatres royal. For example, a theatre royal opened on Finkle Street in Hull on 3 October 1768 with a production of *Love In a Village*. Tate Wilkinson, the manager of the 'York Circuit', recorded the event in *The Wandering Patentee,* his own account of the early days of the York Circuit:

A new, elegant Theatre was opened at Hull; we jogged on quietly on a safe and pleasant easy trot there.

The Brynmor Jones Library holds series of playbills for Hull's Theatre Royal and other local theatres which record sequences of performances from the late eighteenth to the early twentieth centuries. The evidence from the Hull Theatre Royal playbills tells us that the theatre hosted many touring companies. Additionally, it appears that some of the best known actors and actresses of the day such as Mrs Jordan (comedy) and Sarah Siddons (tragedy) appeared as star attractions.

Players could appear in two or three major roles in one night, moving between entirely different parts. Double or even triple bills were the norm. This could lead to an incongruous mix of entertainment. For example, on 23 January 1806 Hull Theatre Royal staged *Macbeth,* starring Mr Melvin in the title role. It was followed by a farce in two Acts called *High Life Below Stairs,* with Mr Melvin as Sir Harry's servant.

Titles which promised scenes of moral decay were evidently popular at this time. With plays like *High Life Below*

Stairs, Provocation Or Spanish Ingratitude and *Inconstant* doing the rounds it seems reasonable to suggest that *Dissipation, a comedy in five acts* (1781) by Miles Peter Andrew (DDHO/20/147) might be typical of the sort of play which was staged in Hull during the late eighteenth century. A printed copy of this play is in the archives. Again collected by Charles Hotham, it was originally written for the Drury Lane Theatre, London, and starred actors such as Mrs Abington and Mr King.

A good example of a comedy, fast moving and witty, it is concerned with courting couples, mistaken identity and the habits of aristocratic society. In the preface the author curses the producer who was the playwright Sheridan:

Mr Sheridan, it must be confessed, has taken away several *witty* things from this comedy... but should he, in his *great dearth* of genius, ever venture to introduce them in any further production of his own, and the audience should not immediately perceive the *difference*, the original author will certainly put in his claim to all the merit they possess.

The petty politics evident here between dramatists is mirrored in the political comedy which proliferates in the play. Politicians it seems were just as hypocritical in 1781 as they are today!:

Charles (looking at the paper): I see your Lordship has been speaking against the Budget.

Lord: Against the Budget! No, *against* it! O yes, yes, so I was; I did not recollect immediately; but you know its all the same thing with us.

Charles: Really my Lord!

Lady: Why you grave creature, ha! ha! ha! are you going to be surprised because a man of fashion forgets which side he took, or thinks politicks a mere matter of amusement?

It should not be forgotten that grievances aired in public frequently have the beneficial effect of attracting publicity. Whilst play-wrights were launching vicious attacks on the quality of each other's work, front house managers went to great lengths to court audiences with promises of novelty, urban sophistication and ever more dramatic innovation. For example the playbill advertising Farquar's play *Inconstant* wooed its audience with the promise of 'alterations, as performed in London'. Those who went to see *Provocation Or Spanish Ingratitude* were promised 'An ENGAGEMENT between Four Spanish Frigates and Four English; during the Engagement one of the Spanish Ships blows up. - Rule Britannia in full Chorus'.

Theatre playbills give us valuable insight into the social concerns and pleasures of the day. On 22 January 1790 Hull Theatre Royal staged a new opera called *The Iron Mask* with libretto by the Hon. John St John and music by Thomas Shaw. The first English opera to be inspired by the fall of the Bastile (July 1789) it promised topical scenes: 'A dungeon in that prison, the hotel de ville at paris, ruins of the BASTILE'.

The enthusiasm of this opera for the French Revolution can be adduced from the playbill's promise that the work would 'conclude with the rising of the temple and genius of liberty'. Yet, such revolutionary fervour is carefully balanced by the tragedy which precedes it the same evening. The anonymously written Percy, it is announced, will include 'Stand to your Guns, my Hearts of Oak', by Mr Mitchell.

As well as reacting and responding to political events, the playbills show a theatrical world responding to fads and popular themes, as we can see in those of the Alexandra Theatre (1909-1922), Hull Assembly Rooms (1845-1872) and Hull Grand Theatre (1896-1900).

Towards the end of the nineteenth century images of the American West were all the rage. On 27 June 1898 *The New World* ('a picturesque and realistic Western Romance') by Fred Darcy was performed at the Grand Theatre and Opera House, George Street, Hull.

It was advertised as 'A thrilling story of Pioneer Life in the Goldfields of the Great North-West'. By this time audiences had to be wooed with more than promises of revamped London theatre. The highlight of the play was to occur in Act I where Joe Williams was to be 'Actually hanged in full view of the audience'.

Other novelties were to come. In the early twentieth century cinema also began to be incorporated into the theatre.

On Monday March 8 1909 at the Alexandra Theatre, *The Woman Pays* by Frank M Thorne was to be shown together with 'cinema-tograph pictures... between the acts'.

As we have seen, a wealth of detail can be crammed onto a playbill. In addition, a scene by scene synopsis of the play was often included, with apposite comments on the characters. Local train times were also frequently added. Evidence from the playbills suggests that moral themes continued to make good theatre throughout the nineteenth and early twentieth centuries. *The White Girl Slave* by Joseph Warncliffe was put on at the Alexandra Theatre, Charlotte Street, Hull, on 22 June 1914.

This was a theatre where 'the sliding roof renders the atmosphere at all times clear and agreeable'! Warncliffe was author of other moral dramas such as *Foiled by a Woman, The Woman of Death,* and *Through Thick and Thin.* Perhaps not surprisingly therefore the playbill emphasises the feminine content of the play rather than the evils of slavery. 'Knowledge is power' shrieks the playbill, 'and the knowledge of the real deadly danger which menaces English Girlhood to-day at the hands of the White Slave traders, will give girls the power to guard against danger when it threatens'.

The scene by scene synopsis tells us that we will be transported from Eva Lennard's house in Manchester to Buenos Aires where it is enigmatically stated that 'England is aroused'.

In conclusion, Hull's drama-related holdings are a well kept secret. This article has focused on early archival holdings. It would take another article to describe and present all the twentieth century material that is available. As well as playbills the twentieth century archives includes 1930s drama by the sons of landed gentry (unperformed) and work by the young Philip Larkin and Alan Plater. The dust is waiting to be swept from the boards once more!

Chapter 10

The Hind and the Panther

The Hind and the Panther was published in 1687, and is said to have been written at Rushton in Northamptonshire, a sylvan neighbourhood. If Dryden's conversion does not present any psychological difficulties, it also seems natural that he should have speedily proceeded to explain to the world a position not new to it, but strange and, therefore, in a sense, new, to himself. That *The Hind and the Panther* cannot be harmonised with *Religio Laici* is, of course, part of the situation, although the two poems are not inconsistent with each other as stages of a mental evolution. To suggest that the later work was written to ensure the favour of James II (from whom it does not appear what Dryden had to expect beyond punctuality), is to ignore a very plain historical consideration.

In April, 1687,—a fortnight before the publication of the poem,—James II put forth the declaration for liberty of conscience, which extended to nonconformists in general, and was, in fact, the catholic king's bid for the support of the protestant dissenters in his struggle with the establishment. On the other hand, the convert Dryden's personal confession of faith was, at the same time, an *eirenicon* to the church of England from the catholic side, and a summons to her to join hands with the church of Rome against the protestant nonconformists.

Inasmuch as a similar royal declaration had been issued in Scotland two months earlier, and the dispensing power had received a solemn judicial affirmation in the previous year, Dryden could not have been taken by surprise by the king's recent action. He could, therefore, hardly have put forth a "libel of policy" less likely to commend itself to the king and those who advised him in accordance with his wishes, or have given a more palpable proof either of obtuseness—a quality not characteristic of him—or of candour.

The poem is far the longest of Dryden's original productions in verse; but it is carried on with unmistakable vigour to its somewhat abrupt close, and, in its concluding, as well as in its opening, part, displays the reverse of a falling off in power of either invention or expression. Criticism has chiefly directed itself against the plan of the work, which Johnson, for instance, terms injudicious and incommodious, rather than to the conduct of the arguments, which cannot be described as inadequate or uneven.

The Hind and the Panther (as would be obvious, even were it not made additionally clear by the first lines of part III) does not pretend to be more than a fable, a product of an artificial stage of poetry, which confines its attention to human nature and introduces animals merely in a parabolical way: so animals would have spoken or acted, had they been men. All references, however interesting, to the beast-epos, an independent literary cycle, into which satirical meanings and types were not introduced till a comparatively late date, are, therefore, more or less out of place in this connection. Still less can there be any question here of the transfer of a whole world of human sentiment and character into the outward conditions of animal life—as in Edmond Rostand's *Chantecler*—not for purposes of analogy, but in order to read a poetical significance into the whole system of animated nature.

The Hind and the Panther is allegorical only in its *mise-en-scène* and distribution of characters; as a fable, its fault is that it falls short of the moderate amount of imaginary verisimilitude required by this literary species. On the face of it, therefore, Prior and Charles Montague, the authors of *The Hind and the Panther Transvers'd to the Story of the Country Mouse and the City Mouse* (1687), were justified in ridiculing in the preface to their squib the incongruity of animals indulging in theological controversy and Biblical criticism, as was Johnson in repeating the same cavil in different words.

But Dryden had often, in regard both to the drama and to other branches of literature, defended the cause of "English freedom"; and, in his free use of the machinery of the fable for satirical and didactic purposes, he was following the examples of Chaucer and Spenser. Still, poetry and theological controversy are ill-matched associates, and Dryden was at little pains to mitigate the harshness of the union, dropping the fabulous vestment which he had cast round his disputants so soon as he chose, in order to resume it at his convenience.

Of the two justly celebrated "fables" proper included in part III of this poem, the earlier—that of the swallows—attests the independence of Dryden's attitude towards the court, where the censure of father Petre (the Martin), though supposed to be delivered by an adversary, cannot have been welcome. In the story of "the Pigeon's and the Buzzard's love," the character of Burnet (the Buzzard) ranks with the most powerful of the poet's satirical efforts. Unlike Stillingfleet, who is dealt with earlier in the same part of the poem, Burnet, though he is called "invulnerable in his impudence," lay broadly open to attack, and, according to his wont, had voluntarily descended into the arena with his *Reasons against Repealing the Test.*

The Hind and the Panther, for reasons which have been made apparent, could not bring the poet into favour with any party; and critics like Martin Clifford and "Tom" Brown could fall upon him as they pleased. When, in contravention of the hopes uttered in *Britannia Rediviva,* the change of *régime* ensued, and William and Mary held sway in her father's stead, Dryden's places and pensions were taken from him, and Shadwell wore the laurel. It seems to have been about this time that Dryden became indebted to Dorset for substantial support; but he manifestly continued to add to his income by literary labours.

That the vitality and freshness of his powers still remained undiminished is shown by the variety of his productions in these years. Not long before the end of James II's reign, he had written the playful *Letter to Sir George Etherege,* which alone among his complimentary epistles and addresses (extending over many years of his life) are in Hudibrastic metre. In 1690, as has been seen, he successfully resumed work for the stage. There does not seem to have been any indisposition on the part of the new court to show goodwill to him as a playwright; but, in commanding *The Spanish Fryar* to be performed on one of her first appearances in public, queen Mary chose more fortunately for him than for herself.

Meanwhile, the connection between the publisher Jacob Tonson and Dryden was productive of much literary work, though, when there was a pecuniary pressure upon Dryden, the relations between them frequently tried his patience and, at times, roused him to wrath. Besides the translations from classical poets already mentioned as included in the earliest volumes of the *Miscellany*, Dryden, with the assistance of his two elder sons, brought out, in 1693, a complete translation of Juvenal and Persius, prefaced by one of the most delightful of his essays. In its earlier portions, *A Discourse concerning the Original and Progress of Satire* may, after the manner of such *prolegomena*, have been put together so as to suit the amount of information to the appetite of the reader; but the comparison between the three Roman satirists contains some admirable criticism, and the easy and graceful style is enjoyable from beginning to end.

The essay prefixed to Dryden's translation (1695) of Du Fresnoy's *Parallel of Poetry and Painting* (the French prose version printed by the author with his original Latin poem *De Arte Graphica*) is, perhaps, more obviously written to order. It contains an elaboration of the theory that the true imitation of nature consists of the pursuit of the ideal in art—a view on which Dryden had insisted in his early disquisitions on dramatic poetry, but which, though it might have commended itself to Goethe, has until recently been regarded as out of date.

Chapter 11

Absalom and Achitophel

It would not serve any purpose to dwell upon the general morigeration of Dryden, who, in this as in other respects, was "hurried down" the times in which he lived, to the leaders of politics and fashion, to the king's ministers, favourites and mistresses, or upon the flatteries which, in dedications and elsewhere, he heaped upon the king himself, and upon his brother the duke.

The attempts, however, which have been made to show that his pen was "venal"—in any sense beyond that of his having been paid for his compliments, or, at least, for a good many of them—may be said to have broken down; and the fact that he may have received payment from the king for writing *The Medal* does not prove that he was inspired by the expectation of personal profit when he first attacked the future medallist in *Absalom and Achitophel.*

In undertaking the composition of this great satire, whether or not at the request of Charles II, Dryden had found his great literary opportunity; and, of this, he took advantage in a spirit far removed from that of either the hired bravos or the spiteful lampooners of his age. For this opportunity he had been unconsciously preparing himself as a dramatist; and it was in the nature of things, and in accordance with the responsiveness of his genius to the calls made upon it by time and circumstance, that, in the season of a great political crisis, he should have rapidly perceived his chance of decisively influencing public opinion by an exposure of the aims and methods of the party of revolution.

This he proposed to accomplish, not by a poetic summary

of the rights of the case, or by a sermon in verse on the sins of factiousness, corruption and treason, but by holding up to the times and their troubles, with no magisterial air or dictatorial gesture, a mirror in which, under a happily contrived disgvise, the true friends and the real foes of their king and country should be recognised. This was the "Varronian" form of satire afterwards commended by him, with a well warranted self-consciousness, as the species, mixing serious intent with pleasant manner, to which, among the ancients, several of Lucian's *Dialogues* and, among the moderns, the *Encomium Moriae* of Erasmus belong. "Of the same kind is 'Mother Hubberd's Tale'; in Spenser, and (if it be not too vain to mention anything of my own) the poems of 'Absalom' and 'MacFlecknoe.'"

The political question at issue, in the troubled times of which the names "whig" and "tory" still survive as speaking mementoes, was that of the succession of the Catholic heir to the throne, or of his exclusion in favour of some other claimant—perhaps the king's son Monmouth, whom many believed legitimate (the Absalom of the poem). For many months, Shaftesbury, who, after serving and abandoning a succession of governments, had passed into opposition, had seemed to direct the storm. Two parliaments had been called in turn, and twice the Exclusion bill had been rejected by the lords. Then, as the whig leader seemed to have thrown all hesitation to the winds, and was either driving his party or being driven by it into extremities from which there was no return, a tremor of reaction ran through the land, the party round the king gathered confidence, and, evidence supposed sufficient to support the charge having been swept in, Shaftesbury was committed to the Tower on a charge of high treason.

It was at this time of tension, while a similar charge was being actually pressed to the gallows against a humbler agent of faction (the "Protestant joiner" Stephen College), that Dryden's great effort to work upon public opinion was made. Part I of *Absalom and Achitophel,* which seems to have been taken in hand quite early in 1681, was published on 17

November in that year. Shaftesbury, it is known, was then fearing for his life. A week later, in spite of all efforts to the contrary, the bill was ignored by the Middlesex grand jury. Great popular rejoicing followed, and a medal was struck in Shaftesbury's honour, representing the sun emerging from the clouds, with the legend *Laetamur*. But, this momentary triumph notwithstanding, the game was all but up; and, within a few months, Monmouth, in his turn, was under arrest, and Shaftesbury a fugitive in Holland.

Without a mention of this well known sequence of events, the fact might, perhaps, be overlooked that part I of *Absalom and Achitophel* is complete in itself, being intended to help in producing a direct result at a given moment, and that it is in no sense to be regarded as a mere instalment of a larger whole, or as an introduction to it. Part II was a mere afterthought, and, being only to a relatively small extent by Dryden, should, in the first instance, be left out of consideration.

Absalom and Achitophel veils its political satire under the transparent disguise of one of the most familiar episodes of Old Testament history, which the existing crisis in English affairs resembled sufficiently to make the allegory apposite and its interpretation easy. The attention of the English public, and, more especially, that of the citizens of London, with whom the decision of the immediate political issue lay, was sure to be arrested by a series of characters whose names and distinctive features were borrowed from the Old Testament; and the analogy between Charles II's and David's early exile and final triumphant establishment on the throne was a commonplace of restoration poetry.

Indeed, the actual notion of an adaptation of the story of Achitophel's wiles as "the Picture of a wicked Politician" was not new to English controversial literature; in 1680, a tract entitled *Absalom's Conspiracy* had dealt with the supposed intentions of Monmouth; and a satire published in 1681, only a few months before Dryden's poem, had applied the name Achitophel, with some other opprobrious names, to Shaftesbury. For the rest, Dryden, with the *grandezza* habitual to him, was careless about fitting the secondary figures of his satire exactly with their Scriptural *aliases,* or boring the reader by a scrupulous fidelity or even consistency of detail.

Absalom and Achitophel remains the greatest political satire in our literature, partly because it is frankly political, and not intended, like *Hudibras,* by means of a mass of accumulated detail, to convey a general impression of the vices and follies, defects and extravagances, of a particular section or particular sections of the nation. With Dryden, every hit is calculated, and every stroke goes home; in each character brought on the scene, those features only are selected for exposure or praise which are of direct significance for the purpose in hand.

It is not a satirical narrative complete in itself which is attempted; the real *dénouement* of the piece falls not within, but outside, its compass; in other words, the poem was to lead up, as to an unavoidable *sequitur,* to the trial and conviction of its hero. The satirist, after the fashion of a great parliamentary orator, has his subject and his treatment of it well in hand; through all the force of the invective and the fervour of the praise, there runs a consciousness of the possibility that the political situation may change.

This causes a constant self-control and wariness in the author, who is always alive to his inspiration and never unmindful of his cue. Instead of pouring forth a stream of Aristophanic vituperation or boyish fun in the vein of Canning, he so nicely adapts the relations of the more important of his characters to the immediate issue that the treatment, both of the tempter Achitophel and of the tempted Absalom, admitted of manipulation when, before the appearance of the poem in a second edition, the condition of affairs had changed.

Chapter and verse could, without difficulty, be found for every item in Johnson's well known panegyric of *Absalom and Achitophel* in his *Life of Dryden.* The incomparable brilliancy of its diction and versification are merits which, to be acknowledged, need only to be mentioned. Still, its supreme excellence lies in its descriptions of character, which, no doubt, owed something to his dramatic practice, and more to the development which this kind of writing had experienced during a whole generation of English prose literature, reaching its full height in Clarendon. Dryden's exquisite etchings cannot be compared with the finest of the full-length portraits from the hand of the great historical writer; but, thanks, no doubt, in part, to the Damascene brightness and keenness into which the poet had tempered his literary instrument, and thanks, also, to the imaginative insight which, in him, the literary follower of the Stewarts, was substituted for the unequalled experience of their chosen adviser, Clarendon, the characters of the poem live in the memory with unequalled tenacity.

How unmistakably is the pre-eminence of Achitophel among the opponents of the royal government signalised by his being commissioned, like his prototype when charged with the temptation and corruption of mankind, to master the shaken virtue of Absalom!

Yet, when the satire proceeds from the leader to the followers, what composite body of malcontents was ever analysed, even by a minister driven to bay, with surer discernment and more perfect insight? The honest whigs, the utilitarian radicals, the speculators who use party for their private ends, the demagogues and mob-orators who are the natural product of faction—all are there; but so, too, are the republicans on principle, headed by survivors of the fanatics who believed in their own theocracy.

Of course, the numerical strength of the party is made up by the unthinking crowd that takes up a cry—in this case, the cry "No Popery." Of the chiefs of the faction, for the most part, a few incisive lines, or even a damning epithet, suffice to dispose; but there are exceptions, suggested by public or by private considerations. In the latter class, Dryden's own statement obliges us to include Zimri (Buckingham)—a character which he declares to be "worth the whole poem."

What he says of his intentions in devising this masterpiece of wit, and of his success in carrying them into execution, illustrates at once the discretion with which he applied his satirical powers, and the limitation which his nature, as well as his judgment, imposed upon their use.

Moral indignation was not part of Dryden's satirical stock. Even the hideously true likeness of Titus Oates (Corah) preserves the accent of sarcasm which had suited the malicious sketch of Shimei, the inhospitable sheriff of the city; it is as if the poet's blame could never come with so full a tone as the praise which, in the latter part of the poem, is gracefully distributed among the chief supporters of the crown. The poem ends with a speech from king David, only in part reproducing the speech of Charles II to the Oxford parliament (March, 1681), of which the king is said to have suggested the insertion.

Chapter 12

Didactic Poetry: *Religio Laici*

Religio Laici, which, for reasons easily guessed, was not reprinted by Dryden in his lifetime after the third edition (1683), is classed (by Scott) among his political and historical poems; but its primary interest is personal, as must have been his primary motive in composing it. He wished to know where, in the matter of religion, he stood. Now, for Dryden, there was but one way of realising any position which he held or any line of conduct on which he had determined.

This was to place it before himself with the aid of his pen, at whose bidding, if the expression may be allowed, his thoughts at once fell into lucid order, ready for argumentative battle. Though Johnson's wish may, in some degree, be father to the thought, when he declares *Religio Laici* to be almost the only poem by Dryden which may be regarded as a voluntary effusion, Saintsbury has rightly insisted on the spontaneous character of the poem. This spontaneity is, indeed, all but essential to the conception of the work; nor was there any possible motive or reason for simulating it.

The title, of course, was anything but original. Lord Herbert of Cherbury's treatise *De Religione Laici* had been published in 1633, Sir Thomas Browne's *Religio Medici* ten years later. With Dryden, though not with Browne, the emphasis rests on the second noun of the title. Amidst the disputations and controversies of learned theologians, a plain word seems not uncalled for from one who can contribute nothing but common-sense and goodwill, unalloyed by self-opinionatedness.

Thus, the layman's religion is expounded with the

requisite brevity, and with notable directness and force, lighted up by a few of the satirical flashes which had become second nature to the writer, but not by any outburst of uncontrollable fervour. He takes his stand on revelation, but is careful to summarise the natural proofs of the truth of Christianity.

The old objection to supernatural religion, that it has not been revealed to all men, he is content to answer by a pious hope, expressed in words both forcible and beautiful. He puts aside the difficulty of the damnatory clauses of the Athanasian creed by conjecturing a very human explanation of their origin, and, after citing a liberal French priest in support of the contention that the authority of the Bible is weakened by mistakes of transcribers and commentators, approaches the crucial question, what authority, then, is to decide? An infallible authority it must be, and the only church which makes such a claim fails to satisfy the tests of infallibility or omniscience. Better, therefore, accept authority where it is ancient, universal and unsuspected, and leave aside matters which cannot be thus settled—

For points obscure are of small use to learn,
But common quiet is the world's concern.

Religio Laici, it is needless to demonstrate at length, represents merely a halfway house on the road which Dryden was following. Reverence for authority was an instinct implanted in his nature; his observation of the conflicts of public life had disgusted him with the contrary principle of resistance, and, at the same time, had impressed upon him the necessity of waiving minor difficulties for the sake of the things that really mattered. If the layman's simple creed should fail, in the long run, to satisfy the layman himself, it could easily be relinquished; for, as the designedly pedestrian conclusion of the poem avers, it was meant merely for what it was—a plain personal utterance.

And, thus, the reader of Dryden's writings in their sequence is not startled on reaching the passage in his biography which has given rise to much angry comment and anxious apology, without, in truth, calling for anything of either. In February, 1685, Charles II died. Dryden's literary services had materially contributed to carry safely through some of the most dangerous stages of the conflict the cause of the legitimate succession, on which Charles had gone near to staking the stability of his throne. The poet's efforts against the party which he had again and again denounced as revolutionary had estranged from him old literary associates—some of them more pliable than himself—and had left him, more than ever, a reserved and, probably, a more or less lonely man.

But, whatever the king's personal interest in Dryden's literary activity, the royal bounty flowed but very intermittently, and neither the three hundred a year due to the poet laureate nor an additional pension of one hundred (granted some time before 1679) was paid with any approach to regularity.

Not until 1684, after he had addressed a letter of complaint to Rochester (Laurence Hyde) at the treasury, was a portion of the arrears paid, while he was appointed to a collectorship of the customs, with a minute salary but (probably) a more substantial amount of fees. In these circumstances, Dryden, whose play-writing had usually been a labour of necessity, and for whom, as a political satirist, there was no opening in the period of reaction following the *esclandre* of the Rye House plot, had to do such taskwork as came to his hand—prefaces, like that to a new translation of Plutarch; prose translations of his own, like that of Maimbourg's *History* already mentioned; and verse translation, from Ovid, Vergil, Horace and Theocritus, inserted in the first volume of *Miscellany Poems* printed in 1684 and 1685 (the latter under the title *Sylvae*). The hope long cherished by Dryden of writing an epic poem, for which he had already been in search of subjects, receded more and more into the background; and, of the muses whom he was constrained to serve, we may well believe that— little was their Hire, and light their Gain.

Chapter 13

Conversion to the Church of Rome

Before the publication of this poem, in which are to be found many allusions to the doctrines of the Church of Rome together with a reference to the "still impending Test," Dryden had himself become a Roman Catholic. As already hinted, the supposition that this step was, or might have been expected by him to be, to the advantage of his wordly interests is not worth discussing.

The intellectual process which led to it, and to the ultimate completion of which *Religio Laici* points, was neither unprecedented nor unparalleled; moreover, whatever they may have expected (which nobody can tell) neither Dryden nor his wife or eldest son (if, as is supposed but not proved, they had become Roman Catholics before him) gained anything by their conversion. That he should have chosen a time for joining the church of Rome when the prospects of her adherents in England seemed bright was in keeping with his disposition; for he had, as an acute critic says, "a sovereign intellect but a subject will."

But there is no single known fact in his life to support the conclusion that he changed his faith for the sake of gain. Nor can his consistent adherence to the church which had now received him be explained away by the insinuation that another change would not have been of any use to him. It is sometimes forgotten that his political was consistent with his religious loyalty, and that, under the new *régime,* he declined to take the oaths which might have secured to him the continuance of at least a measure of royal favour.

The effect of Dryden's conversion upon his spiritual life

lies beyond the range of literary criticism. It is, however, certain that, to the aspiration "good life be now my task," there corresponds, at a time very near that of his change of faith, a confession which, in depth of feeling, and in severity of self-judgment, stands almost alone in his published writings. The spring and force of by far the most beautiful among his longer lyrics, the ode *To the Pious Memory of the Accomplisht Young Lady, Mrs. Anne Killigrew* (printed in 1686, the year after that of her death), are characteristic of Dryden's genius; but, in the spirit of the poem, especially of the well known fourth stanza, we recognise that it was composed at a time when his whole nature was moved by unwonted impulses.

A fainter recurrence of these may, perhaps, be traceable in some passages of his later writings; on the other hand, it cannot be averred that, in these writings, as a whole, there is any indication, as there is certainly no pretence, of a change which purifies what is intentionally impure, or refines what is intentionally gross.

The new king was not in a position to disdain the aid of any fresh ally; and the services of Dryden's pen were speedily claimed by the side which he had joined. But the desired version of the *Histoire de l'Hérésie* (1374 to 1569) by Antoine Varillas, never saw the light—hardly, as Burnet contended, because of his criticisms of the French historian and publicist. Dryden's assistance was also engaged in defence of a paper written by Anne Hyde, duchess of York, giving reasons for her conversion to the Church of Rome, which James II had published with two statements found among his deceased royal brother's papers, acknowledging the authority of that church.

Stilling fleet had commented on the publication as a whole, and now replied in a *Vindication* on which, in his turn, Dryden, denounced by Stilling fleet as a "grim logician," commented in an *apologia* of an altogether novel description.

DON SEBASTIAN AND CLEOMENES

After the close of king James II's reign, however, two plays were produced by Dryden, which may be regarded as a worthy consummation of his dramatic development. Yet *Don Sebastian* (acted 1690) is incorrectly regarded as marking his emancipation from the traditions either of tragi-comedy or of the heroic play, though it is blank verse which, in this piece, alternates with prose.

On the contrary, the serious action of *Don Sebastian* is a romantic fiction—an attempt to account by a love-story, ending with a most astonishing recognition, both for the well known disappearance of Don Sebastian in the battle of Alcazar and for the rumour that he lived for some time afterwards as an anchorite. The comic action of the mufti is repulsive, though noticeable as illustrating Dryden's *animus* against all kinds of clergy.

The only real attempt at drawing character is to be found in the figure of Dorax, particularly in a scene which has met with universal praise. Although the tragedy *Cleomenes, the Spartan Hero* (acted 1692) is not usually deemed equal to its predecessor, it is finely conceived, and, on the whole, finely carried out on the lines of French classical tragedy, without any comic or other adventitious admixture. The character of the hero (performed by Betterton), though probably modelled on Hengo in Fletcher's *Bonduca,* is drawn with vivacity, and, in the earlier part of the rather long-drawn-out catastrophe, with pathos.

Plutarch's abundant material is supplemented from other sources; and, though, viewing Dryden's dramatic work as a whole, it is impossible to regret that he should not earlier have engaged in a whole-hearted imitation of French tragedy, his one complete attempt in that direction must be pronounced a noble play.

With it, our survey of his career as a dramatist may fitly end; for it is unnecessary to do more than refer to the *Secular Masque* written by him, together with a prologue and epilogue, to grace the revival, for his own benefit, of Fletcher's *Pilgrim,* which actually took place in June, 1700, little more than a fortnight after the beneficiary's death. The tone of gentle pessimism audible in the masque recurs in the epilogue, where, without the acrimony with which he had assailed "Quack

Maurus" (Sir Richard Blackmore) in the prologue, he defends himself against the censures preferred against the contemporary drama in Jeremy Collier's *Short View of the Immorality and Profanity of the English Stage* (1698). Dryden's defence—truthful so far as it goes (which is not very far)—is the evil influence of ways of thought and life brought over by a "banished court"; a far nobler attitude than this of uneasy apology was the open avowal of shame made by him many years earlier in the ode *To the Pious Memory of Mrs. Anne Killigrew* (1686).

Chapter 14

Dryden's Work as a Dramatist

Dryden's association with the stage was not a source of pride to himself, and can be regarded only with qualified satisfaction by the admirers of his poetic genius. That he attained to a very notable degree of success in almost every branch of dramatic literature which he essayed cannot be held surprising; but it was only in the heroic play, in which he strained every nerve to "surpass the life," that he distanced all his rivals and followers.

Although, at times, carried away by the impetus of his own genius, Dryden could not often put his heart into his dramatic composition, least of all into the comic side of it. He wearied of playwriting from the outset—frequently passing from one kind of play to another, and back again, but rarely satisfied with any phase of his endeavours.

When, after a long interval of absence he returned to the arena in whose contests he had taken a prominent part, about whose theory and practice he had speculated widely and written at length, but which, at times, like Ben Jonson he was led to call the "loathèd stage," it was with a sense of fatigued unwillingness which even the most overworked and *blasé* of modern playwrights, "still condemned to dig in those exhausted mines," would be slow to avow.

This, of course, is not to say that Dryden failed to enrich English dramatic literature by much magnificent writing—more especially in his heroic plays—or to deny that at least one comedy (as we may call *The Spanish Fryar*) and one tragedy (*All for Love*) from his hand permanently hold their own among dramatic masterpieces of their respective kinds. It is of greater importance that, in Taine's words, Dryden's work as a dramatist "purified and clarified his own style" by teaching him closeness of dialectics and precision in the use of words; that, in it and by it, under the guidance of Corneille, he learnt the art of political oratory and debate, and, at the same time, attained to that mastery of the heroic couplet of which he was to make superb use in his satirical poems. Dryden, who, in these poems, was to show an unsurpassed power of drawing character, rightly recognised in its presentation the supreme function of the dramatist; but, the secret of exhibiting the development of character by action he was not able, unless exceptionally, to compass, and it was thus that he came to fall short of the highest dramatic excellence.

THE GROUNDS OF CRITICISM IN TRAGEDY

With this attempt, which must be classed among Dryden's dramatic failures, was printed the remarkable *Preface concerning the Grounds of Criticism in Tragedy,* which, although not actually the last of Dryden's contributions to dramatic criticism, may be said to complete their cycle. Here, at last, we find a plain and reasonable application of the fundamental Aristotelian theory of tragedy to the practice of the English drama. Shakespeare and Fletcher—the former in particular—are set down as deficient in "the mechanic beauties" of the plot, but, in the "manners" of their plays, in which the characters delineated in them are comprehended, the two great masters of the English drama are extolled at the expense of their French rivals.

Although exception must be taken to the distinction between Shakespeare and Fletcher as excelling respectively in the depiction of the more manly and the softer passions, "to conclude all," we are told, "Fletcher was a limb of Shakespeare"—in other words, the less is included in the greater. Thus, though neither of much length nor very clearly arranged, this essay signally attests the soundness of Dryden's critical judgment, with his insight into the fact that the most satisfactory dramatic theory is that which is abstracted from the best dramatic practice. It was not given to him to exemplify by his own dramatic works the supreme freedom claimed by the greatest masters of the art; but he was not to end his theatrical career without having come nearer than he had as yet approached to his own ideals.

From this point of view, two tragedies may be passed by in which the unbalanced, but not wholly uninspired, powers of Lee co-operated with the skill and experience of Dryden. *Oedipus* (acted 1678), though provided with an underplot, threw down a futile challenge to both Sophocles and Corneille. In *The Duke of Guise* (acted in December, 1682), Dryden's share seems to have been mainly confined to the furbishing up of what he had written many years before. Whatever he might say in the elaborate *Vindication of the Duke of Guise* (printed in 1683), the political intention of the play, as a picture of the now discomfited intrigues of Shaftesbury in favour of Monmouth, was palpable, and not disproved by the fact that the authority of Davila had been more or less closely followed, or by the other fact that the parallel might, in some respects, have been pressed further than would have been pleasing to king Charles.

In *Albion and Albanius,* Dryden committed himself to a still lower descent—hardly to be excused by the "thought-depressing" quality of opera mentioned by Dryden (who, on this head, agreed with St. Évremond) in the interesting preface which gives a short account of the early history of musical drama. After many delays, the chief of them being due to the death of Charles II, in compliment to whom the opera had been first put together, it was at last performed on 3 June, 1685. Ten days later, the news arrived of Monmouth's landing at Lyme, and the unlucky piece, with its jingling rimes, French music and all, was finally withdrawn.

Saintsbury describes it as, to all intents and purposes, a masque; but it lacks all the beauties of which that kind of composition is capable, and which are not made up for by the grotesquely ridiculous supernatural machinery to which here, as in *The Duke of Guise,* the author condescended to have recourse. Dryden was not, however, deterred from carrying out his intention of writing the "dramatic opera" of *King Arthur or The British Worthy,* to which *Albion and Albanius* had been designed as a prelude. It was produced in 1691, with music by Purcell; but, notwithstanding the claim put forth in the preface, little or no proof is furnished of Dryden's familiarity with Arthurian romance; and, in spite of the magic, there is not much fire in the piece, while the figure of the blind Emmeline is an unpleasing experiment. Perhaps, as the tag suggests, the poet was, for once, almost losing heart.

Chapter 15

Essay *of Heroick Plays*

Dryden's apologetic *Essay of Heroick Plays* was preceded in date of publication by his *Essay of Dramatick Poesie* (1668), written in reply to Sir Robert Howard's preface to his *Foure New Plays* (1665). The earlier essay is in that dialogue form which had preserved its popularity in the literatures of Europe since it had been revived by Erasmus and others in the renascence period, with which Dryden's age was familiar from both Spanish and French precedents, and which was practised by many contemporary English writers, including Clarendon and Burnet.

But there can be little doubt that Dryden derived the most direct impulse to the composition of the essays in dramatic and other literary criticism with which he enriched the library of English prose from the three *Discours* severally prefixed by Corneille to the three volumes of the 1660 collection of his plays, and the *Examens* which, in the same edition, preceded each drama.

Dryden's famous essay is written with great spirit, and with a fusion of vigour and ease altogether different from the vivacity by which literary critics appealing to a wider public at times strive to hide their thoroughness, or the want of it, as the case may be. The dialogue form is employed with Platonic grace, the *venue* being laid under the sound of the guns discharged in the battle of Solebay, and audible in the Thames "like the noise of distant thunder or swallows in a chimney." The conclusions reached may be described as eclectic and, at the same time, as based upon experience, albeit the latter was, necessarily, of a very limited range.

As a matter of fact, Dryden's opinions on most subjects—and not the least on dramatic theory—were sufficiently fluid to respond without reluctance to the demands of common-sense; nor did he ever take pride in a *doctrinaire* consistency—even with himself.

The arguments, in this *Essay*, of Neander (who represents Dryden's own views) lead to the conclusion that observance of the time-honoured laws of dramatic composition, as reasonably modified by experience—in other words, adherence to the principle of the unities as severally interpreted by Corneille—is reconcilable with the greater freedom of treatment assumed by the masters of the English drama; while the plea for the use of the rimed couplet, based on its dramatic capabilities, especially in tragedy, comes in as a sort of corollary.

The immediate occasion for Dryden's *Essay* had been the confession of a doubt by Sir Robert Howard (who, as Crites, reproduces it in the dialogue) with regard to the appropriateness of the use, in which he had formerly taken part, of the rimed couplet in dramatic verse.

Howard having replied to Dryden's answer in the preface to his play *The Great Favourite, or The Duke of Lerma* (1668), without losing his temper—as why should he have done, except to give grounds for the persistent misrepresentation of a literary difference as a personal quarrel?—Dryden wound up the controversy by *A Defence of an Essay of Dramatick Poesie* (1668), prefixed to the second edition of *The Indian Emperor,* from later editions of which, however, he omitted it.

This piece, which is an admirable example of light raillery, though with just a suspicion of a sting, adds little to the previous force of his argument; but the incidental remark that "poetry only instructs as it delights" explains the failure of many attempts made in defiance of the truth conveyed by the saying.

The Conquest of Granada (1669–70) may be justly described as the heroic play *par excellence,* and exhibits Dryden as exultantly carrying through a prolonged effort such as only the splendid vigour of his peculiar genius could have sustained throughout at so tremendous a pitch as is here essayed. The colouring of the whole is gorgeous, and the hero, Almanzor, combines, on Dryden's own showing, the imposing features of the Achilles of the *Iliad,* Tasso's Rinaldo and the Artaban of La Calprenède's *Cléopâtre.*

Dryden had now reached the height of his popularity—it was in the year 1670 that he was appointed poet laureate. With an arrogance which Almanzor himself could hardly have surpassed—though it is hidden behind the pretence that not the poet, but the age is praised—the *Epilogue to the Second Part* declares the dramatist superior to all his predecessors, including Jonson, in "wit" and power of diction. The poets of the past could not reply; but, among the critics of the day who took up the challenge, Rochester, for one, retorted with a rough *tu quoque* which is not wholly without point.

Other protests may have ensued; at all events, Dryden did not allow the hot iron time to cool, but followed up his rodomontade (for it really deserves the name) by *A Defence of the Epilogue, or An Essay on the Dramatick Poetry of the last Age* (1672), which cannot be called one of the happiest, and is certainly one of the least broadly conceived, of his critical efforts.

Finding fault with a series of passagés in the chief Elizabethan and Jacobean dramatists was not the way to make good the general contention on which he had ventured. He appealed once more to his own generation against its predecessors; but he was wise enough not to appeal to posterity.

Meanwhile (in December, 1671), the nemesis provoked by the arrogance of success had descended upon Dryden, though in no more august shape than in that of a burlesque dramatic concoction by a heterogeneous body of wits. *The Rehearsal,* as the mock play with its running commentary was called, had gone through a period of incubation spread over nine or ten years, and among the contributors to the joke were the duke of Buckingham, Thomas Sprat (already mentioned), Martin Clifford, master of the Charterhouse, a very learned and foul-mouthed writer, and, it is said, though without proof, Samuel

Butler. They included in their ridicule anything which seemed to offer them a chance in any of Dryden's plays; but they also impartially ransacked the productions of other dramatists; indeed, it would seem that, before Dryden, D'Avenant and Sir Robert Howard, had, in turn, been thought of as the central figure of the farce, and that it was only the triumphant success of *The Conquest of Granada* which had concentrated the attack upon its author.

The recent appointment of Dryden to the poet laureateship, of course, suggested the name Bayes, which the lampooners continued to apply to him for the rest of his literary career.

The Rehearsal, which, if the long line of its descendants, including Sheridan's *Critic,* be taken into account, proved an important contribution to the literature of the stage, is an amusing *revue* of now for the most part forgotten productions, diversified by humorous sallies of which the spirit of burlesque always keeps a store for use.

Its satire against heroic plays is incidental, except in so far as they carried artificiality, exaggeration and bombast further than had any other of the species of plays ridiculed. Its satire against Dryden himself glanced off, practically harmless, from a personality in which there was nothing to provoke derision, and from a genius to which no adversary could seriously impute poverty of invention or sameness of workmanship.

Thus, he was able to treat the satire, so far as it concerned him personally, with more or less good-humoured contempt; and his *revanche* on Buckingham, when it came, was free from spite.

As for heroic plays, he certainly did not leave off writing them because of *The Rehearsal;* nor did it deter him from publishing a reasoned essay in defence of the species. But he could not expect to outdo his chief effort of the kind; and no other playwright was likely to seek to surpass him in a combination of treatment and form which he had made peculiarly his own.

In 1672, *The Conquest of Granada* was published in

company with a prefatory essay *Of Heroick Plays*. The essay opens with the assertion—the latter half of which Dryden was afterwards himself to help to refute—that heroic verse was already in possession of the stage, and that "very few tragedies, in this age," would be "received without it."

For the rest, this essay only develops propositions previously advanced, besides fearlessly engaging in a defence of the *non plus ultra* of the heroic character-type, Almanzor, the Drawcansir of *The Rehearsal*.

Chapter 16

The Satire of *The Rehearsal*

The latter (1670–6) was, no doubt, partly due to the appearance of *The Rehearsal* (1670). Although that celebrated burlesque cannot be said to have killed heroic plays, there can be no doubt that, notwithstanding the brilliant features which some of these plays displayed, the elements of vitality were wanting in the species.

The list of plays which, as written partly or wholly in the rimed couplet, have any claim at all to be reckoned as heroic, is small in itself, and, if reduced by certain obvious omissions, contains, with the exception of Dryden's, few works of even secondary significance. In a word, Dryden completely dominates the English heroic play.

Like *The Indian Emperor, Tyrannick Love* treats with much freedom a theme out of the common track—in this case, the persecution of the Christians by Maximin and the martyrdom of St. Catharine. The argument of *Aureng-Zebe* deals, again quite freely, with a notability of the writer's day, though largely following the course of Racine's *Mithridate,* and borrowing the matter of one scene from *Le Grand Cyrus.*

On the other hand, the most important and the most typical of Dryden's heroic plays, *The Conquest of Granada,* is essentially based on Madeleine de Scudéry's *Almahide,* while one of its episodes is taken from her *Le Grand Cyrus* and another from her *Ibrahim.* But the important point is that these subjects, as treated in the plays in question, all resemble one another in their substance, and, more or less, in its adjuncts.

The plays are all of them "heroic" plays and the metre which they employ is called the "heroic" couplet, because they follow and imitate the example of "heroic" romance, as set forth by Ariosto himself. Their themes, like those of heroic poetry and fiction in general, are the "emprises" and conflicts of absorbing human passions—love, jealousy and honour—all raised to a transnormal height and expressed with a transnormal intensity. Their men and women are, if the term may be thus applied, "supermen" and "superwomen," and their master passions are superlove and superhonour. From these out-of-the-way premisses flow a number of out-of-the-way results.

The actions must be suited to the motives; their conditions must be unexpected changes and chances and tumultuous backgrounds, their complications must be insoluble except by violent means, and deaths as numerous as leaves in Vallombrosa. Furthermore, the personages of these dramas must conduct themselves in a manner wholly unlike the usages obtaining in the daily round of life; it must be a manner appropriate to spheres into which the imagination alone can transplant us—ancient Rome, Jerusalem, or Troy, or, still better, because still less familiar, Mexico or the east Indies. Finally, the verse, as well as the words, must be suited to the action, and the "heroic" couplet must serve the purpose of a sort of "cothurnated," which is interpreted "stilted," speech.

It was inevitable that a succession of plays of this type should soon pall upon the spectator, because of the sameness of their method (one of Dryden's most persistent assailants, Martin Clifford, accused him of "stealing from himself"), unless each new production sought to force the pace, and to outvie its predecessors. The interest in the action, cut adrift, as it was, from probability and from the sympathy which probability begets, had to be sustained by all sorts of adventitious expedients—supernatural apparitions and magic processes, with fantastic songs, serenades and dances. But, notwithstanding the resources of Dryden's rhetorical genius, and the wonderful mental buoyancy with which he carried out any task undertaken by him, the species was doomed to self-exhaustion, nor can its master long have deceived himself on this head.

THE HEROIC COUPLET IN DRAMA

It does not seem to be necessary here to enter into a reexamination of the question of the suitableness, or unsuitableness, of the heroic couplet as a form of dramatic verse. Not only in certain kinds of romantic comedy, for which it has been claimed as a suitable vehicle, but, also, for various eccentric species which have been or may be invented—such as pantomime, burlesque or extravaganza—it may readily be allowed to be both well fitted and effective.

As to its use, however, for the purposes of the regular tragic or comic drama, the case is altered. Partly, of course, the objection lies in the tendency of the couplet, as treated by Dryden and his successors, to make against continuity of flow, to shut up the sense within fixed limits and, because of the consequent demand for precision of statement, to impart to dialogue or soliloquy a didactic rather than dramatic colouring. And, further, with regard to the use of rime itself in English dramatic verse, the *caveat* of Taine cannot be put aside, that "rime is a different thing for different races": the Englishman being transported by it into a world remote from the actual, whereas, for the Frenchman, it is nothing more than a conventional costume. The heroic couplet, as used in Dryden's plays and those which followed their example, therefore, operates against, instead of in favour of, theatrical illusion and the sway of the imagination on the stage, and helps to urge the dramatist who employs it in the direction of conventionalism and artificiality.

Against this general result, it is useless to argue that passion, and even mere eloquence, at times gets the better of the outward form, and, by its driving force, moves and disturbs the hearer in spite of himself. No sooner had Dryden, in *The Rival-Ladies,* produced a tragi-comedy, containing an element of rimed verse, in which he had made successful use of his gift of poetical rhetoric, than he was characteristically ready to take a leading part in evolving an ulterior dramatic species not precisely new, but with features of its own so marked as to differentiate it from tragicomedy proper. The tragi-comedy bequeathed to him and the restoration dramatists in general by their predecessors was wont to possess a double plot, consisting, to use Dryden's own phraseology, of "one main design," serious in kind, carried on in verse, and "an underplot or second walk of comical characters and adventures subservient to the chief fable, yet carried along under it and helping to it"; although, in point of fact, the connection between the two was frequently very slight. At different stages of his career, he produced three more plays, of various merit, which belonged to this class.

Secret Love, or The Maiden Queen (acted 1667), of which—probably because of the frank gaiety of Nell Gwynn's scenes in it—Charles II approved so greatly as to dub it "his play," is founded, as to its main plot, on *Le Grand Cyrus,* and, as to its comic underplot, partly on that romance and partly on the same novelist's *Ibrahim, ou L'illustre Bassa.* The interest in the serious plot is impaired by the quite unheroic character of Philocles (intended, as Dryden says, to represent queen Christina of Sweden's favourite Magnus de la Garide); and the chief attraction of the play consists in the "discoursive" passages between Celadon and Florimel.

In *The Spanish Fryar, or The Double Discovery,* again (acted and printed 1681), which seems certainly to have been designed as a tragi-comedy by Dryden, the comic effect preponderates over that of the serious plot, though the latter cannot be said to be without interest. The interweaving of the two has been praised—perhaps overpraised—by more than one eminent critic. The comic dialogue of this play is excellent, and the character of the friar by no means a *replica* of Fletcher's *Spanish Curate* (though there are points of resemblance in the two plays), but a new variety of an unctuous type which, from Chaucer to Dickens, has afforded unfailing delight to the public, and which it must have given Dryden, who hated priests and parsons with a consistent hatred, much satisfaction to elaborate. His last tragi-comedy, *Love Triumphant, or Nature will Prevail* (acted 1694), in which there is a large admixture of rime, merely repeated in its main plot that of *Marriage-à-la-Mode,* and the play justly proved a failure.

Chapter 17

The Wild Gallant and other Comedies

In the actual year of the restoration, or, at all events, within a few months from that date, Dryden, perhaps stimulated by the use made in the commonwealth period of quasi-dramatic dialogue as a vehicle of political satire or invective, proposed to himself to read a political lesson to the public by means of a historical tragedy, *The Duke of Guise,* applying the doubtful parallel of the Catholic league to the recent memories of puritan ascendency.

But the attempt was not thought successful by judicious advisers, and what had been written of the play was left over to be utilised by the author in the tragedy which, many years later, in 1682, he produced in conjunction with Lee. Thus, the first play by Dryden produced on the stage was *The Wild Gallant,* first acted in February, 1663.

It has no further claim to be singled out among the comedies, at the same time extravagant and coarse, in which the period of dramatic decline abounds; though there are some traces of the witty dialogue, often carried on by a flirting couple, in which Dryden came to excel. The statement in the prologue that the author was "endangered by a Spanish plot" (*i.e.* a rival "Spanish" play) has been perverted to the direct opposite of its meaning, and the most humorous incident in the piece is conveyed straight from Ben Jonson.

The play did not find favour, except, apparently, with lady Castlemaine; and, in the sequel, Dryden only intermittently returned to comedy proper. He wrote of himself, early in his dramatic career, that he was "not so fitted by nature to write comedy" as certain other kinds of drama; "he wanted," he confesses, "that gaiety of humour which is required to it;" and he also wanted, as he might have added, the facility of invention—whether of situations or of characters—which relieves the productions of a comic dramatist from the sameness which is noticeable in this class of Dryden's plays.

He consoled himself with the notion that "a reputation gained from comedy" was hardly worth the seeking; "for I think it is, in its own nature, inferior to all sorts of dramatic writing." Thus, he only returned to it from time to time, and wholly eschewed "farce, which consists principally of grimaces," and from which he naturally shrank, devoid as he may generally be asserted to have been of any inclination to what was grotesque, or even merely odd or quaint. And, in the critical essays and excursuses which illustrated his practice, he discusses the comic drama with comparative rarity.

The Wild Gallant was written in prose, as was *Sir Martin Mar-All, or The Feigned Innocence* (1667, printed 1668), an adaptation by Dryden, whose name was not attached to it till thirty years later, of the duke of Newcastle's translation of Molière's early comedy *L'Étourdi,* with certain touches suggested by two plays by Quinault. The translation is not close, nor the treatment refined; but the play was very successful. Also in prose is the main portion of *The Assignation or Love in a Nunnery* (1672, printed 1673), worthless, except where in some blank verse passages it rises to a higher literary level. *Marriage-à-la-Mode* (produced at the same dates), which, unlike *The Assignation,* greatly pleased the town, thanks to the admirably drawn coquette Melantha, presents the same mixture of prose and blank verse.

Of Dryden's remaining comedies, *Limberham, or The Kind Keeper* (acted in 1678), which is entirely in prose, has unmistakable dramatic merits; but it was speedily withdrawn, having been judged a gross libel on a well known public personage, generally supposed to be Lauderdale. Dryden's last comedy, *Amphitryon* (produced so late as 1690), for which both Plautus and Molière were put under contribution, is, again, a mixture of prose and blank verse; none of Dryden's plays more brilliantly attest his literary gift, and none have more of the wantonness to which he afterwards pleaded guilty.

In Dryden's second acted play, *The Rival-Ladies* (acted 1664), he had already passed from comedy into tragi-comedy, where his genius was more at home. Its complicated plot (two ladies disguise themselves as pages in order to take service with a gallant whose affections are set on a third) caused it to be supposed, rightly or wrongly, to have a Spanish origin; its dialogue falls into the stagey antithesis which, though it was as old as Shakespeare, *The Rehearsal* and Butler were to ridicule without mercy. What, however, is most noticeable in this play is the first, though still tentative, use of rime as a proper feature of dramatic verse. This use is defended in a dedication to lord Orrery—the earliest of Dryden's critical excursions.

It should be remembered that, since Fletcher's short preface to his *Faithfull Shepheardesse* (printed 1609 or 1610), such discussions of dramatic problems as these had fallen out of use, and that the public was now neither "railed into approbation," as it had formerly been by Ben Jonson, nor gently led on to acquiescence in the precepts of its critical guides. Following the example of Corneille, Dryden took advantage of the revived interest in the stage to address its patrons, as it were *ex cathedra*, but without any assumption of academical solemnity or rigour.

To the subject of the dramatic use of the heroic couplet which he here broached, he afterwards returned at greater length, both in his *Essay of Dramatick Poesie* and in his *Essay of Heroick Plays;* but he did not claim the innovation as primarily his own, and he recalled the fact that the rimed five foot couplet, in a form approaching as near as possible to that which it owed to Waller, had been first applied to its "noblest use" by D'Avenant in the quasi-dramatic *Siege of Rhodes* (1656, enlarged 1662).

Dryden, however, was the first to employ the rimed couplet in the dialogue of an ordinary stage play, though he, too, only introduced the innovation tentatively. Etherege went a step further, and, in *The Comical Revenge, or Love in a Tub* (acted and printed 1664), put the whole serious part of the play into heroic couplets.

Inasmuch, however, as, in the same year 1664, lord Orrery's *Henry V,* which is entirely in heroic couplets, was performed, Etherege and he must be left to "divide the crown" of having introduced the innovation with Dryden and D'Avenant. If it could be proved that Orrery's "first play," mentioned in king Charles's letter of 22 February, 1662, was *Henry V,* there would be no doubt as to Orrery's priority over Etherege.

Influence of French Tragicomedy and Romance [mh]

Inasmuch as the primary object of the London stage, when re-established with the monarchy, was to please the king, his court and its surroundings, and, inasmuch as, in that court, many besides the king himself had acquired a personal familiarity with the French stage and its literature which, at all events in his case, dated back to the earlier years of his exile, French influence upon the English drama in the restoration age was, almost as a matter of course, both strong and enduring.

But it is equally certain that the basis from which the English drama started on the reopening of the theatres was no other than the old English drama, at the point which it had reached at the time of their closing.

Beaumont and Fletcher, and the drama of tragi-comic romance which, through them, had, for a generation before the closing of the theatres, established their supremacy on the English stage, were the favourites there when the theatres reopened; nor had either Jonson or Shakespeare been forgotten, and the former was still, though the flow of humour among his followers had begun to run dry, regarded as the acknowledged master of comedy. The dominant power on the French stage down to about the middle of the fourth decade of the seventeenth century had been that of Hardy, whose most celebrated play, *Mariamne,* dates from 1610, and whose *vogue* did not begin to give way till after his death in 1631.

Now, Hardy, like the dramatists who gave the tone to English dramatic literature in the generation before the closing of the theatres, kept the French stage popular by means of the mixed species of tragi-comedy, and thus prevented it from falling back on the academical lines of Senecan tragedy represented by Garnier. It is true that he was warming in his bosom the great reformer of both French tragedy and French comedy, who said of himself that, in his earlier plays, he had no guidance "but a little common-sense and the examples supplied to him by Hardy"; but Corneille's epochal production of *Le Cid* did not take place till 1636 (*Médée* appeared only a year earlier); and *Le Menteur,* which stands in much the same relation to the development of French comedy as that held by *Le Cid* to the progress of French tragedy, was not produced till 1642.

Thus, though Part I of *Le Cid* was brought out in an English translation (by Joseph Rutter) in 1637 and Part II (in a version in which Richard Sackville, afterwards earl of Dorset, is said to have had a share) in 1640, both being republished in 1650, it seems clear that the main influence exercised by the French upon the English drama was due to Hardy and tragi-comedy, which dominated all the French dramatists—including Rotrou, whose work synchronised with Corneille's earlier dramatic labours—rather than to Corneille in the maturity of his creative genius.

When, however, the perennial conflict was renewed under new conditions and on reasoned principles by Corneille, a loftier and more logical conception of tragedy approved itself to the French critical public; and, perfected in practice by the singularly refined and sensitive genius of Racine, French classical tragedy reached its consummation as a distinct species of dramatic literature.

The beginnings of Molière (though more than one of his plays have an earlier date) may, for our present purpose, be placed in 1658, when, both as actor and writer, he first appeared before Louis XIV and his court. It was not long before the English drama, in the hands of Dryden and others, revealed the impression made on it by these new developments, the effects of which, whether direct or indirect, will be summarised in later chapters; but they should not be regarded as what in no sense they were, the starting-points of our post-restoration drama.

Of special importance for the progress of the English drama, both before and after the closing of the theatres, was the influence of prose fiction, operating either directly or through plays for which it had furnished material. The two literatures which here particularly come into question are the Spanish and the French—of popular Italian fiction, the heyday seemed to have passed away, as, in the seventeenth century, artificiality of taste established its sway. Concerning Spanish influence, more will be said below; while it is not unfrequently difficult to substantiate a traditional derivation from a Spanish play, the direct indebtedness of English dramatists to Spanish prose fiction was, beyond doubt, considerable in extent, both before and after the restoration.

French prose fiction, on the other hand, in the course of the seventeenth century, passed through an entirely new phase in its history; and, inasmuch as this very directly influenced an English dramatic species with which Dryden was, for a time, identified, reference must be made to it here. With the *Astrée* of Honoré d'Urfé (1610–2) began a literary movement representing, in the first instance, a reaction towards a refinement of sentiment and expression which had been incompatible with the turbulence of a long epoch of civil war.

This movement culminated in the school of romance associated with the name of La Calprenède and, still more largely, with that of Madeleine de Scudéry, the authoress of *Le Grand Cyrus*. Gomberville and the comtesse de La Fayette belong to the same group, but that lady's last and most celebrated novel, *La Princesse de Clèves*, is already differentiated from the creations of Mlle. de Scudéry by being, to some extent, based upon historical fact, towards which, as a writer of memoirs, the authoress had a leaning. The romances of this school invariably turned on the pivot of "heroic" love, or love in more than the usual number of dimensions, and, though dealing with the deepest of human emotions, they never fell out of the tone of elaborate conventional formality.

They were, in some instances, translated into English or

imitated by English writers, from the commonwealth times onwards, when, no doubt, they had been welcomed, in many quarters, as alternatives to the drab dulness of everyday life; and, after the restoration, as will be seen, they supplied themes to dramatic writers whose object it was to heighten and intensify the characteristics of stage romance. While prose fiction, of this class, continued to attract English readers to within the last quarter of the century, in France, a reaction had already set in towards simplicity, on the one hand, and satire, on the other; but, in these directions, English dramatists were not, at all events at this time, prepared to follow.

It was, then, under these influences, that Dryden gradually settled down to the particular forms of dramatic composition which he chose from time to time, and in no regular succession, to make his own, and which he frequently illustrated by signally suggestive prose commentaries, written with consummate grace and ease in the form of dedications, prefaces or essays, thus bringing his dramatic productions into harmony with rules of good sense and good taste evolved from established theory and, still more largely, from approved practice. Dryden's plays would often lose much, if not most, of their interest if read without reference to their prefaces and other critical apparatus; neither, however, is it advisable, except in a few special instances, to detach these from the texts which gave rise to them.

HEROICK STANZAS ON CROMWELL

When, in 1657 or 1658, Dryden took up his abode in London, to which, with the exception of occasional visits to Northamptonshire and other easily accessible parts of the country, he remained faithful during the rest of his life, Cromwell's rule had, for some years, been firmly established, and Sir Gilbert Pickering was in full possession of the great man's favour. That the young Dryden actually became "clerk" or secretary to his influential kinsman rests only on the late evidence of Shadwell's lampoon. But no special connection of the kind with the protector's court or person is needed to account for Dryden's first public appearance as a writer with

A Poem upon the Death of His Late Highness, Oliver, Lord Protector of England, Scotland and Ireland, first published separately early in 1659, and reprinted in the same year, in company with an ode on the same subject by Thomas Sprat (afterwards dean of Westminster and bishop of Rochester) and some lines by Waller *Upon the late Storme and Death of the Protector.*

Sprat's is a not undignified effort in a style in which he acquitted himself so well as to become known as "Pindaric Sprat," and contains a daring figure afterwards appropriated by the master of the species, "the incomparable Dr. Cowley." Waller's lines, as usual with him, beat out the gold of a single thought into very thin leaf. Dryden, on the contrary, whose poem was again reprinted in 1659, revised, and under the title of *Heroick Stanzas consecrated to the Memory,* etc., surveyed his theme with not less circumspection than ardour, and chose his topics of eulogy not only, as Scott says, with attention to truth, but, also, with a manifest desire to avoid hyperbole. Even the fine passage

Such was our Prince, yet owned a soul above
The highest acts it could produce to show

cannot be censured as an exaggeration, except by those who deny that Cromwell was a great man and, as such, necessarily greater than his deeds. The poem, though still studded with far-fetched and not always appropriate conceits (*e.g.* "War, our consumption," st. XII; "Bolognia's walls," st. XVI; the death of Tarpeia, st. XXXIV), shows Dryden already controlling the form chosen by him with a certainty not to be found in his juvenile efforts, and master of an overpowering directness which was to become one of his most notable characteristics. Thus, the *Heroick Stanzas,* though, necessarily, they attracted little attention at a time when the immediate future absorbed public interest, and though their author, naturally, was willing to allow them to be forgotten, hold a permanent place among his poetical achievements.

Dryden's working days in the service of the muses had now begun. With his very modest income, and without any family interest that could be of use to him, he can have looked the world in the face in no very sanguine mood; and, indeed, a certain reserve and lack of satisfaction in life and in the work which he had to do in it is noticeable in his writings, as it seems to have been in his personal bearing. Shadwell's sneer that Dryden had "turn'd journeyman to a bookseller" probably applies to a rather later period of his career, and may be an ill-natured perversion of an insignificant fact.

But, in any case, Dryden, till he had studied his brief and taken up his pen, was devoid of the political, and, still more, of the religious, enthusiasm which might have sufficed to inspire him as a writer; and few poets have ever been less manifestly moved by spontaneous lyric impulse. What he wrote in the earlier part of his literary career was, as it were, automatically suggested by the great changes in contemporary public life, to which his literary powers, growing surer of themselves in each successive trial, responded without any apparent hesitation.

ANNUS MIRABILIS

The whole of the first group of Dryden's poems may be said to be brought to a close by *Annus Mirabilis, or The Year of Wonders* (1666); but, before the production of this work, he had already brought out several plays. It was, not improbably, in this way that he was brought into contact with Sir Robert Howard, a younger son of the earl of Berkshire, who had long been connected with the Stewart court and whose wife was a daughter of the great lord Burghley. On 1 December, 1663, Dryden married lord Berkshire's daughter Elizabeth, then twenty-five years of age.

The marriage took place with her father's consent, and lady Elizabeth seems, sooner or later, to have brought her husband some addition to his estate. She was, no doubt, his superior in rank, but not in any unusual measure. That Dryden was not, at this time, leading the life of a bookseller's hack is shown, *inter alia,* by his election, in November, 1662, as a fellow of the Royal Society, in its early days often as much of a social as of a scientific honour.

The circumstances of Dryden's marriage and wedded life, whether actual or fictitious, were an inexhaustible fund of scandal to the malevolent. One story ran that lady Elizabeth's brothers had bullied Dryden into the match; another, that it was made up to cover a *faux pas* on the part of the lady with another man.

It is clear that she had led no cloistered life; but Dryden seems to have been throughout on easy terms with Sir Robert Howard, even during their literary controversy, and sufficiently acknowledges his personal goodwill. The general character of Dryden's long married life remains obscure; it has been freely described as unhappy, and, in its last period, cannot but have been darkened by his wife's mental decay; on the other hand, there are indications in their correspondence of pleasant relations between them.

That the husband provoked or requited the wife's infirmities of mind or temper by infidelities is a conjecture resting on an assumption; for the assertion that "Dryden was a libertine" remains unproved. *Annus Mirabilis,* though not written in the heroic couplet with which Dryden had already familiarised himself in both dramatic and non-dramatic composition, offers unmistakable proof of the ease and self-confidence which by this time he had already acquired as a writer of verse.

The stanza form of decasyllabic quatrains here adopted had already been used by Sir John Davies in his philosophical poem *Nosce Teipsum* (1599), where it well suits both theme and treatment, and had been revived by D'Avenant in *Gondibert* (1656), where the poet, in order to satisfy his principle that each quatrain "should contain a period," often becomes prosy in consequence. For the rest, *Gondibert,* though composed under the critical eye of Hobbes, and compared by him to the *Aeneid* and the *Iliad,* notwithstanding the advantage which accrued to these as dating from "what is called old time, but is young time," contained little that invited imitation; while the long and not uninteresting critical *Preface,* though it may have helped to suggest the writing of those critical essays of which Dryden composed the earliest in the year before that in which *Annus Mirabilis* appeared, clearly did not serve as a model for them.

Like *Gondibert, Annus Mirabilis* was the fruit of exile; but, while part of the former was written at the Louvre, Dryden had been driven from London, by the great plague and the great fire commemorated in his poem to take refuge at his father-in-law's country seat at Charlton in Wiltshire. In *An Account of the Ensuing Poem, in a letter to Sir Robert Howard,* dated November, 1666, Dryden, although he utters some heterodox opinions about Vergil, declares that "he has been my master in this poem," which, indeed, is distinguished by a masculinity of tone and a richness of imagery which lend force to the assertion. The admirably chosen title was not original, though the application seems to have been new.

Dryden describes *Annus Mirabilis* as a historical poem, apparently implying that it does not make any pretensions to being an epos, for which it lacks both the requisite unity and the requisite length of action. On the other hand, it treats its twofold theme, the Dutch war and the fire of London, with great skill, both in the selection of topics, and in the management of the transitions which give coherency to the whole.

As for the war, its final cause lay in the commercial jealousy between the two nations, which made itself felt wherever English mercantile enterprise was seeking to compete with that of a more successful rival, and which, of course, came home most nearly to the city of London. But it was also due to a general antipathy on the part of the English against the Dutch, as of the naturally stronger, to the actually wealthier, community. Dryden, accordingly, takes care to dwell on the strength of England, as contrasted with the meanness, baseness and so forth, of Holland.

Moreover, the upper class of English society was offended by Dutch burgherism and republicanism, while the court resented the act excluding the house of Orange from the stadholdership. When, therefore, war was declared, a good deal of enthusiasm (of a kind), especially among the gentry, hailed the event; and Evelyn gives an amusing description of the outbreak of a universal passion for taking service in the fleet. Dryden, in his preface, describes that part of his poem which treats of the war as "but a due expiation" on his part for "not serving his King and country in it." The navy, as the favourite service of both the king and his brother the duke of York, was, at this time, extremely popular; and Dryden's confessed anxiety to have his sea terms correct was pedantry in season.

Altogether, his account of the progress of the war—from the dearly-bought victory of Solebay to the barren triumph off the North Foreland—is full of fire and spirit; and it was not any part of the poet's business to expound how, when the campaign of 1666 came to an end, the feeling began to spread that, with or without further naval victories, the situation of the country, against which France was intriguing in every part of the king's dominions, would, before long, become untenable. Thus, when Dryden represents the terrible visitation of September, 1666,—the destruction of the far greater part of London by fire,—as having befallen England at a season of undiminished confidence, and as a nemesis of this national pride—he is putting a gloss of his own upon the actual sequence of affairs.

He had, moreover, omitted any account of the plague, whose ravages were at their height at a date considerably earlier than that of the events described in the introductory part of his poem, and had thus made it easier to represent the fire as a calamity which overtook the nation when "palled" with the long succession of its "joys." The fury of the fire at its height is depicted with splendid energy, and the daring figure of the witches' sabbath, danced by the ghosts of traitors who have descended from London Bridge, is not less apposite to the wild scene than that of the divine extinguisher by which the fire is put out is preposterous.

The poet's prophecy that a "greater and more august" London would arise "from her fires" was fulfilled; but the companion political prophecy had a lamer ending in the peace of 1667, which was all that England gained from the glories of the "wonderful" year.

Yet the literary achievement itself was wonderful. Without the assurance to be derived from any great previous success,

Dryden had undertaken a task so full of pitfalls that nothing but a most extraordinary impetus could have carried his course past these to its goal—and this, though he had hampered himself with a metrical form which, as he knew and confessed, had made a far more exacting claim upon his ingenuity and skill than the couplet already familiar to him.

The courage and dash of the whole performance, which cast into the shade its lesser features, its far-fetched conceits and other reminiscences of poetic schools that were nearing their end, could not but apprise the critical world, including king and court, that a combatant had descended into the arena who was unlikely to find an equal there.

Chapter 18

Tercentary Essays

The tercentenary of Dryden's death is appropriately celebrated by the publication of two further volumes in Paul Hammond's and David Hopkins's sumptuous and, it must be said, expensive, new edition, by a volume of essays on him and by a monograph on his Aeneis. Dryden has always been popular especially with English poets: Keats and Byron, not usually in agreement on anything, agreed to find Dryden great. Scott (not an English poet) edited him, and wrote his life, Wordsworth and Tennyson were admirers and both wrote memorably about him.

Eliot and Auden agreed to praise him. So why is he so unread today? None of the august contributors to the Tercentenary Essays puts the question in terms as vulgarly direct as this. Indeed few write as if there were any such question to be asked. I find a general lack of urgency about the whole enterprise. Most contributors seem to be writing to impress one another. Indeed, the writer of one essay here takes up so many acres in footnotes in commenting on others' essays, as to provide a complete bibliography of the subject, which was not, I think, the intention.

The new edition is beyond praise for its amplitude and accuracy of annotation, and its elegance of design. One apparent convention worries me: this edition does not use italics when Dryden does, except in prose, and when quoting other contemporary writers in the notes. I had hoped to find illumination from David Hopkins's brisk essay on 'Re-presenting Dryden's Poetry in 2000', which draws on his own experiences in editing the present volumes, but he doesn't deal with the subject of italicization in full. Judging from his edition of Pope's Epistles to Several Persons, F. W. Bateson, the founding editor of the series in which the present volumes of Dryden appear, was against any sort of 'antiquated' printing practice whatever, and his views may have influenced the present editors.

The contents of Volume III do not show Dryden at his best. It is largely taken up with The Hind and the Panther, Dryden's most absurd poem, and various prologues and epilogues to his dramatic works, but it lightens up towards the end with the influential 'Discourse concerning Satire'. Volume IV takes up this theme with the translations from Juvenal and Persius, works which show Dryden finding his true voice as a poet. His mock epic masterpiece, the translation of Juvenal's Sixth Satire (with Messalina the epic heroine).

Harold Love is an authority in early music, and his essay on 'Dryden and Purcell' is an all-too-brief survey of the all-too-brief(Hammond conjectures that their direct relationship began in 1690) relationship. They went to the same school and both held editorial positions under their respective publishers (Playford and Tonson). Purcell set a number of Dryden's plays, masques and songs, including the exquisite song 'I Attempt from Love's Sickness to Fly'.

Dryden's translations from Greek have been unjustly neglected (perhaps because they were thought 'low', or eclipsed by Pope's?) In a welcome and spirited essay James A. Winn attempts to rehabilitate Dryden's Ilias Book 1. Following on this theme of translations from Greek, Robin Sowerby cites some illuminating parallels from translations by Knightly Chetwood, and others, including Racine, in his examination of 'The Last Parting of Hector and Andromarche'.

Jennifer Brady's essay 'Dryden and Congreve's Collaboration in "The Double Dealer"', one of three essays here on Dryden's plays promises, in its title, more than the subsequent essay delivers. However, it ends with the intriguing suggestion that Dryden's death may have contributed to Congreve's decision to 'quit the stage'.

The best single essay in the collection is a close

examination of 'Alexander's Feast', an essay of passionate engagement by Tom Mason and Adam Rounce, which looks at early readings of this wonderful poem, examining its language in some detail, and the poem's afterlife in later poems of the eighteenth and nineteenth centuries.

The professional relationship between Dryden and Tonson was to become a model for such relationships between writer and publisher until quite recent times, and it is right to have it commemorated in the most substantial essay here in John Barnard's long-meditated 'Dryden, Tonson, and the Patrons of "The Works of Virgil"'.

Morton's thesis is simple: Dryden subtly alters Virgil to 'speak such English, as he [...] wou'd have spoken, if he had been born [...] in the present Age', and we might add with the mind set of the 'present age'. Can this be accurately described as 'Enlightenment'? The decade 1691-1700 has been called strange things, a decade that produced fewer great works of literature than any other, but never, to my knowledge, Enlightenment. The book is pleasantly rambling, and contains a lot of observations on Dryden's practises in translating the Aeneid.

AMBIVALENT COLONIALISM IN DRYDEN'S *AMBOYNA*

For a play called by its author "scarcely [worth] a serious perusal" and once deemed by its editors "beneath criticism" and "utterly worthless" (by Sir Walter Scott and George Saintsbury, respectively), John Dryden's *Amboyna, or The Cruelties of the Dutch to the English Merchants: A Tragedy* (1673) has received a good deal of critical attention in the last fifteen or so years. The reasons are related to the reason Dryden wrote the play in the first place: a wide-spread and timely fascination with colonialism and empire building.

According to most modern accounts, however, Dryden applauds English empire building in his play, while readings like those of J. Douglas Canfield, Bridgett Orr, Robert Markley, and Shankar Raman deplore it. Such readings seem to spring from a valuable deconstructive or postcolonial orientation that allows us to "read through" a text's apparent pernicious, coherently propagandistic intentions. What I would suggest instead is that *Amboyna*–particularly in those aspects of the play that have been neglected or confused in recent scholarship–displays Dryden's *own* ambivalence toward unalloyed jingoism and imperialism. My project, then, is to reassess Dryden's supposedly unilateral, if wrongheaded, propagandistic stance *vis a vis* his subject, and in so doing to link the relatively inconsequential *Amboyna* to Dryden's more famous works, to his religious evolution, and to the arc of Restoration history.

Among the aspects of *Amboyna* which I will revisit are these:

The passage in which Dryden condemns *Amboyna* occurs in his dedication to Thomas Clifford, the Lord Treasurer. It reads:

To this Retirement of your Lordship, I wish I could bring a better Entertainment, than this *Play*; which, though it succeeded on the Stage, will scarcely bear a serious perusal, it being contriv'd and written in a Moneth [sic], the Subject barren, the Persons low, and the Writing not heightned with many laboured scenes.

Notable in Dryden's apology is his deeming his "Subject barren" and his "Persons low." This is at odds with many commentaries which have focused on the topicality of the "Subject"–read as a jingoistic rehashing of the Dutch "massacre" of English merchants in the Molucca islands in 1623—and its propagandistic relevance in the 70's when the English were engaged in the Third Dutch War. Such commentators have emphasized Dryden's strenuous efforts to elevate his merchant "Persons" by attributing to them the manners and ideals of the English gentry, as opposed to the materialistic Dutch "boors" (2.1.393)–overemphasized, I feel, since we shall see that Dryden's valorizing of the English is not absolute.

Further, in addressing his dedication to Clifford, Dryden is making his apologies to a dead man: On August 18, 1673, Clifford, a Catholic, had reportedly hanged himself in his

"Retirement," having felt compelled to resign from the government after the passage in March of the Test Act requiring all office-holders to deny that transubstantiation occurs during the Eucharist. Estimates for the premier of *Amboyna* vary from June 1672 to May 1673, but the play was not published, with its dedication, until November 24, 1673 (Dearing 257-58; 277 n.3; Gardiner 18-27), three months after Clifford's death.

Thus, while Clifford's supposed suicide cannot have inspired Dryden's original composition of the play (though it may have had some impact on the published version), it is interesting that its tragic climax begins with a long debate between the play's hero and heroine as to whether suicide can be moral; finally, they decide it can. Their debate is deeply concerned with issues of Providence, a topic to which Dryden doggedly returns throughout his career. Notably, however, none of the recent discussions of *Amboyna* have mentioned this debate, much less investigated its relevance to whatever values Dryden is espousing.

Also under- or misrepresented in recent discussions is the ambiguous handling of the play's secondary couple: the Spaniard Perez and his wife Julia. Julia, also courted by an Englishman and a Dutchman, is usually treated as a symbol of contested colonies previously Iberian, but her nationality, her worth, and her allegiance require further investigation, as do the heroism or venality of Perez, and his motives.

To show how such matters suggest that Dryden's endorsement of the colonial project is considerably less than wholehearted, let me begin by sketching the plot of *Amboyna* in relation to its immediate political occasion, and its relevance to the larger cultural context of its composition.

By the opening of the seventeenth century, the Dutch had driven the Portuguese out of the Moluccas (islands lying between modern Borneo and New Guinea) and were attempting to expel the English. "Outgunned and out financed" (Markley 5), the British signed a treaty in 1619 which "allowed the Dutch to have two-thirds of the trade in the east, and the English one third, both companies [the Dutch East

India Company or VOC, and the English East India Company] agreeing to fight as equal partners in declared and undeclared war on the Spanish and Portuguese" (Dearing 260). The event at Amboyna (now Ambon, the provincial capital of Seram) occurred when the Dutch accused the English there of conspiring with Japanese soldiers and Moluccan islanders (the Ternatans and Bandanese) to seize their fort, murder them, and use Amboyna as a stronghold from which to prey on VOC trade; they tortured and executed the English merchants.

Dryden had read two pamphlets by a shareholder in the East India Company, Sir Dudly Digges, both published in 1624: *A True Relation of the Unjust, Cruell, and Barbarous Proceedings Against the English at Amboyna* (reprinted in 1651 and 1672– and hence used as propaganda to fuel the second and third wars against the Dutch as well as the first) and *The Answere unto the Dutch Pamphlet, Made in Defense of the Unjust and Barbarous Proceedings against the English at Amboyna, in the East-Indies, by the Hollanders There.* He had also read John Darrell's 1665 pamphlet, *A True and Compendious Narration; Or (the Second Part of Amboyna) of Sundry Notorious or Remarkable Injuries, Insolences, and Acts of Hostility which the HOLLANDERS Have Exercised from time to time against THE ENGLISH NATION in the East Indies* (Markley 5-6).

Dryden was motivated to dramatize the events described in his sources to gain support for the Third Dutch War (1672-74). Referring to the first earl of Shatesbury's contention that "a War was absolutely necessary and unavoidable," Blair Hoxby tells us that "What Shaftesbury strove to do in Parliament [that is, argue that a 'a War was absolutelyl necessary and unavoidable'], Dryden tried to accomplish on stage" (180). Vinton Dearing, the editor of *Amboyna* in the California *Works,* remarks that Charles II's councellors wished to pass off [the war], political at root, as commercial in essence [and Dryden was] following the official line.

He was, after all, poet laureate and historiographer royal, and Thomas Clifford, the Lord Treasurer, who had conceived the idea of suspending treasury payments except for the war effort, saw to it that Dryden got his full salary in 1672 and

1673. It may be that the play was another of Clifford's ideas, as it was later said to be. "Political at root" refers to the fact that Clifford was one of only two councellors to whom Charles had confided the terms of the secret Treaty of Dover with Louis XIV (1670), which withdrew England from the Triple Alliance with Holland and Sweden against France and was intended to "prepare the way for [England's] Catholicization and for French seizure of the Spanish Netherlands [modern Belgium]" (Dearing 263).

An unflattering interpretation of these facts would be that Dryden's motives for writing *Amboyna* as he did were strictly mercenary rather than at least partly principled. Granting that Dryden may have been engaged in political hack work, I maintain that in the play he was unable or unwilling to entirely repress counter-propagandistic positions he expresses in other, better-known works. Hoxby—alone among modern critics—argues that the play has a "divided conscience"—which she sees primarily in the brutal treatment of the Amboynese heroine, a contention that I would like to amplify significantly. In any case, how far Dryden's qualifications of the "official line" in *Amboyna* are conscious or unconscious and how far the speed of his composition (a month) may have contributed to the ambiguity of his treatment are unclear.

However, it is worth noting here one relevant detail concerning Dryden's political orientation: Though he evinced "almost unmitigated dislike" for the Dutch throughout his life (Dearing 265-68), in *Absalom and Achitophel* (1681) Dryden would make the breaking of the Triple Alliance with Holland and Sweden (the "Triple Bond") one more crime of the Earl of Shaftesbury, who argued for it in Parliament.

So what sort of play did Dryden make of his openly propagandistic sources? Dearing writes that the historical event occurred "very much as Dryden describes it", and in relation to the "Persons Represented" he notes:

Gabriel Towerson, (John) Beamont (Beomont), (Edward) Collins, (Augustine) Perez, Harman Senior (Harman van Speult), and the Fiscal (Izaak de Brune) were real people. Their full names appear in *True Relation* (1624), in *Answer*, issued as part of *True Relation,* and in *Acts,* issued as part of *Remonstrance* (1632).

The play opens with Harman Senior (the Governor), the Fiscal, and Van Herring (a Dutch merchant) plotting to falsely accuse the English. The English merchants Beamont and Collins enter to announce the return of the English "General" Towerson to Amboyna after an absence of three years.

Towerson has rescued Harman Junior from pirates at sea, but Harman's debt of gratitude is soon cancelled by his desire for the Amboynese woman Ysabinda, Towerson's betrothed. Perez, a Spaniard (historically a Portuguese in service of the Dutch) who has not been paid by Towerson for fighting with him against the pirates, is hired by the Fiscal to murder Towerson.

Perez is reluctant to leave his wife Julia, who is being courted both by the Fiscal and by Beamont; but when he goes to Towerson's lodgings and finds his memorandum to reward Perez for his service, he leaves Towerson alive with the note "Thy Vertue sav'd thy life." The Fiscal then enlists Harman Junior in the plot to kill Towerson. After the wedding of Towerson and Ysabinda, an English woman appears to report that the Dutch have waylaid English mariners and colonists from neighboring islands and that she is the only survivor. The Dutch, of course, deny the charge. The Fiscal and Perez lure Towerson and Ysabinda separately into a wood. Perez, aware of the plot against Towerson, attacks Harman Junior, but Harman is saved by Towerson, though neither is certain of the other's identity.

Harman Junior accosts Ysabinda, ties her to a tree, and rapes her. When Towerson frees her, both decide to commit suicide after their revenge has been accomplished. Towerson and Harman Junior fight and Harman Junior is killed, but Towerson is then wounded by the Fiscal. The Fiscal swears that Towerson is guilty of murder and that he and the rest of the English have conspired to capture the Dutch fort. The English (with women and children) are tortured and executed along with Perez, but Julia manages to have Beamont freed. The play ends with the condemned Towerson prophesying

"Universal Ruine" for the Dutch. Dryden's main additions to the historical event, then, are the love plots: "high," involving Ysabinda, Towerson, and Harman Junior; and "low," involving Julia, Perez, the Fiscal, and Beamont. The women of both plots are not so much invented as drastically altered and embellished from what "sources" exist. Ysabinda takes her name from Tsabinda, a Japanese soldier named in Digges' *True Relation* (Summers 563 n. 352).

"Julia" is an invented name for an anonymous woman; of her, Dearing notes: "According to *True Relation* Perez 'had, by the perswasion of the Dutch Gouernour, taken [a wife] in that countrey [i.e., Amboyna] (p. 28); *Acts* says she was one of the slaves, given to him by the Dutch to engage his loyalty and repossessed by them after his death". So one thing Dryden has done is bring women centrally into the action. But to what purpose?

The obvious purpose that suggests itself is to make the play more attractive to audiences; I can think of no tragedy by Dryden–or indeed any during the Restoration–that does not include an element of love in peril and, in the case of Ysabinda, the love plot may be intended to make Towerson's doom doubly "moving," as the term was in those days. This strategy fails miserably with modern readers like Orr, who calls the Ysabinda-Towerson pairing "a degraded version of a heroic amour" or Markley, who calls it a "redaction of the Pocahontas myth".

The latter phrase suggests a reason for including the women more commonly argued today, and I have already touched upon it in relation to Julia, above: that both women represent the period's contested colonies and that both prefer their English suitors (or colonizers) to any others; as Hoxby remarks, "*Amboyna* repeatedly equates sexual relations with commercial ones". Put plainly, possession of Ysabinda is a "synecdoche for the possession of Amboyna" (Orr 158), and Julia represents "Iberian colonial possessions in general" now being claimed by the English and Dutch (Raman 201). I have reservations about such equations.

To pursue Julia first, commentators always point to her

remarks on finding the Fiscal with Perez, in which she explicitly announces the emblematic nature of the subplot:

If my *English* lover *Beamont*, my *Dutch* Love the *Fiscall*, and my *Spanish* Husband, were Painted in a piece with me amongst 'em, they wou'd make a Pretty Emblem of the two Nations, that Cuckold his Catholick Majesty in his *Indies*. (2.1.226-30)

A little further on in the same scene, with Beamont's entrance, we have an exchange that seems to confirm such emblematic readings:

Beam. Now Mr. *Fiscall*, you are the happy Man with the Ladies, and have got the precedence of Traffick here too; you've the *Indies* in your Arms, yet I hope a poor *English* Man may come in for a third part of the Merchandise.

Fisc. Oh, Sir, in these Commodities, here's enough for both, here's Mace for you, and Nutmegg for me in the same Fruit; and yet the owner has to spare for other friends too.

Jul. My Husbands Plantation's like to thrive well betwixt you. (2.1.281-88)

Granting the significance of such exchanges, I would like, however, to take note of some complicating factors. First, Dryden's handling of Julia's nationality (and therefore of her symbolic function) is at least ambiguous: Orr and Raman wrongly assume Julia is a Spanish woman (Orr 159; Raman 201); Canfield says that Dryden "seems to portray [her] as more European"; and Dearing, attempting to explain Beamont's reference to Spain as "your [Julia's] nation" (2.1.301), is compelled to suggest.

We have three possibilities. Perhaps this is another mark of lack of "labour" on Dryden's part. Perhaps he regarded the wife as taking her husband's nationality by marriage. Perhaps there is an element of irony here, though the audience would have no sense of it unless Julia and Ysabinda were somehow costumed similarly and in some way differently from English women. (295-6 n. 301).

Given the difficulty modern commentators have had with Julia's nationality, it seems reasonable to suggest that audiences might not have recognized that Julia is a native of

Amboyna until near the very end of the play, when Perez suddenly announces before his execution, [. . .] my *English* friends, I'm not asham'd of death, while I have you for part'ners; I know you innocent, and so am I, of this pretended plot; but I am guilty of a greater crime; For, being married in another Country, the Governors perswasions, and my love to that ill Woman, made me leave the first, and make this fatal choice. I'm justly punish'd, for her sake I dye; the *Fiscal* to enjoy her has accused me. (5.1.439-45)

The details of Perez's bigamy and Julia's native status are found in the *True Relation* (Dearing 317 n. 439-445), but they are dramatically a rather bizarre insertion and raise the issue of just how Julia is "ill" or whether she is indeed desirable. That Julia is *desired* is not at issue, but that she is desirable is called into question in the remarks the Dutch Fiscal and English Beamont whisper between themselves, comparing Julia to a "little kind of venture," a "drudgery," and a carrier of venereal disease (2.1.291-299).

And since these remarks appear to satirize Julia as a Spaniard, they further problematize any clear equation between Julia and a valuable, contested colonial space. The character of Julia, her value to the various colonizers, and her valuation of *them* is also complicated by Julia's insisting that her condemned husband is her "dear sweet Man" (5.1.29), that she only consents to marry the Fiscal on the condition that he spare Beamont's life, and that she parts with Perez saying "Farewel, my dearest, I may have many Husbands, but never one like thee" (5.1.437-38). Orr sees in Beamont and the Fiscal's remarks at Julia's expense evidence of miscegenation:

This contempt for miscegenation, repressed in the Towerson-Ysabinda alliance (in which the heroine, though an Amboyner, is emphatically aristocratic, and hence superior to the boorish Dutch), resurfaces in the casual bonding of the North European rivals over a Spanish woman [*sic*] whose "easy virtue" they read as a function of her tainted blood.

The issue of how to assess Julia's value (as a representative of the colonies) in the play is indicative, perhaps, of European ambivalence toward colonial Others–simultaneous desire for and contempt for colonial persons and spaces is commonplace in texts of the period. England's expansion into "exotic or savage" cultures for profit carried with it the threat of colonists' degeneration. My point is that the character of Julia and her contested status is anything but clear cut along propagandistic, pro-colonial lines and this suggests that Dryden was at least conflicted about such lines. At the very least, *Amboyna* "qualifies [. . .]as an attempt to register the costs and imagine the responsibities of a trade empire" (Hoxby 190).

More evidence of such conflict on the playwright's part may be found in relation to the genuine representative of Spain–Perez–whose portrayal by Dryden is relatively flattering. True, Perez agrees to assassinate Towerson, and his "moral reformation" upon learning of the Englishman's intended reward might thus be seen as "a function of his sudden wealth" (Markley 14), but this is too simple. Perez, though attempting to convince himself that his "revenge" is "noble", honorable (2.1.205), and fair, admits to himself that it is "Satan[ic]" before discovering Towerson's intentions and readily repents. He says of himself:

[. . .] hadst thou done it, thou hadst been worse then damn'd; Heav'n took more care of me, then I of him, to expose this paper to my timely view. Sleep on thou Honourable *Englishman*, I'll sooner now, pierce my own breast then thine [. . . .] (3.2.4-7)

He then returns the blood money, and the Fiscal says Perez "had too much of honesty" for the murder (3.2.45). To list of positives this may be added Perez's intervention in the Fiscal-Harman Jr. attempt to kill Towerson, and his heroic farewell to his English "partners" in death, already cited.

Political readings of the Julia-Fiscal-Beamont-Perez plot are also complicated by the issue of how we are to value its English representative. In demonstrating Dryden's vilification of the Dutch, Orr misattributes a line cited above—exposing the sexual/colonial possession trope ("Y'ave the Indies in your arms")–to the Dutch villain Harman Junior, when it is in fact spoken by the English "hero" Beamont. In that exchange, the Dutch Fiscal voices the principles of "an idealized mercantile vision of an unencumbered 'Traffick'"(Raman 204) in stores of inexhaustible bounty, while the Englishman seems anxious to secure his share in a limited supply. It seems to me that this suggests Dryden's reservations about the legitimacy of valorizing one nation's mercantile aspirations while demonizing another's.

And there are other ways in which the characterization of Beamont is not unilaterally flattering to English identity or ambitions. Beamont apparently is drunk at the wedding celebration, which accounts for his fomenting bad blood on that occasion; and his besottedness, Julia believes, makes him incapable of sexual possession (4.2.35). Dearing argues that Beamont's drunkenness may have been suggested by that of Abel Price (301.n.27-35). Price was "a drunken debauched sot," according to Digges' *Answer to the Dutch Pamphlet*, an English surgeon who drank and gambled with the Japanese and "other Blacks" and threatened to burn down a Dutch home, poisoning relations between the English and the Dutch. Markley claims that "Price is absent from Dryden's tragedy [. . .] because he threatens to complicate the play's binary logic of demonizing the other as a strategy of self-definition [. . . .] The construction of national identity in Dryden's play [. . .] thus discloses itself as an act of idealization designed to banish [. . .] the Abel Prices of the world [. . . .]".

However, insofar as Beamont is, at the very least, unimpressive in relation to the low plot, his characterization suggests that Dryden's project is not so unilaterally "an act of idealization" of the English—not simply "a stoic hero in the tradition of Hercules" (Hoxby 186). The "low" plot does not unproblematically heroicize colonialism or the English role in it; a critical attitude toward the colonial project may be fostered in the play *not* despite Dryden's (unsuccessful) attempts to whitewash it, but because of Dryden's own ambivalence toward it.

By contrast to his character in the low plot, however, Beamont's behavior in the high plot appears so different as to be nearly schizophrenic, and Dryden's handling of this plot–the Ysabinda-Towerson-Harman triangle and the "massacre" itself–seems to aim at entirely different effects. Let me now turn, then, to examine these sections of the play.

Raman identifies a "buried tension" in the high plot: "Gabriel Towerson, who bears the burden of English honor and the English colonial cause, is as much a merchant as any of the Dutch against whom he contends"; Towerson is thus "inappropriate for heroic representation" (Orr 157). Canfield notes that Towerson "was at best a ship's purser". Yet, Markley argues, in order to portray a "manichean politics of Dutch vice and English virtue," to stage the essential clash between "gentlemanly virtue and lower-class money-grubbing," Dryden "conflates the values of absolute honor and mercantile compromise in the person of a hero dedicated to the gentlemanly extension of English power. This hybrid, the heroic merchant, both constitutes and is constituted by the discourse of nationalism".

Looked at this way, Beamont would be essential to Dryden's project of elevating Towerson. In the high plot, and according to convention, Beamont becomes the hero's friend and panegyricist–Dollabella to Towerson's Antony, Cleanthes to Towerson's Cleomenes.

We first hear of Towerson from Beamont–in quite a different rhetoric than that Beamont is given in the Julia-Fiscal scenes:

Were I to chuse of all mankind, a Man, on whom I would relie for Faith and Counsel, or more, whose personal aid I wou'd invite, in any worthy cause to second me, it shou'd be only *Gabriel Towerson*; daring he is, and thereto fortunate: yet soft and apt to pitty the distress'd; and liberal to relieve 'em: I have seen him not alone to pardon Foes, but by his bounty win 'em to his love: if he has any fault, 'tis only that to which great minds can only subject be, he thinks all honest, 'cause himself is so , and therefore none suspects. (1.1.129-134)

Beamont is also available to support the testimony of the abused Englishwoman, to protest Towerson's innocence from the charge of murdering Harman, to suffer torture stoicially (*until* he begs to die at the very end [370-73]), and, upon being freed, to hear Towerson's heroic leave-taking: "A long and last farewel; I take my death with the more chearfulness because thou livst behind me [. . . .] Last, there's my heart, I give it in this kiss–[*Kisses him.*] Do not answer me; Friendship's a tender thing, and it would ill become me now to weep" (5.1.396-406). Beamont, then, is a hinge that links the low to the high plot, and his drastic inconsistency may be an index of the deeply ambivalent stance Dryden takes toward his material.

To elaborate, let me return to the "woman as land" trope, here in relation to Ysabinda. In relation to the "high" love plot, Raman explains:

[. . .] the "Indian woman" becomes a site of a direct struggle between the two European powers who have taken over the mantle once worn by Spain/Portugal. The struggle between Towerson and Harman for Ysabinda aims, first, to make explicit the qualitative difference between their respective desires, and, second, to establish the ethical superiority of the English position.

Raman cites the East India Company's claims that the natives of two Moluccan islands had surrendered their lands to England "entirely [by] their own motion" and outlines the process' three principal components: "first, the [temporal] priority of England's colonial rights; second, the voluntary surrender on the parts of the natives; and finally, symbolic confirmation [. . .]." All three are satisfied in regard to Towerson's contract with Ysabinda, which was established three years before, has included Ysabinda's voluntary conversion to Christianity, and is confirmed by their marriage ceremony.

The analogy of woman and land is made explicit in readings of lines like those in which the Dutch Harman Junior rationalizes his rape:

You are a Woman; have enough of Love for him [Towerson] and me; I know the plenteous Harvest all is his: he has so much of joy, that he must labor under it. In charity you may allow some gleanings to a Friend. (4.3.31-34)

But several commentators have argued that–despite Dryden's intentions—such lines rebound upon the English colonizer hero as well as the Dutch villain. Canfield feels that

Harman's speech "sounds eerily like Towerson's rationale for shared trade":

> [. . .] what mean these endless jars of Trading Nations? 'tis true, the World was never large enough for Avarice or Ambition; but those who can be please'd with moderate gain, may have the ends of Nature, not to want: nay, even its Luxuries may be supply'd from her o'erflowing bounties in these parts; from whence she yearly sends Spices, and Gums, the food of Heaven in Sacrifice: And besides these, her Gems of richest value, for Ornament, more than necessity. (1.1.220-27)

Orr adds that Dryden's hero Towerson tries to deny the synecdochical relation Harman Jr. identifies between Ysabinda and the island ("You've the Indies in your arms" [2.1.325]) by disclaiming any pecuniary motives for his marriage [. . . .] Nevertheless [. . .] after the rape he reassures Ysabinda that she is still "Paradise," "still as fragrant as your Eastern Groves" [. . . .] (158)

Raman elaborates on what he sees as Dryden's failure to distinguish adequately between Towerson and Harman Jr.–between "England's legitimate marriage with the (Christianized and assimilated) Eastern other and her brutal rape at the hands of the Dutch colonialist"—by focusing on the epithalamium sung at the wedding, which utilizes the marriage-as-rape trope, and the depiction of Ysabinda's actual rape by Harmon: "[T]he epithalamium conceals the implicit English rape of the colonized by explicitly assigning it elsewhere". In short, such arguments suggest that Dryden tries to construct a "manichean politics of English virtue and Dutch vice" (Markley 9), but his attempts are, at least to modern readers, unsuccessful.

I have already suggested that, at least in relation to the English Beamont (who calls *Julia* "the Indies"), an uncomplicated "manichean politics" does not seem to be precisely what Dryden is after, and I would like to adjust readings like those above. First, as regards the epithalamium, Dearing notes that Dryden based it "On the Latin of Joannes Secundus (Jan Everaerts, a Dutchman), first as appropriate to a celebration provided by Harman [Senior], and second, in its picture of the groom raping the bride, as appropriate to Harman Junior's character and foreshadowing what he will do" (300 n. 1-24).

Secondly, the impropriety and brutality of the *Dutch* song is underscored by Beamont, who says "Come let me have *The Sea Fight,* I like that better than a thousand of *your* [my emphasis] wanton Epithalamiums" (3.3.27-28). Towerson worries that the song celebrating an English naval victory will "breed ill blood," and in fact it does. Harman Junior grumbles, "See the insolence of these *English,* they cannot do a brave Action in an Age, but presently they must put it into Meter, to upbraid us with their benefits" (3.3.60-83).

The scene, then, seems intended to underscore the difference between the two nations through these samples of their art. However, as I have already pointed out, Beamont's request is a drunken and antagonizing one, and I might add that the difference is only between sexual and martial lustiness, and after all, lust is lust–a truism, by now, of postcolonial studies, and one Dryden seems to have recognized in relation to his low plot.

To pursue what Orr calls "the linkage between love and acquisition, love and location", I would note that in his defense against Harman's second attempted assault, Towerson claims, "[. . .] this Sword Heaven draws against thee, and here has plac'd me like a fiery Cherub, to guard this Paradice from any second Violation". Whereas Harman Junior depicts Ysabinda as a "Harvest," Towerson names her a "Paradice"–an attempt on Dryden's part, some argue, to distinguish between the rapacious commercial nature of Dutch colonialism and the (supposedly) pious stewardship of the English. If that were his strategy–which I question–it would be no great success since depictions of colonized lands and peoples as Edenic, accompanied by admissions of willingness to exploit these "Edens" are common in colonial literature. One thinks, for instance, of Aphra Behn's description of the Indians of Surinam in *Oroonoko* as "like our first Parents before the Fall", and a few paragraphs later, remarking that these same Indians "supply the parts of Hounds" to the English colonizers.

More obviously, however, Towerson's claim is just one instance of Dryden's characteristic interest in religious matters, an interest that manifests itself in this play in the action surrounding Ysabinda's rape.

The theme of the role of Providence in the fates of individuals and of nations is first announced when Ysabinda greets Towerson after their three year separation: "Now I shall love your God, because I see that he takes care of Lovers [. . .]" (2.1.277-78). Her reliance on Providence is emphasized in the rape scene, when she calls on assistance from Heaven four times in thirty lines and urges Harman to "tremble at a power above, who sees, and surely will revenge it" (4.3.62-63). Granting that a possible parallel between the villain and the hero may lurk in this exchange-

Ysab. Does thou not fear a Heaven?

Harm. No, I hope to find one in you. (4.3.55-56)

–more forcefully Dryden wishes to call attention to issues of divine justice, when, for instance, Towerson frees Ysabinda:

Ysab. [Harman] forc'd me to an Act, so base and Brutall, Heaven knows my Innocence:but, Why do I call that to Witness? Heaven saw, stood silent: Not one flash of Lightning shot from the Conscious Firmament to shew its Justice: Oh had it struck us both, it had sav'd me!

Towers. Heaven suffer'd more in that then you, or I: Where-fore have I been faithful to my trust, true to my Love, and tender to th'opprest? Am I condemn'd to be the second man, who e'er complain'd, he vertue serv'd in vain? (4.5.24-32)

Of Towerson's lines, Dearing remarks, "Exactly what Towerson has in mind is not clear; perhaps he feels that God's reputation has suffered, or perhaps he means that a loving God feels the sorrows of his world even more than it does" and "Apparently 'the second' means 'another' (*OED*), though the normal meaning of 'who e'r' goes awkwardly with such an interpretation" (307 n. 29-31). On the points Dearing raises, I am equally puzzled, but more interesting to me in this exchange is Dryden's clear interest in a higher court of "justice" than those man-made ones, inevitably tainted by extra-legal private agendas, that come into conflict in the play's denouement, when Towerson insists to the Dutch governor "you have no right to judge me" (5.1.255).

Dearing calls this "a major theme of the play" (308.n.227), one also sounded in 4.1.227, 5.1.56-57, and 5.1.132-33, and adds that the matter of which nation's law should govern in Amboyna was very much at issue historically, with each side claiming its law should govern (310 n.63-67). This scene raises that theme to a metaphysical level, as Towerson and Ysabinda debate the intention and judgement of "th'Eternal Mind" (4.5.46).

Concerning suicide, Dryden's handling of it throughout his career–in *Aureng Zebe* (1676), *All for Love* (1678), *Don Sebastian* (1690) and *Cleomenes* (1692), for instance—seems to suggest that his view is the one voiced by Towerson: "Self-homicide, which was in Heathens honour, in us is onely sin" (44-45). In this play, though, the Christians finally decide that in their case, too, suicide is "honorable" and no sin. Ysabinda argues that as God has "given us will to choose, and reason to direct us in our choice [. . .] why should he tie us up from dying, when death's the greater good" (47-48). Towerson counters with the "greatest Law" of nature, "to preserve our beings". Then Dryden has Ysabinda say something rather remarkable:

I grant, it is its great and general Law: But as Kings, who are, or should be above Laws, dispence with 'em when levell'd at themselves; Even so may man, without offence to Heaven, dispense with what concerns himself alone [. . . .] .

This is noteworthy since Dryden's habitual position seems to be that the monarchy itself is bound by law and that this principle underlines monarchical right and the rights of those governed. As he puts it in *Absalom and Achitophel*, "Laws are vain, by which we Right enjoy, / If Kings unquestiond can those laws destroy" (763-64). Just as remarkable is Towerson's reply. After weakly suggesting that "Heaven may give [Ysabinda] succour yet," he points to himself, and Ysabinda dismisses this ("'Tis too late, you shou'd have come before"). Towerson then concedes that suicide, even for Christians, is justified:

You have convinc'd my reason, nor am I asham'd to learn from you. To Heavens Tribunal my appeal I make; if as a Governor he sets me here, to guard this weak built Cittadel of Life, when 'tis no longer to be held, I may with honour quit the Fort. But first I'll both revenge my self and you.

The term "quit the Fort" calls attention to itself as "the fort" is the site of dispute in *Amboyna* and since Towerson's status as a "Publick Person, intrusted by my King and my Employers" (2.1.111-12) was earlier produced by him as justification for refusing to hazard his life in a duel with Harman. His speech upon being condemned by the Dutch likewise focuses on the obligations incurred by one "set" in a position of national trust: "give to my brave Employers of the *East India* Company, the last remembrance of my faithful service; tell 'em I Seal that Service with my Blood [. . .]" (5.1.399-401).

One might add that Towerson takes leave of Ysabinda "in haste" since "time [. . .] would divide my Love 'twixt Heaven and you" (5.1.411-13) and that he urges Ysabinda to survive him; she resolves on death not by active means but by starvation. As with Ysabinda's speech above, the metaphysical questing has occasioned secular theorizing at odds with Dryden's apparent positions elsewhere. It is surely curious that in this play our merchant hero should provide, couched in religious terms, a rationale to "quit the fort." But religious and political issues (here, especially in relation to trade) are inevitably intertwined in Dryden's work–in this instance in a way that links the relatively inconsequential *Amboyna* to three of Dryden's more famous poems, and to his religious development in the context of Restoration history.

Dryden's *Amboyna,* linked to the Third Dutch War, was, on some level, meant to serve as a piece of topical and royalist anti-Dutch propaganda (undercut, I believe, by Dryden's inability to wholeheartedly prostitute himself); to a lesser extent, so was the more ambitious *Annus Mirabilis, The Year of Wonders, 1666* (1667), linked to the Second Dutch War. Edward Niles Hooker and H. T. Swedenberg, Jr. describe the latter as "a piece of inspired journalism, written to sway public opinion in favor of the royal government, which dreaded a revolution [. . . .] Dryden suggested at every point through the poem that heaven and Providence had favored the King's party" (258-59).

In *Annus Mirabilis*, Dryden suggests a theory of the "mercantile state" which Hooker and Swedenberg sum up thus:

A healthy state seeks power and wealth; wealth flows in from the expansion of foreign trade; trade is the means of enriching the public treasury, and the nation's treasury alone has the resources to wage modern war; a strong king is needed to foster and protect trade, and to lead his people in war; and by victory in war the expansion of wealth and power is guaranteed.

In other words, whether synergy, a vicious cycle, or both, Dryden's theory of the mercantile state is an extension of his staunch royalism and allegiance to the Stuarts, the same allegiance that likely led him to compose *Amboyna*.

Securing support for the Third Dutch War was important to Charles II. In June 1672 Louis XIV's army had invaded Holland, resisted by Prince William of Orange; also in that month was published a pamphlet revealing the true contents of the secret Treaty of Dover (1670) negotiated between Charles and Louis, which "withdrew England from the Triple Alliance [with Holland and Sweden against France] and was intended to prepare the way for its Catholicization [. . .]" (Dearing 263).

When *Amboyna* and other attempts to secure support failed, Charles was forced by Parliament, in exchange for financial war supplies, to withdraw the Declaration of Indulgence which he had issued earlier that year and which had suspended all laws previously enforced against Dissenters and Catholics. Encouraged by success, the Parliamentary majority passed the Test Act, for which Shaftesbury argued, and which led to Clifford's resignation and, soon after, to his suicide.

As Winn explains, "On Easter Sunday, the day after Parliament recessed, the Duke of York [later James II] failed to take Anglican communion, in effect officially declaring his

Catholicism; since he remained the heir apparent, the Anglican interests now victorious in the Parliament had to face the prospect that a Papist would eventually inherit the throne" . It is this prospect, of course, that led to the Exclusion Crisis and to *Absalom and Achitophel.*

The Test Act is also integral to the occasion of Dryden's equally famous and longest poem, *The Hind and the Panther* (1687). Earl Miner calls that poem, published "more or less under James [II]'s aegis," a "salvo in the controversy of the day". James had "vainly expected the Anglican bishops to nullify" the Test Act, and began to seek the support of Dissenters with his own Declaration of Indulgence in 1687; "[t]he question became one of whether the King or the bishops could persuade the Sects that they shared common interests, and on whose side James's son-in-law, William of Orange, would come down" (327-28).

History tells us, of course, on whose side–Dutch William of Orange became William III of England; and Dryden, Catholic since 1685, lost his public posts, putting him, as Winn believes Dryden was acutely aware, in the position of Clifford fifteen years earlier. Dryden's response, in *Don Sebastian, Amphitryon,* and *Cleomenes,* was to continue writing plays that radically explore the role of Providence in human history.

It is interesting, then, that in *The Hind and the Panther,* Dryden returns to a charge against the Dutch *and* the English leveled in *Amboyna.* In the prologue, and the epilogue of the play, Dryden "specifically refutes the arguments of those reluctant to attack the Dutch on the grounds of a common religion [. . .]" (Winn 316), but he does it by accusing both the Dutch and the English of irreligiousity; he says to his English audiences that the Dutch "have no more Religion, faith–than you [. . .]" (prologue 18). In the later poem, he says the Dutch "on gain, their onely God, rely: / And set a publick price on piety" (II.569-70), but just as Dryden's charge in the prologue to *Amboyna* rebounds upon his own countrymen, so he savages British colonialism in *The Hind and the Panther*:

Our sayling ships like common shoars we use,
And through our distant colonies diffuse

The draughts of Dungeons, and the stench of stews;
Whom, when their home-bred honesty is lost,
We disembogue on some far Indian coast:
Thieves, Pandars, Palliards, sins of ev'ry sort,
Those are the manufactures we export;
And these the Missionaires our zeal has made:
For, with my country's pardon be it said,
Religion is the least of all our trade. (II.558-67)

I have argued that Dryden's stance toward colonialism in *Amboyna* is not as unilaterally–if wrongheadedly–pro-English as recent commentators have presented it to be. I would close with an observation by Canfield that does, I think, come close to representing the effect of the play–with this crucial difference: Canfield sees *Amboyna* as a "paean to Brittania" and what he regards as a single exceptional moment he believes to be unintentional; I see Dryden's attitudes as expressed in the entire play as considerably more ambivalent. Canfield remarks that [. . .] sticking out like a sore thumb is Ysabinda's plea to Towerson after her rape: "[F]or my sake, fly this detested Isle, where horrid Ills so black and fatal dwell, as *Indians* cou'd not guess, till *Europe* taught (IV.v.15-17). "*Europe*" includes not only the cruel Spanish and Dutch but the English as well. A minor note, surely not intended by Dryden to undercut his paean. Yet it as surely sounds, however diminished, in the ear of the attentive spectator.

The difference amounts to this: as an "attentive spectator," I believe that in *Amboyna,* Dryden once again demonstrates–however intentionally—his characteristic complexity of mind, here, in relation to the propagandistic purposes he was under pressure to serve.

Chapter 19

John Dryden and John Denham

In 1692, more than two decades after the death of John Denham, John Dryden paid homage to the poet as he recalled a conversation he had had "about Twenty Years ago" with Sir George Mackenzie:

He asked me why I did not imitate in my Verses, the turns of Mr. Waller, and Sir John Denham; of which, he repeated many to me: I had often read with pleasure, and with some profit, those two Fathers of our English Poetry; but had not seriously consider'd those Beauties which give the last perfection to their Works."

The largesse of this tribute, the labeling of Denham and Waller as "Fathers of our English Poetry," is, on first appearances, startling considering the discrepancy between Denham's slight reputation today and the fact that throughout the 1690s Dryden is concerned—to the point of obsession—with cementing an English poetic tradition and establishing poetic genealogies.

Also startling, however, is what an examination of the number and nature of allusions to Denham pervading Dryden's works reveals. While Dryden rarely acknowledges his debts to Denham and while critics remark upon them only cursorily, key tenets of Dryden's critical and political stances have their roots in Denham's poetry and critical proclamations. This intricate poetic relationship sheds light on Dryden's criticism and politics—not least a previously unnoted philosophical correlation between them.

The dues owed to Denham's criticism, in particular, point to limitations in existing discussions of Dryden's works. One problem, as Jennifer Brady notes, is the tendency to isolate Dryden: "Our institutional praxis of respecting the discreteness of literary periods tends to insulate Dryden and his contemporaries from predecessors who were central to their critical self-awareness."

When critics do contextualize Dryden, they generally look if not to Classical and French influences then to the "big three" English predecessors (Shakespeare, Jonson, and Fletcher) often assuming traditions rather than recognizing where Dryden was creating them. Yet the parallels between Denham's and Dryden's conceptions of problems facing seventeenth-century English literature throw into relief the extent to which Dryden's criticism builds upon English precepts that go beyond Shakespeare and Jonson.

At the heart of Denham's influence lies his Royalism, even as the neglect of his place in English letters is a result of the limiting of his importance to Coopers Hill. Certainly, this famous poem signals but does not circumscribe Denham's accomplishment as a Royalist poet: one searching for a rhetoric at a time when aesthetics and politics became indistinguishable and political turmoil rendered inherently unstable any personal or public stance. Willy nilly, Dryden found in Denham not only a kindred poetic spirit and English precedent for many of his own critical and poetical declarations, but a methodology that enabled him, throughout his career, to confront political chaos in an open-ended fashion while promulgating English traditions in a seemingly teleological fashion.

Phillip Harth has thoroughly explicated the nature of Dryden's skepticism by showing how he contrasts his "natural diffidence" or "skeptical way of reasoning" with a "Magisterial" or "dogmatical" manner. Yet Harth traces the roots of Dryden's philosophy to that of the Royal Society, whose influences, he contends, were everywhere evident to him. Further arguing that attention must therefore be paid to the specific contexts of Dryden's thought, Harth follows this skepticism through the particular theological and political debates that challenged him. The defining features of Dryden's skepticism—through which he deeply probes English tradition and monarchic authority while providing reassurances of their stability—are, however, also a natural consequence of his participation in a Royalist poetics, the spadework of which is owing to Denham.

Dryden's allegiance to Denham thus also writes larger Howard Weinbrot's argument in Britannia's Issue: attention to French influences on Dryden's works has overshadowed his conscious development of an English literary tradition. While Weinbrot's discussion of the Essay of Dramatick Poesie's "poetics of nationalism" makes a convincing case for Dryden's early efforts to establish English supremacy over French literature and the neoclassicism that dominated it, Dryden's relationship with Denham points not only to his lifelong efforts toward an English and Royalist poetics but also to the consistency of an oeuvre much maligned for its inconsistency.

To begin with the seldom-remarked translation theory of both poets, much of what Dryden is praised for as the father of English literary criticism (and of English translation theory) has its roots in Denham's small body of works. T. R. Steiner's history of English translation theory is typical in positing Dryden at the beginning of an English tradition. While Dryden is renowned for his division of translation into three main types (metaphrase, paraphrase, and imitation), Steiner notes, critics rarely acknowledge him as "as the spring of the Drydenian rules which we find in their essays." Nonetheless, he continues, "much circumstantial evidence supports the idea that Dryden was the chief lawgiver."

Steiner sees Dryden as in fact synthesizing two traditions of translation, one a French tradition that emphasized the decorum of literary language and the other an English tradition that emphasized the poetic spirit of the original. He does not fully allow, however, that the essential elements of Dryden's famous theories from his first essay on the topic to his last can be found in Denham's two brief essays on translation: his "To Sir Richard Fanshaw Upon his Translation of Pastor Fido" (probably 1643-1644) and his Preface to "The Destruction of Troy" (1656).

This fundamentally English context in fact provides the seedbed for the central tenet of Dryden's thoroughly modern and on-first-appearances innovative critical theory: the idea that poets of all ages are contemporaries. Denham's translation theory, furthermore, first formulates the associated notion of a "transfusion" of poetical spirit and so the metaphor that, as Brady argues, becomes the common thread linking Dryden's many reflections on poetical relationships, ultimately "emerg[ing] as the dominant metaphor of the preface to Fables, Ancient and Modern," his last work.

This transfusion of spirit from one poet to another entirely complemented the two poets' Royalist sensibilities as they sought to raise aesthetics above political turmoil while directly confronting it. For, such poetic commerce insures poetic continuity—and so stabilization of tradition—even as historical particulars are transcended. In his Preface to Ovid's Epistles (1680), his first discussion of translation, Dryden indicates but does not explicitly acknowledge the impact Denham had on him. Several times he refers to Denham's theories, twice quoting from him at some length.

The first quotation comes as he reiterates the Horatian warning against word for word translation: "Too faithfully is indeed pedantically: 'tis a faith like that which proceeds from Superstition, blind and zealous: Take it in the Expression of Sir John Denham, to Sir Rich. Fanshaw, on his Version of Pastor Fido." He then quotes the relevant lines from Denham's poem:

That servile path, thou nobly do'st decline, Of tracing word by word and Line by Line; A new and nobler way thou do'st pursue, To make Translations and Translators too: They but preserve the Ashes, thou the Flame, True to his Sense, but truer to his Fame. (1:115)

Just as Dryden downplays the originality of Denham's theory here, so several paragraphs later he praises his insights only to disagree with him. As he denounces imitation, he argues,

To state it fairly, Imitation of an Authour is the most advantageous way for a Translator to shew himself, but the greatest wrong which can be done to the Memory and

Reputation of the dead. Sir John Denham (who advis'd more Liberty than he took himself,) gives this Reason for his Innovation, in his admirable Preface before the Translation of the second AEneid: "Poetry is of so subtil a Spirit, that in pouring out of one Language into another, it will all Evaporate; and if a new Spirit be not added in the transfusion, there will remain nothing but a Caput Mortuum."

I confess this Argument holds good against a litteral Translation, but who defends it? Imitation and verbal Version are in my Opinion the two Extreams, which ought to be avoided. (1:117-18)

Steiner takes seriously Dryden's disapproval of Denham, claiming that "Dryden's first major work of translation, the Ovid's Epistles of 1680, marked his revolt against Cowley and Denham." While he later concedes that as Dryden "developed, he moved somewhat toward the freer style and the loose regulations of Cowley and Denham," (12) he is typical in failing to recognize that Denham here supplies the kernel for the emphasis on spiritual communion (the "transfusion" of one poetical "Spirit" into another) that quickly comes to dominate Dryden's discussion of poetical relationships.

Already in this first essay, however, both verbal echoes of Denham and Dryden's conceptualization of translation reveal Denham's creeping influence on him. Dryden's discussion of metaphrase, for a start, owes a double (unacknowledged) debt to Denham. After the first quote from Denham cited above, Dryden continues in his own voice: "'Tis almost impossible to Translate verbally, and well, at the same time; For the Latin, (a most severe and Compendious Language) often expresses that in one word which either the Barbarity, or the narrowness of modern Tongues cannot supply in more" (1:115). He then twice states that "gracefulness" is missing from such a "servile, literal translation" (1:116).

Both his choice of vocabulary and his basic points regarding the differences between languages and the need to supply the translation with a certain "grace" repeat Denham's warning against metaphrase: there are, Denham says, "certain

Graces and Happinesses peculiar to every Language, which gives life and energy to the words; and whosoever...

The ongoing emphasis in literary studies on the work of literature as cultural artifact, or as one in a number of "texts," literary and otherwise, that derive meaning only from their interdependence, has had surprisingly little impact on Restoration and eighteenth-century theater studies, particularly the discussion of plays themselves. Since the playwright's script is but one factor in any performance, concern for intertextuality should lead to exploration of the mutability of any durable play's meaning, especially in a theater world that constantly evolves, as this one did. Yet, whether located in aesthetics, in political or social issues, or even in the circumstances or personalities around which a play is written, the meaning or significance assigned to that play is almost invariably a fixed one.

This critical tendency neglects two remarkable features of drama in the so-called long eighteenth century: the extent to which audiences dictated the content and mood of plays, and the extent to which audiences, theaters, and new plays differed from each other. In prologue after prologue as well as in critical commentaries, playwrights and theater connoisseurs lament that the tastes of audiences—on which a play's success depended—debase the fare proffered. Such objections (and the sheer number of them) point to the subordination of the playwright's aesthetic concerns to audience expectations about a play.

This raises interesting questions about those plays that had any longevity during this period but that do not have a readily apprehensible universality of the kind generally attributed to, say, Shakespearian drama. If, as they did, audience demands kept pace with the rapidly changing political and cultural milieus and theater personnel and atmospheres, then in order to appeal to these ever-changing demands the durable plays of this period must be endowed with qualities that are incompatible with the fixed meanings sought for them.

An outstanding example of a play with a critical history

as remarkable as its endurance on the eighteenth-century stage is one that in fact kept a Shakespearian play from the boards throughout the entire period.

John Dryden's All For Love (also known in its own time as Antony and Cleopatra) replaced Shakespeare's Antony and Cleopatra until 1813. Howard Weinbrot long ago showed the futility of looking to Shakespeare for the key to All for Love, leaving critics still pondering the reason for the endurance of this starkly neoclassical play—one formal to a degree that even Dryden himself expressed nervousness about.

The critical dilemma has been confounded by the doggedly traditional approach, however: attention has focused not on those qualities that allowed it to survive chameleon stages and fickle audiences from the Restoration to the Regency, but on uncovering a particular moral, aesthetic, historical, or political meaning.

The red herring was perhaps thrown out by Dryden himself: the "excellency of the Moral" promised in the preface. Pursuit of this moral, or at least of some pinpointable meaning that makes sense of it, has led to titles like "The Significance of All For Love" (1970) and to assurances that "the value system of the play" lies in a circumscribed historical context (2000).

The result of such searches for a single encompassing meaning is that the only consistency amongst the criticism of All for Love is, as Harry Solomon notes, its inconsistency. The play's elusiveness is itself, however, the key to its durability. In light of its stage history, All For Love clearly has an openness and flexibility that, even as they have remained resistant to critical analysis, allowed the play to adapt to quite different theaters and audience needs.

It was able to please audiences of the 1670s and 1680s who were directed in their responses by Charles II, his libertine courtiers, and the political and philosophical issues that riveted the Restoration.

In the first part of the eighteenth century, it was equally able to attract more finicky audiences who loved to sympathize with characters and weep over heroines in distress, and who were profoundly interested in women's issues. The play also drew audiences to the cavernous Regency theaters, where the preferred fare was spectacle and the sense of intimacy between audience and actors that the earlier period had enjoyed was lost due to the physical nature of the playhouses. For each of these eras of production All For Love's significance simply cannot have been the same.

Nor, clearly, was its appeal similar from one dramatic season to another, as it catered to ever-changing moral tastes as well as to different social ranks. In the early eighteenth century, John Dennis saw All For Love as part of the libertinism of the former age: "Certainly never could the Design of an Author square more exactly with the Design of White-Hall, at the time when it was written, which was by debauching the People absolutely to enslave them."

The aristocratic women of the second and third decades of the eighteenth century most certainly were not offended by the play's moral content (as they were by other Restoration plays), however, for it was then frequently acted "At the Desire of several Ladies of Quality" and even "By Their Royal Highness's Command."

At the same time, the various benefit performances for actors and actresses, who relied upon All For Love to fill up a playhouse, are testimony to its undiminished popular appeal. This is not to say that it was a fallback for theater companies; David Vieth has counted 123 performances from 1700 to 1800, and several London Stage entries note that it had not been performed for a number of years.

Yet, over a 150-year period of major and minor evolutions of the London stage, Dryden's neoclassical play was a staple in a repertory that rejected even David Garrick's attempt at Shakespeare's Antony and Cleopatra. Any discussion of this play (and of the other durable plays from this period) must, then, take a holistic approach.

All for Love's significance to the audience is located primarily in the moment of production, and the relationship between the play and the world to which it is addressed during any given performance depends upon a number of complex elements. This fact poses, of course, the difficulty, indeed the "impossibility" as Paula Backscheider has observed, of "reconstructing a past event (performance), of determining what appealed to a long-dead audience (what needs and desires were met, what specifically triggered strong responses), and of articulating the complex relationship between social life and works of art.... "Yet, as Backscheider continues, despite the lacunae, a "wealth of evidence survives that permits new discoveries about how [plays] were experienced."

This is particularly true of information about actors and actresses and their onstage and offstage personalities, and critics generally agree that the soul of drama from the Restoration well into the eighteenth century is dynamic interaction between audience and players. Robert D. Hume's The London Theatre World long ago pointed out how the physical nature itself of the playhouses demanded a close audience/actor relationship, while Lisa Freeman's recent argument about cultural identity and theatricality pivots on the absence in the theater of "a 'fourth wall' that could create the double illusion of separation and transparency between spectacle and spectator."

Kristina Straub has also argued convincingly that Restoration and eighteenth-century audiences were affected in their response to characters by their knowledge of the actors' private lives and personal traits. In this type of theater, actors contribute as much, if not more, to the meaning of any performance as the playwright does. Or, as Peter Holland puts it, to "find out how the audience understood the play that they watched, a study of Thomas Betterton is as important as one of John Dryden."

The purpose of this essay, accordingly, is to consider a few different actors who played the key roles in All for Love between 1677 and 1813, and to place their performances within a cultural context. The paucity of information about circumstances of production means that any judgment concerning likely audience response to the play is obviously speculation.

Yet in addition to what is known about the major actors

who played Dryden's characters and about audience expectations of them, there are some givens concerning certain periods of eighteenth-century life. It is clear, for example, that in years of political turmoil, theatrical presentations of kingship or political strife were viewed as commentary on contemporary problems.

Similarly, in particular years, certain cultural issues—say, interest in women's writing and women's social roles or the ambiguity surrounding heroism in a mercantile world—permeate the theater as much as any other medium. In order best to highlight the differences between performances, which is the main focus here, this essay draws upon what is known, choosing the most studied dramatic periods as test cases for the probable significance of All For Love during these times.

It begins by investigating the Restoration origins of the play, tracing the play's versatility to self-contradictions within both drama itself and a culture that clung to aristocratic ideals even as it rejected them. It then examines two sets of productions staged in the decades immediately before and after the turn of the century.

The Elizabeth Barry/Thomas Betterton and Anne Oldfield/Barton Booth versions of the play shared emphases that distinguish them from the Restoration productions; however, new cultural factors feeding into the Booth and Oldfield performances further transformed All for Love's original focus on civic duty.

The essay looks finally at late-eighteenth-century renditions of the play, arguing that its significance then derived from the taste for spectacle and pageantry that went hand-in-hand with larger theaters. The intention here is not to define the play's meaning for any of these performances, nor is it to trace the development of the play's impact on audiences over the period.

It is rather to highlight the possibilities of meaning given the theatrical and cultural variables at a given moment, and to demonstrate what qualities ensured durability on the eighteenth-century stage.

Paradoxically, given its adaptability over the century, All

For Love was, as much as other plays of its period, the product of a particular cultural moment.

Beginning with, if not before, John Dennis and his complaint about its immorality (cited above), numerous critics have shown the various ways in which it is an artifact of the court of Charles II. The extent to which this is true explains its remarkable survival.

Despite his famous claim that this was the only play he wrote for himself, Dryden wrote into it the paradoxes of the theatrical and political stages, which, as Backscheider has shown so convincingly, were inextricably intertwined.

Chapter 20

Gendered Desire, Political Occasion, and Dryden and Lee's Oedipus

Let me begin with three common observations about the 1678 Oedipus of Dryden and Lee. First, more than their predecessor versions by Sophocles, Seneca, and Corneille, the Restoration playwrights emphasize the erotic nature of the incestuous relationship between Oedipus and Jocasta. Second, Creon is transformed from the relatively ambitionless playboy prince of Sophocles' original to the physically and morally twisted precipitator of the crisis, analogous to "the figure of Shaftesbury seen through royalist eyes and representations" (Novak, "Commentary to Oedipus"462).

Third, as the previous suggests, Dryden and Lee's play, while offering no strict allegory, has relevance to contemporary events-the Popish Plot and the gathering Exclusion Crisis-not least in that, with its added subplot, their version focuses more than others on issues of legitimacy and succession.3 My focus here is the link between the first observation-the exaggerated eroticism of the play-and the others, a link that exists since a patriarchal, monarchical society transmits its power and property through the body of a woman. That eroticism has usually been attributed to Lee's tendencies toward the sensationalistic, by contrast to Dryden's judicial and metaphysical emphases.4 Insofar as that may be true, and I will severely qualify its applicability, I would argue that in the collaboration, especially in the depiction of Jocasta, if these are Lee's means, they nevertheless serve-in a complex way-Dryden's ends.

We should begin by placing the composition of Dryden and Lee's Oedipus in its historical context. Max Novak has written that in 1678 "the political theater of the Popish Plot [had] . . . distracted . . . theatergoers from the beauties of the legitimate stage" ("Commentary to Troilus and Cressida"497). The Popish Plot, of course, was a series of alleged Catholic-backed plots that involved the planned assassination of Charles II by Jesuits, the installation of James on the throne, and a Catholic invasion. The Earl of Shaftesbury led the Whigs in exploiting the supposed danger by pressing for the exclusion of James from the succession and the legitimization of the Duke of Monmouth, Charles's bastard-and Protestant-son. The larger issue, of course, was a Parliamentary struggle to reverse the flow of power, to restructure both constitutional laws and historic notions of kingship, which was accomplished, finally, with the Glorious Revolution.

But Novak's term the "legitimate stage" posits a drama untainted by politics-arguably untrue of all theater, as indeed of all art. A most explicitly political work is Dryden's own Absalom and Achitophel, published in 1681during Shaftesbury's trial, the climax of the "Plot." Dryden first published it anonymously-a transparent attempt at distancing himself from his argument, but an attempt all the same. The relation of Oedipus to contemporary events is more oblique. In choosing to adapt so well known a play, Dryden and Lee could do implicitly what Dryden later did explicitly in the later political crisis, the Glorious Revolution, when he claimed, somewhat disingenuously, that his plays were not political commentaries but "plain stor [ies] " (Cleomenes 79). Dramatically, the collaborators would wait until 1683, with The Duke of Guise and its "Vindication," to make contemporary relevance more plain. Yet Oedipus does have at least broad relevance to the Popish Plot in that guilt is unexpectedly uncovered and innocence falsely accused. (It may be telling, too, that Dryden's next play, Troilus andCressida [1679], is subtitled The Truth Found Too Late.)

Since Dryden, according to his own declaration, composed the whole design of Oedipus as well as writing Acts I and III ("Vindication" 344), it is worthwhile to review his personal involvement in contemporary events. In 1681, he claimed that he had "seen through" the Plot from the start (Winn 317). Be that as it may, as early as 1677, Dryden would have been aware and personally concerned with its developing implications. He would have followed the marriage of William of Orange to Mary, with its potential repercussions to adherents of James II, and in the dedication of All for Love he attacks Shaftesbury and Buckingham, asserts that "subverters of Governments" are no friends to the arts and equates Shaftesbury with Satan-a strategy he would return to in Absalom and Achitophel (Winn 304-05).

In 1673, enemies had damned one of Dryden's plays as a "Catholic intrigue"; and in 1676 Catholic mass were said illegally only steps from Dryden's home. An actor who might have expected to participate in Oedipus, Matthew Medbourne, a Roman Catholic, was committed to Newgate on Titus Oates's testimony and died there in March (Novak, "Commentary to Oedipus"444). Dryden's brother-in-law Charles, second Earl of Berkshire, who had written compromising letters to a "conspirator," fled to France in 1678 and died there in 1679 (Winn 315). Also in 1679, Dryden himself was beaten senseless with cudgels by three thugs, in all probability for a "lampoon" touching upon some members of the Opposition-which he had not even authored.

And certain specific passages in Oedipus's apparatus do indicate Dryden's orientation to the issues raised by the plot. In the prologue, for example, he urges that audiences not "pell mell to damning fall, / Like true born Brittains who ne'er think at all" and, more pointedly, warns against headlong, potentially disastrous commitment to action, like William of Orange's assault on Mons -relevant since England was close to being drawn into a war with France and Holland, with Shaftesbury arguing strenuously for a war Charles opposed.

The prologue closes with a similar caution against the "private spirit" of "Fanaticks", that "numerous Host of dreaming Saints" Dryden describes in Absalom and Achitophel as joining with the Whigs in pressing for the exclusion of James. Similarly, the epilogue tells audiences, "We know not what you can desire or hope, / To please you more, but burning of a Pope". Odai Johnson describes the Pope-Burning Pageants between 1673 and 1682 as "Whig theater [. . .] that sought by performative strategies to politicize the crowd as a stable subject of the Whig Party [. . .] a propagandized extension of the Whig party".

Dryden's strategy too is to camouflage politics in aesthetics, but that is a gauzy tactic when aesthetic matters are political matters and, in the 1670s, 80s, and 90s, dovetail with religious and metaphysical matters-a point to which I will return later.

Let us turn now to examine two of the broader analogues between politics and play: the representation of the Theban citizenry and of Creon. In Sophocles and in Seneca, the Theban chorus are almost unshakably loyal to their king. In Sophocles, at the peak of Oedipus's paranoiac rage against Creon, the Chorus only tells him "Sir, I have said before and I say again-be sure that I would have been proved a madman, bankrupt in sane council, if I should put you away [. . . .]" Even after the truth of parricide and incest is revealed, the chorus's response is more empathie than condemnatory: "To speak directly, I drew my breath / from you at the first, and so now I lull / my mouth to sleep with your name".

In Dryden and Lee's play, the citizenry is portrayed quite differently. They are a "people prone, as in all general ills / To sudden change" (1.1.75-76), like the "headstrong [.. .] race" of the Jews (English) in Absalom and Achitophel. When Tiresias chides them for "Rebellion" and reminds them of their oath of loyalty to Oedipus, one citizen grumbles, "This is true; but it's a hard World Neighbors, if a mans Oath must be his master" (1.1.285-86). As Oedipus has become king of Thebes "By publick voice elected", so in Absalom and Achitophel the citizenry whose "Humour more than Loyalty exprest, / Now, wondered why, so long, they had obey'd / An Idoll Monarch which their hands had made".

Their characterization, with the characterization of the English in the prologue and epilogue, reminds us that the propagandized posturing surrounding the Popish Plot was "responsible for the creation of a popular political entity outside the court-the crowd-not as a subject produced by the monarch (the rabble), but as participants of the Whig party [. . .] a construct of the Whigs designed to publicly demonstrate against the king the City of London's popular support of Exclusion" (Johnson 14).

The head of the drive toward Exclusion is Shaftesbury in history, Creon in the play, and Achitophel in the poem. As Shaftesbury's ostensible opposition was to the succession of Charles's brotherjames, so Creon initially and necessarily opposes not the king himself, but Oedipus's likely successor, his "step-daughter," Eurydice, who resists marriage to Creon, which would make him the next king of Thebes. Novak considers the representation in Creon of "the figure of Shaftesbury seen though royalist eyes and representations" Dryden and Lee's "crucial" alteration of their sources ("Commentary to Oedipus"462). In Act I, Creon describes his deformity thus:

Am I to blame if Nature threw my body
In so perverse a could? Yet when she cast
Her envious hand upon my supple joints,
Unable to resist, and rumpled 'em
On heaps in their dark lodging, to revenge
Her bungled work she stamped my mind more fair:
As for Chaos, huddled and deformed,
The God strake fire, and lighted up the Lamps
That beautify the sky, so he informed
This ill-shaped body with a daring soul:
And making less than man, he made me more. (1.1.145-55)

This passage certainly forecasts Dryden's description in Absalom and Achitophel of Shaftesbury's "huddled Notions," his "Pigmy Body" reproduced in his son, "born a shapeless lump, like Anarchy". Creon, of course, aims to rule himself, and Dryden makes the same accusation against Achitophel, "Resolved to Ruin or to Rule the State".

The most interesting parallel between Creon and Achitophel extends the emphasis upon those characters' twisted bodies. Creon admits "My body opens inward to my soul, /And lets in day to make my Vices seen / By all discerning eyes, but the blind vulgar" (1.1.179-81), so Creon's ambition is not really a compensation for his deformity, but an extension of it. Likewise, in his relentless plotting, Achitophel "Punishe [d] a Body which he [can] not please". Creon's frustration manifests itself in misogynist statements like this:

These Women are such cunning Purveyors!
Mark where their Appetites have once been pleased,
The same resemblance in a younger Lover
Lyes brooding in their Fancies the same Pleasures,
And urges their remembrance to desire.

Or this: "That thoughtless Sex is caught by outward form / And empty noise, and loves it self in man". Achitophel is likewise misogynistic, arguing that Charles "By Force [...] wishes to be gained, like women's Lechery". Where Creon plans to take Eurydice by blackmail or force, and afterwards to discard her, Achitophel urges Absalom to "commit a pleasing rape upon the Crown". Charles's petitioners are "Unsatiate as the barren Womb or Grave". In the villains of both Oedipus and Absalom and Achitophel, sexuality is either debased, sterile, or brutal. Problematized representations of sexuality, however, are certainly not limited to the villains-not in this play-which leads us to consider Dryden and Lee's depiction of Oedipus himself and, especially, Jocasta.

Specifically, I want to emphasize two points: first, Dryden's contributions in Acts I and III and the whole "design" accentuate the psycho-sexual complexities especially apparent in this version of the Oedipus story as much as, if not more than Lee's; second, these complexities, too, are particularly relevant to the political context of the collaboration.

There is a tremendous emphasis on carnality, even animality, from the outset of play. Act I.i, written by Dryden, insists on the drive-often brutal-toward sex and procreation. Alcander recommends that Oedipus (absent) "bring the Wives and Children / of conquer'd Argians to renew his Thebes".

Creon says Jocasta remarried in haste since she "Fear'd to lye single", and he attempts to seduce Eurydice "For when the Gods destroy so fast, 'tis time/ We should renew the Race" even "in the midst of horrour".

Eurydice retorts by describing Creon's monstrous birth, at which "The Midwife stood aghast [....] And knew not, if to burn thee in the flames / Were not the holier work", calling him only fit to mate with monsters like himself. Further, Act I introduces two occasions for incest, not one: the consummated incest of Oedipus and Jocasta, mother-son incest; and the potential, though ultimately unperformed, incest between Creon and Eurydice, uncle-niece incest. Likewise, there are two triangles: Oedipus/Lajus/Jocastaand Creon/Adrastus/Eurydice.

The obvious difference is that Creon's rival is not his kin, whereas Oedipus's is. Oedipal incest, of course, involves the replacement of father with son; or, to put it another way, the son, in seeking to displace and replace his sire, to some degree becomes his sire, becomes husband/father. Thus, the Oedipal version of parricide and incest conflates identification and difference; they meet at the crossroads, if you will.

Dryden represents this meeting, the doubled nature of the incestuous desire, in two early and crucial rhetorical moments: the plague and its consequentmeteorological manifestations is described in a figure that would seem to conflate Oedipus with Lajus, and Oedipus's earlier career with his ultimate fate: "Blind Winter meets the Summer / In his Midway, and seeing not his livery, / Has driven him headlong back". Let me unpack these lines.

Every one of the spectators, and each of us readers, though not the characters at this moment, would recognize in the passage the image of Oedipus driving Lajus back at the crossroads, not having recognized his "Livery"-that is, his status as king and father (positions analogous in the contemporary, though embattled, political theory of Dryden's time). It is not going too far to see in Oedipus's and Lajus's jostling for primacy to pass through the "narrowway", the "verge" (perhaps recalled in the famous line Lee gives Oedipus at his moment of discovery: "Gods meet Gods, andjustle in the dark!), the contest for primacy in the passage to Jocasta's womb.

As Jeffrey Rusten has detailed, "the juncture of three roads (double into single) figures the female genital region [. . .]"; the Greek word that designates "crossroads" is etymologically closely related to the word for "crack," defined as "the vulva" in Rufus of Ephesus On Medical Terminology, and Rüsten traces such associations in, for instance, Aristophanes's Wasps. Thus, usten concludes, "the crossroads may double as a designation for sexual territory, territory that is simultaneously the threshold of emergence into life and of accession to political power. That a woman's body may become the terrain of sexual and generational rivalry is especially overt in the case of Jocasta [. . .]".

This initial impression of how the lines mean, however, is complicated, in that the Oedipal figure is "Blind," a forecast, also easily recognizable, of Oedipus's literal blindness to come. Essentially, the figure overlays the image of Oedipus in the play's past (at the crossroads) with the image of Oedipus in the play's future (blinded). And this rhetorical palimpsest goes further in that Oedipus, the youthful son, would here be "Blind Winter" (my emphasis), while the older Lajus would be "Summer." A later image similarly conflates Oedipus with Lajus, particularly in the attribution of blindness, not to the young but to the old. Oedipus sees an omen:

A young Stork,
That bore his aged Parent on his back;
Till weary with the weight, he shook him off,
And peck'd out both his eyes. (3.1.384-87)

The effect of such complex figures (Dryden's, I would remind us) is to hint at the problematic identification/difference paradox at the heart of the Oedipal crisis.

The second rhetorical moment I think crucial will position Jocasta at the Oedipus/Lajus juncture, and this moment involves Creon's theorizing with his supporters about feminine desire:

More straightforwardly than the previous passage, these lines stress the identification of Lajus and Oedipus and particularly injocasta's perception, wherein "remembrance" is confused with "desire."7 But they also hint at the association of female sexual desire with narcissism, another version of the confusion of other with self, which Creon makes clearer in his reading of Eurydice's desire for Adrastus: "That thoughtless Sex is caught by outward form / And empty noise, and loves itself in man".

In Act III, when Eurydice is condemned (since the murderer is supposed to be "the first of Lajus'blood" and Oedipus's paternity is not yet known), Creon's description of what death will bring further emphasizes what he sees as female narcissism. Eurydice's spirit will enter

What is notable here is that while the "object of desire" in these lines is Eurydice's body and those who desire it in the play are Creon and Adrastus, this image makes the one desiring as well as the desired Eurydice herself. She is agent and object; female eroticism, here even after death, is auto-eroticism.

My point in all of this is to suggest that the insistent identification/difference trope in relation to Oedipus and Lajus-their permeability, or interchangeability-ultimately impacts on Jocasta, as does the issue of narcissism, the latter as Jocasta, not Eurydice, is the primary object of the play's examination of female desire, and thus even utterances not about her per se accrue to her characterization. More than other versions, Dryden and Lee's play obsessively returns to the question, as a colleague of mine phrased it, "What does Jocasta know, when did she know it, and what has she been telling herself all these years?"

For in Dryden and Lee's version, Jocasta's culpability is certainly more at issue than in Sophocles, Seneca, or Corneille, and more likely to be condemned than Oedipus's own. In his preface, Dryden, claiming that he follows Sophocles's example, takes Corneille's version to task particularly for "miserably fail [ing] in the Character of his Hero":

if he desir'd that Oedipus should be pitied, he shou'd have made him a better man. He forgot that Sophocles had taken care to shew him in his first entrance, a just, a merciful, a successful, a Religious Prince, and in short, a Father of his Country: instead of these, he has drawn him suspicious, designing, more anxious of keeping the Theban Crown, than solicitous for the safety of his People: Hector'd by Theseus, contem'd by Dirce, and scarce maintaining a second part in his own Tragedie.

Dryden's self-proclaimed faithfulness to Sophocles's conception of Oedipus's character is not dogged, however. Whereas Sophocles's Oedipus is groundlessly hostile toward Creon, Dryden's Creon is groundlessly hostile toward his Oedipus. In so reversing the flow, Dryden diverts at least part of the culpability of his hero toward his villain and his cronies, who busy themselves in attempts to destroy all of the major admirable characters in both plots, which, Novak feels, makes Oedipus's tardiness in solving the mystery of his birth more plausible ("Commentary to Oedipus" 459-60). Dryden further mitigates the guilt that might accrue to his hero for the sins he does commit in all versions (murder and incest) by including the ghost of Lajus. Dryden provides Lajus with a warning before the birth of Oedipus. Lajus says the gods

In providing this detail, Dryden allots some of the guilt to Lajus by his own admission and reinscribes Oedipus's virtuous nature and his victimhood. In fact, Dryden later wondered if he had made Oedipus "too good a man" (in the Parallel between Painting and Poetry, qtd. in Novak, "Commentary to Oedipus"470-71 n.115:17-19).

The guilt, then, is partly extenuated in relation to Oedipus, but, I would argue, exacerbated in relation to Jocasta. At her first entrance, Jocasta's wish that Heaven "bring the effects of these [Oedipus's] pious prayers / On you, and me, and all" (1.1.502-503) is ill-timed as Oedipus has been cursing the murderer of Lajus, and his "Unkind" rebuke to her evokes this, the first of many explicit references to their incest (not to be found in sources):

Such lines may be thought to work paradoxically. They keep the horror and revulsion toward their incest that the characters will have to admit in the forefront of our reckoning of their guilt; yet they suggest that Oedipus's and Jocasta's actions are, in fact, unwitting and thus-insofar as that matters to us-innocent. For why should the remarks on physical likeness and the incestuous rhetorical figures be so glibly and publicly given voice by the couple and their enemies if the implications of these were consciously recognized? But insofar as this is how these lines work, they work less efficiently in term of Jocasta, since immediately after this exchange Jocasta sues that Oedipus allow the marriage of Creon and Eurydice.

Oedipus, at least, sees the uncle/niece union as incestuous and forbids even mention of it ("I know not why, it shakes me / When I but think on Incest" [558-59]), to which Jocasta reluctantly agrees. Jocasta's understanding of the prohibition against incest is, at least in the case of Creon and Eurydice, more elastic than that of her husband. Moreover, since, I have argued, the moral and psychological valence of Eurydice also impacts upon Jocasta as the play's major representative of female desire (and "like mother, like daughter"), it is relevant that Eurydice does not seem to consider a union with Creon incestuous, only unwelcome-she never raises the issue of kinship in her rejections of him.

We might also note that in the passage above, despite the problematic terms, Oedipus characterizes his love for Jocasta as "pious," she characterizes hers as "tender" and speaks of his being "in [her] arms." More of the implications of forbidden desire accrue to Jocasta than to her husband. We might pause for a moment to consider that Eurydice was promised to Creon by Jocasta early, when her daughter was "at Nurse" and that after Lajus's death Jocasta "Fear'd to lye single."

The latter suggests a voracious female sexual appetite combined with timidity at being alone, but also latent in these details is the matter of the succession to the throne of Thebes. Creon and his followers seem to assume that if Jocasta had remained unmarried, Creon would have ascended to the throne after Lajus's death. As Diocles remarks, "Had merit, not her dotage, been consider'd, / Then Creon had been King". The implication is that Jocasta, unmarried, would not have been permitted to rule alone; her power would have been effaced.

Under these circumstances, one motive for the hasty marriage to Oedipus, then, may have been the preservation of Jocasta's position as queen. It is instructive to remember that up to Dryden and Lee's day, with the exceptions of Elizabeth I and "Bloody" Mary I, all British monarchs had been male.

The cultural moment for a female monarch would not arrive until Mary II (and the operative monarch, her husband, William III) and following her, Ann, in 1685 and 1702, respectively. If in the details of the Restoration Oedipus we choose to ascribe such a motive to Jocasta-the preservation of female monarchical power-the response to such a motive during Dryden and Lee's day would likely have been negative.

From politically based suspicion to visceral horror is but a short step in this play, and Lee takes it immediately in opening Act II with prodigies: "blood on the moon" and gigantic figures of Oedipus andjocasta against the sky. While the other spectators comment on the astronomical manifestations as astronomical (shooting stars, comets, lightning and so on), Oedipus sees a monstrous birth, one in which he will assist:

Ha! My Jocasta', look! The Silver Moon!
A selling Crimson stains her beauteous Face!
She's all o're Blood! And look, behold again,
What mean the mistick Heav'ns, she journeyes on?
A bast Eclipse darkens the labouring Planet.
Sound there, sound all our Instruments of War;
Clarions and Trumpets, Silver, Brass, and Iron,
And beat a thousand Drums to help her Labour. (2.1.37-44)

The monstrous birth recalls, of course, Oedipus's own and the "birth" to come of his recognizing his true identity. He offers his life as a sacrifice to the angry gods, but when Jocasta enters and the prodigies vanish, he retreats into erotic (and, he insists, innocent) imaginings:

Yes, I will dye, O Thebes, to save thee!
Draw from my heart my blood, with more content
Than e're I wore the Crown. Yet, O Jocasta
By all the indearments of miraculous love,

By all our languishings, our fears in pleasure,
Which oft have made us wonder; here I swear
On thy fair hand, upon thy breast I swear,
I cannot call to mind, from budding Childhood
To blooming youth, a Crime by me committed,
For which the awful Gods should doom my death.

What is interesting about this is that in the midst of denying criminality, Oedipus mentions misgivings about sexual pleasure and attributes these to Jocasta as well as himself. Jocasta takes the opportunity to sooth Oedipus's fears and proclaim his and her own innocence; her "perhaps" is notable: "Were you, which is impossible, the man, / Perhaps my Ponyard first should drink your blood; / But you are innocent, as jour Jocasta [. . .]". Oedipus, however, elaborates on his habitual aversion to (as well as attraction to) sexual intercourse with Jocasta after sending her reluctantly to bed:

Nay, she is beauteous too; yet, mighty Love!
I never offer'd to obey thy Laws,
But an unusual chillness came upon me;
An unknown hand still check'd my forward joy,
Dashed me with blushes, tho' no light was near:
That ev'n the Act became a violation.

In the next scene, Oedipus is seen sleepwalking, dreaming that the Jocasta he approaches in bed is his supposed mother, Merope, and that he has killed his supposed father, Polybus, two acts whose criminality he clearly ranks:

Yet what most shocks the niceness of my temper,
Even far beyond the killing of my Father,
And my own death, is, that this horrid sleep
Dashed my sick fancy with an act of Incest:
I dreamt, Jocasta, that thou were my Mother [. . . .] (384-88)

Jocasta's response is interesting. Essentially, she accuses Oedipus of loathing her ill-timed, distracting, and "vile" sexual appetite; and her effect is to determine Oedipus to "act [his] joys".

In the next Act, Dryden elaborates a hint in Sophocles to damning affect. As in Sophocles, Jocasta attempts to counter mounting evidence by discounting prophecies, but the brevity, the peremptoriness of her responses to Oedipus's anguished questions is striking. To the rumor that Oedipus was not Polypus's son, she says only "T'was somewhat odd"; to the Delphic prophecy of parricide and incest, "Vain, vain oracles"; to Oedipus's determination to avoid these, only "Too nice a fear".

(Notably, Jocasta's later discounting of oracles has something of a feminist cast, when she says "If we must pray [. . .]/ Let Virgin hands adorn the Sacrifice; / And not a gray-beard forging Priest come near . . . [4.198.201, my emphasis].) It does not help that Jocasta has just emphasized to Oedipus his suspicious physical resemblance to Lajus:

JOCASTA: bate but his years, You are his picture

OEDIPUS aside: Pray Heaven he drew me not!-Am I his picture?

JOCASTA: So I have often told you.

OEDIPUS: True, you have [. . . .]

We may add to this Jocasta's extreme reluctance to produce Forbes, the shepherd who was supposed to murder the infant Oedipus. Jocasta recognizes the truth about the murder and marriage even before Forbes is, finally, produced and, having recognized it, seeks to dissuade Oedipus from questioning him-presumably she would continue in the incestuous relationship if her son remained ignorant of its true nature. Or is recognition not so much of the truth as it is a recognition of the imminence of exposure of a fact she has suspected or even known all long? The play maintains ambiguity, but the weight of evidence in Dryden and Lee's version allows, perhaps even impels spectators and readers to suspect the latter.

In fact, looked at this way, the motto for Oedipus's and Jocasta's relationship may be found in his line to her, "O, thou wilt kill me with thy Love's excess!" "Thy Love's excess"-the lines return us from what Jocasta knew to what Jocasta is: a woman. I have already argued in relation to Eurydice that other characters' psychological/moral valence accrues to Jocasta as she is the play's primary study of female desire; now I would like to reverse the flow and suggest thatjocasta's psychological/moral valence accrues to other characters-to begin with, to Oedipus's supposed mother, Merope. When the news arrives that Polypus has died of natural causes, Oedipus's consideration of his supposed mother's widowhood undergoes an extreme shift:

AEGEAN: Your Royal Mother Merope, as if She had no Soul since you forsook the Land, Waves all the neighboring Princes that adore her.

OEDIPUS: Waves all the Princes! Poor heart! For what? O speak.

AEGEAN: She, tho' in full-blown flower of glorious beauty, Grows cold, even in the Summer of her Age: And, for your sake, has sworn to dye unmerry.

OEDIPUS: How! For my sake, dye, and not marry! O My fit returns.

AEGEAN: This Diamond, with a thousand kisses blest, With thousand sighs and wishes for your safety, She charged me give you, with the general homage Of our Corinthian Lords.

OEDIPUS: There's Magic in it, take it from my sight; There's not a beam it darts, but carried Hell, hot flashing lust, and Necromantick Incest: Take it from these sick eyes, Oh hide it from me.

As we recognize, and as Oedipus is informed, Merope is not his mother and thus not guilty of "Necromantick Incest," but the emphasis on her languishing, on her desirability, on her "thousand kisses" all make the charge of "hot lust" at least momentarily plausible and add to the play's depiction of the insatiability and transgressiveness of female sexuality. We also hear that Merope has "had no Soul," which leads us to consider the play's handling of the laws of Heaven versus the appetites of Earth, or, in another formulation, the Apollonian versus the Dionysian, the latter term of both formulations being identified as female. In Tiresias's oracular terms, Heaven "sees" while Earth births: "Then hear me Heaven, / For blushing thou hast seen it: hear me Earth, /Whose hollow womb cou'd not contain this murder [...] ".

Accordingly, the ceremony in the grove that brings

Oedipus's guilt to light is earthbound, performed in a trench, rather than at an altar; the sacrifice involves a "barren Heyfer," who, when opened in Seneca "proves [. . .] to contain a fetus even though it is unmated [. . .] allegorically representing the incestuous issue of Oedipus and Jocasta" (Novak, "Commentary to Oedipus"483 n. 274); the grove is dedicated to the furies, violent female deities transformed and demoted by the Olympian Apollo in TheEunpides. Oedipus, one might say, seeks to ally himself with law and with heaven against these feminized forces, to deny them in himself. In Act I, considering the plague and the murder of Lajus, he rails at the Corinthian crowd:

Novak explains that this is [p]artly because Thebes was the birthplace and a cult center of Dionysus, a god of the earth and underworld. Oedipus supposes himself of Corinth, whose principle cultwas that of Olympian Aphrodite. The opposition between underworld and Olympian deities recurs in Oedipus' curse, I, i, 496 and in II, i, 266-70. ("Commentary to Oedipus"477 n. 452-55)

Novak further, in commenting on Jocasta's murder of all her children ("swift and wild, / As a robb'd Tygress bounding o're the Woods [5.1.402-03]), points out that Dryden and Lee may have in mind Seneca's Oedipus, "where Jocasta's final entrance is marked by likening her to another Theban matron, Agave, who killed her son in a frenzy . . ., and did so on the wooded slopes of Mount Cithaeron, where she and her fellow Bacchants roamed with and like animals [. . .]" (494 n.402-07).

After the discovery, Oedipus vacillates between cursing Jocasta as "thou far worse than worst / Of damning Charmers" (5.1.174-74) and yearning toward her:

For her part, Jocasta alternates between deferring to Lajus's prohibitive ghost (226-32) and attempting to "fright" the Gods and reclaim her husband (whom she alternately imagines as Oedipus and Lajus). Oedipus wishes for sight to see her "mouth the Heav'ns, and mate the Gods . . .". Novak glosses "mouth" as "declaim against" and "mate" "in the sense of rival or vie with, especially presumed superiors". I would add that the phrase keeps intact Jocasta's defiance of

Apollonian law and her voracious sexuality. And, if Dryden and Lee had contemplated writing a sequel, the suicides of Oedipus and Jocasta and the murders of the rest of the royal family would have made impossible an Antigone, in which the Apollonian laws are upheld by a woman.

Novak and others have pointed out Dryden's making Oedipus "too good a man" may have stemmed from his acceptance of certain principles of Thomas Rymer:

> We are to presume the greatest vertues, where we find the highest of rewards; and though it is not necessary that all Heroes should be Kings, yet undoubtedly all crown'd heads by Poetical right are Heroes. This Character is a flower, a prerogative, so certain, so inseparably annex'd to the Crown, as by no Poet, no Parliament of Poets, ever to be invaded, (qtd. in Novak, "Commentary to Oedipus"485-86 n. 363-65)

Hence, the problem Oedipus would pose for a Restoration playwright: Oedipus both kills a king and is a king; he commits parricide and incest but must be a "Heroe. "And it is a truism by now that political theory during the Restoration (and modern literary criticism-particularly New Historicism) exploits the analogies of state and family, of father and king. At the time Dryden and Lee were writing, moreover, contemporary political theory as well as the brute facts of government and power was in crisis. In relation to Absalom and Achitophel, Susan Greenfield explains,

> [Political theorists] assume that discourses about the body and state overlap, and they recognize that any representation of conception is thus a political act. This sense of integration was obviously influenced by their own system of government, figured in the body of a ruler who passed his power through genetic descent. At the same time, though, recent historical events-most importantly the execution of Charles I-had proved that the royal succession could be broken. The classic seventeenth-century patriarchalism that linked monarchal and paternal creative power would not endure.

Richard A. McCabe has discussed the relevance of incest to such embattled political theorizing in his Incest, Drama and Nature's Law: 1550-1700: "Perversions in the sexual politics of the family provide ready analogies for corruptions in the power politics of the state or the ideological politics of church and academy" J. Douglas Canfield is more specific:

The majority of Restoration political tragedies polemically defend Stuart monarchial theory of hereditary succession, especially at the time of the most severe political crisis of the era, 1678-88, from the Popish Plot through the Exclusion Crisis to the Glorious Revolution. A handful of plays offer a counter ideology-or at least expose the fatal Oedipal crisis lurking at the heart of monarchial ideology.

Given the dilemma inherent in the Oedipus story they had inherited and given Dryden's (at least) staunch royalist convictions, Dryden and Lee could do neither one of these, exactly. The uneasy nature of what they did do has been largely explained by commentators insisting on the strict division of labor, forte, and intention between Dryden and Lee. McCabe, for instance, says that "Dryden is intent upon the tragedy of fate [. . .] Lee upon a tragedy of desire":

Lee was interested in the psychological Oedipus, Dryden in the political, in the virtuous "Father of his Country" overcome by circumstance, and his part of the play duly reflects the moral and political confusion of the age through the strategy of oblique allusion at which he excelled [....] In this play, if anywhere, Dryden evokes something of Sir Robert Filmer's atavistic respect for the king as patriarch [....]

So, according to McCabe, Lee's additions "[undermine] Dryden's insistence upon [Oedipus's] purity of motive in wedding Jocasta". But, as my analysis of the play has shown, Dryden's parts too question "purity of motive"; Dryden too is interested in the "tragedy of desire" and the "psychological Oedipus." There is more coherence in the two playwrights' efforts than divisionary analyses suggest. Moreover, both playwrights are interested in "purity of motive," "desire," and the "psychological" in relation to Jocasta as much as, perhaps even more than, in relation to Oedipus.

The role of Jocasta, and by extension the depiction of woman, does much of the cultural work that would be required of royalist playwrights. Greenfield has argued in relation to Absalom and Achitophel that the poem's "emphasis on [David's] promiscuity has been effaced by increasing references to a feminine sexual desire and productivity so dangerous that the king appears reliable by contrast". Jocasta's characterization in Oedipus functions similarly: in deflecting much of the attention, perhaps condemnatory attention to issues of desire and agency as depicted in the female, the playwrights do not excuse Oedipus, who is, when all is said and done, inexcusable; but they do manage to mitigate it as much as possible under the circumstances. As Greenfield concludes in relation to Absalom and Achitophel.

In many respects Dryden at first seems remarkably sensitive to the mothers, reflecting what James Winn has described as his "more than occasion insight into the hard lot of ... women." But this insight is, as Winn notes of other works, also balanced by Dryden's tendency to lapse into misogynistic conventions. Ultimately [. . .] by the end only the standard negative implications about female sexuality persist.

As much as I would like to soften this judgment in relation to Dryden and Lee in regard to Oedipus, it seems to me disturbingly true. Novak states in his "Commentary to Oedipus" that the playwrights' insistence upon the continuing sexuality of [the protagonists'] relationship-they are, it should be remembered, more recently married, both seem younger than they are in other versions-constitutes the principle addition of Dryden and Lee to the story they inherited. These mutual endearments might distantly derive from Seneca's interpretation of the myth-maximum Thebis scelus- / maternus amor est- but Seneca permits no caressing by the unfortunate couple and, like Sophocles and Corneille, is far from allowing the recidivism we find in Dryden and Lee when, even after the full discovery, blind Oedipus andjocasta melt toward each other.

Brown remarks on the play's reputation for "lurid emotionalism"; Canfield also notes that its "surprisingly" open expression of erotic desire sets it apart from earlier versions. Charles Segal states that Dryden and Lee "virtually anticipate Freud in the suggestion of a subconscious attraction between

Oedipus andjocasta ...". All citations to act, scenes, and lines from Dryden and Lee's Oedipus come from Novak's edition in The Works of John Dryden, Vol. 13, and all citations from the preface or other prose are to page number. Citations of "Commentary" to the Works are page number, and when relevant, to note number.

The Creon/Shaftesbury link is also noted in George McFadden's Dryden, the Public Writer: 1660. McFadden's is the most specifically developed analysis of political relevance (SOS211). See also Novak's "Commentary to Oedipus" 461-64. Canfield designates Oedipus a "political tragedy".

Hume writes that "Lee's participation is probably responsible for some of the play's excesses, but also for its high emotional temperature. By himself, Dryden tends to be slightly frigid, his designedly emotional scenes too obviously calculated". Brown notes that "Dryden's standard of cool precision is often used to denigrate Lee's more passionate poetry" and ultimately argues that the difference in the playwrights' methods result from Dryden's having "planned the play as a means of extending his investigation into the varieties of tragedy, arranging a side-by-side comparison of Oedipus' irony and pathos with the wildness of his passion". Novak remarks in the "Commentary to Oedipus' that "Terms like 'passionate' for Lee, 'argumentative' for Dryden come unbidden to the mind" and that the playwrights' contemporaries were struck by the "characteristic frenzy" of Lee's style.

All citations of Absalom and Achitophel are to line numbers and are from Swedenberg's edition in The Works of John Dryden, volume 2. All citations of Sophocles's Oedipus are from Grene's translation in The Complete Greek Tragedies. In regard to Seneca's works, Fitch and McElduff remark that "As the Oedipal son's desire mimics that of the father, so the desire of the mother [. . .] toward the son mimics her own earlier desire toward the father, who has become undesirable through age or absence".

Chapter 21

Images of Women in Three Early Eighteenth-Century Plays

"It is a truth universally acknowledged, that a single man in possession of a good fortune must be in want of a wife."

Jane Austen, *Pride and Prejudice*

The progress of humanity and the evolution of societies have been documented through oral traditions, cave paintings, textbooks and news reels. All of these forms of communication show the societies of which they tell, but only creations actually from the era they discuss can reflect an undistorted image. Literature is one of those mirrors - for it reflects not only the author's thoughts, but also the society in which the author lived.

Women's status evolution in society can be traced through literature, specifically through drama. As women began to step out from under their husbands' and fathers' thumbs, society saw an emergence of more dominating, independent female characters. The introduction of more female authors and playwrights gave rise to more dialogue from a feminine point of view and more desirable female roles. However, male writers also began developing their female characters.

In addition to showing the evolution of women's role in society, drama also traced men's reactions to the female's new status. As the women gained higher status and independence, the roles for females written by several of the male playwrights became almost bipolar in relation to each other. Almost as if only together could the roles create one full character. The introduction of stronger female roles led to the extreme purification of feminine characters. The witty, self-reliant woman gained a wicked, bitter edge, and the innocent young daughter became even more devoted and tragic. While the extreme sides of the characters expanded, the middle ground between them seemed to shrink. Even in comedies, the role of the calculating woman became more wicked than humorous. As the character of the wife gained knowledge of her husband's affairs, she became the butt of more jokes and the target of humiliating acts. The biggest change comes about perhaps in the fact that the jokes were no longer at the expense of *all* characters, but at the expense of the newly enlightened woman.

However, the duality of the female characters, even as sexist as they were, must have heartened the actresses of the time because of the new role opportunities. "No doubt the frequency of paired heroines in Restoration tragedy, passionate villainess and 'Ravish'd Virgin', sexually experienced, restless intriguer and passive victim, reflects Restoration theatrical practice in providing parts for specific actresses. . . . But the bifurcation of Dark Lady and female saint, differentiated by the indelible stain of sexual knowledge, has deep psychological root". The root slowly sprouted and only through the passage of time did the change become apparent.

Amphitryon (1690), *The Beggar's Opera* (1728) and *The London Merchant* (1731) are three plays that show the progression and evolution of the characters of the daughter, the wife and the independent, calculating woman through time.

The role of the daughter is represented in dissimilar ways with John Gay's *The Beggar's Opera* and George Lillo's *The London Merchant*. The slightly earlier play (*Opera*) provides Polly as the part of the young innocent daughter. Yet, she possesses a little of the individualism indicative of the independent female with her refusals to blindly obey her parents. Her persistence in marrying Macheath despite her parents wishes contradicts the image of the submissive daughter. Such an attitude, along with Polly's act of marrying for love instead of for parental approval and money demonstrates the change in women's attitudes. The knowledge of self worth and desire to make independent choices are evident in the character of Polly. However, Gay avoids attacking the females and plays more off the humor of the situation instead of the change in the traditional daughter role. "'But hear, me Mother.—If you ever loved—' 'Those cursed play-books she reads have been her ruin. One more word, hussy, and I shall knock your brains out, if you have any'". It is not until later in the play does Gay poke fun directly at Polly and her role as a wife.

Lillo, in contrast, makes his daughter character, Maria, every bit the innocent, submissive and tragic young girl. As if to contrast the independent thinker that was arising in women in the real world, he overemphasizes Maria's obedience to her father. When discussing marriage, Maria says her choice of husband will be the man her father considers best.

THOR. A noble birth and fortune, though they make not a bad man good, yet they are a real advantage to a worthy one, and places his virtues in the fairest light.

MA. I cannot answer for my inclinations, but they shall ever be submitted to your wisdom and authority; and, as you will not compel me to marry where I cannot love, love shall never make me act contrary to my duty.—Sir, have I your permission to retire?.

The daughter character of Maria is similar to that of the wife character, Alcmena, in Dryden's *Amphitryon*. Both are submissive, obedient and eager to please. The role of wife seems to be a mere extension onto that of a daughter. Alcmena is apparently happy as a wife and actually loves her husband (a rarity in those days). "I am the fool of love, and find within me the fondness of a bride without the fear. My whole desires and wishes are in you". While Alcmena is happy with her husband, Amphitryon, the other wife in the play, Bromia is decidedly the opposite with her husband, Sosia. He alternates between insulting her and neglecting her. However, since it is a comedy, the relationship is talked about in jest, while Sosia makes advances on Phaedra.

Sosia: I warrant I was monstrous kind to thee.

Bromia: Yes, monstrous kind indeed. You never said a truer word; for, when I came to kiss you, you pulled away your mouth and turned your cheek to me.

Sosia: Good.

Bromia: How, good! Here's fine impudence. He justifies!

Sosia: Yes, I do justify, that I turned my cheek, like a prudent person, that my breath might not offend thee; for, now I remember, I had eaten garlic.

Gay presents a similar situation with Macheath and his several wives. Polly's devotion is used as a comedic effect and he is made the comic hero at her expense. While both Polly and Lucy lay claim to Macheath, he will only recognize, as his wife, the woman who can help him the most at that time. When he is imprisoned, he refuses Polly as his wife because Lucy can help him get out of the jail.

He respects neither, as his play on words in the last sentence are used to make fun of the institution of marriage that the two women hold so revered: "Be pacified, my dear Lucy—this is all a fetch of Polly's to make me desperate with you in case I get off. If I am hanged, she would fain have the credit of being thought my widow.—Really Polly, this is no time for a dispute of this sort; for whenever you are talking of marriage, I am thinking of hanging".

Polly is a tragic character in *Opera,* because she never moves beyond the doting wife. Lucy, on the other hand, develops into a calculating woman with her plan to poison Polly. *Opera* treads on the middle ground with Lucy; first making her humorous, then embittered and devious, but never evil. It is a perfect balance between the earlier character of Phaedra (*Amphitryon*) and the later character of Ms. Millwood (*Merchant*).

Phaedra is used entirely for comedic effect. Her self-serving antics and devious deals make for several jokes between the characters. But, her lack of sympathy for Bromia as she makes a sexual deal with her husband is relevant. The character is not taken seriously.

Mercury pokes fun at her. Sosia seems half intimidated by her. Phaedra is a woman after her own wants, using her wits and wiles to persuade. However, no one sees her as a real threat. In *Merchant,* Millwood is the reason for the tragic ending. Lillo takes the image of a strong, independent woman and makes her threatening to masculinity. The tragedy comes with her victim, George Barnwell. He is the innocent youth who is overcome by the wiles of the charming older woman. Several females have played the innocent to an older man, yet the situation is more commonly found in a comedy. *Merchant* presents a theme that warns against such woman as Millwood. "The satirist's end, then, is to release men from the power of women by attacking the entire sex. Men need to free themselves from the power of the *sex* [Nussbaum's emphasis]. Ideally men will learn to live without women, who only confuse them, prove them fools, and then destroy them".

Ironically, or perhaps appropriately, it is from the representation of the most threatening woman for men that we find an explanation which blames the males for the actions that they despise most in women. "Woman, by whom you are, the source of joy, with cruel arts you labour to destroy; a thousand ways our ruin you pursue, yet blame in us those arts first taught by you". Millwood becomes the extreme and the vindication of the manipulating woman at the same time.

The roles of wife, daughter, and manipulator evolved through the theater world at the same time they spread through the outside world. *The Beggar's Opera, Amphitryon* and *The London Merchant* reflected the changes of the times through their similar characters. Although the first two are comedies and the latter a tragedy, all present females in certain roles. The time span between the three, especially between *Opera* and *Amphitryon,* contributes to the different representations of the same type characters because of the change in sentiment in the outside world. Lillo, perhaps, faced the varying attitudes the best with his Millwood. Her explanation of her own role, despite the character's evil nature, may have led to a less threatening view of the independent woman. "The path from the whore to the fallen woman leads to greater understanding of the woman's plight, and a shift in blame from her inherent sexual characteristics to her social plight".

Bibliography

Bredvold, Louis Ignatius. The Intellectual Milieu of John Dryden.

Ann Arbor: University of Michigan Press, 1956.

Hooker, Edward Niles, H. T. Swedenberg, Jr., Vinton A Dearing, Earl Miner, et al. eds.

The Works of John Dryden. 18 vols.

Berkeley and Los Angeles: University of California Press, 1956.

Eliot, T. S. Homage to John Dryden.

London: The Hogarth Press, 1924.

Eliot, T. S. John Dryden: The Poet, The Dramatist, The Critic.

New York: Terence & Elsa Holliday, 1932.

(Repr. New York: Haskell House, 1965, 1968)

Frost, William. John Dryden: Dramatist, Satirist, Translator.

New York: AMS Press, 1988.

Gelber, Michael Werth. The Just And The Lively: The Literary Criticism of John Dryden.

Manchester: Manchester University Press, 1999.

Hammond, Paul. John Dryden: A Literary Life.

New York: St. Martin's Press, 1991.

Hammond, Paul and David Hopkins, eds. John Dryden: Tercentenary Essays.

New York: Oxford University Press, 2000.

Hammond, Paul and David Hopkins, eds. The Poems of John Dryden. 4 vols.

New York: Longman, 1995-2000.

Kirsch, Arthur C. Dryden's Heroic Drama.
Princeton, N.J., Princeton University Press, 1965. (Repr. 1972).
Miner, Earl Roy, ed. John Dryden.
London: Bell, 1972.
Myers, William. Dryden.
London: Hutchinson, 1973.
Saintsbury, George. Dryden.
New York, Harper, 1881.
(Repr. London: Macmillan, 1930)
(Repr. New York, AMS Press, 1968)
Scott, Walter, Sir. The Life of John Dryden. Edited with an introd. by Bernard Kreissman.
Lincoln, University of Nebraska Press [1963]
Sutherland, James. John Dryden; The Poet as Orator.
Glasgow: Jackson, Son, 1963.
Van Doren, Mark. John Dryden: A Study of His Poetry.
New York: Henry Holt & Co., 1946.
(Repr. Bloomington & London: Indiana University Press, 1960, 1963, 1967, 1973)
Van Doren, Mark. The Poetry of John Dryden.
New York, Harcourt, Brace and Howe, 1920.
(Repr.& Rev. Ed. Cambridge: Gordon Fraser/The Minority Press, 1931)
(Repr. New York: Haskell House, 1969)
Ward, Charles Eugene. The Life of John Dryden.
Chapel Hill, University of North Carolina Press, [1961].
Winn, James Anderson. John Dryden And His World.
New Haven: Yale University Press, 1987.